Contributions to Political Science

The book series offers an outlet for cutting-edge research in all areas of political science. Contributions to Political Science (CPS) welcomes theoretically sound and empirically robust monographs, edited volumes and handbooks from a variety of disciplines and approaches on topics such as political theory, comparative politics, democracy, European politics, electoral systems and voting behaviour, public policy and administration, political economy, and related fields.

All titles in this series are peer-reviewed. This book series is indexed in Scopus.

Lisa Kriegmair

Responsiveness and Responsibility in the Euro Crisis

Explaining Governments' Blame Avoidance Strategies Under EU Conditionality

Springer

Lisa Kriegmair
Ludwig-Maximilians-Universität München
Munich, Germany

ISSN 2198-7289 ISSN 2198-7297 (electronic)
Contributions to Political Science
ISBN 978-3-031-84472-0 ISBN 978-3-031-84473-7 (eBook)
https://doi.org/10.1007/978-3-031-84473-7

This Springer imprint is published by the registered company Springer Nature Switzerland AG
The registered company address is: Gewerbestrasse 11, 6330 Cham, Switzerland

Acknowledgements

This book is based on my dissertation, which I completed at Ludwig-Maximilians-Universität München (LMU) in 2023. At the time of the outbreak of the European debt crisis, I was just at the beginning of my studies in political science and economics in Munich. Since then, I have always been interested in the impact of this shock on the European Union and on the policies of its member states. For a long time, however, I could not imagine the moment when this book would actually be finished. The task seemed daunting, the goal far away. I am grateful to many people who have accompanied me on this journey.

First of all, I would like to thank my supervisors for their advice and support during the development of my dissertation. Berthold Rittberger has always struck a balance between giving me the freedom to explore ideas and keeping me on track with his wise questions and advice. I am very grateful for his always open door and generous support. I would also like to thank Berhard Zangl for his motivating and constructive advice. I am also grateful for the opportunity to work on the research project 'Public Responsibility Attributions in the European Union'. Not only did I learn a lot from this collaborative work, but it also had a significant influence on the development of this book.

My thanks also go to my former colleagues at the LMU's Geschwister Scholl Institute for Political Science, Benjamin Daßler, Tim Heinkelmann-Wild, Nina Guérin, Stefan Jagdhuber, Vytautas Jankauskas, Andrea Johansen, Raphaela Hobbach, Rainer Hülsse, Christian Kreuder-Sonnen, Andreas Kruck, Hilde Van Meegdenburg, Johannes Müller Gómez, Veronika Ohliger, Sebastian Schindler, Laura Seelkopf, Moritz Weiß and Eva Ziegler. They helped to shape this work at the IR/GG research colloquium and in numerous discussions on and off campus. I would also like to thank Josef Lolacher, Karin Nutzinger, Severin Süß and Simon Zemp for their support. Very special thanks go to Moritz Weiß, who gave me my first insight into scientific work. It was his enthusiasm for research that gave me the idea of doing a PhD.

Working on this book has taken up a lot of space in my life in recent years—often at the expense of my friends and family. I am forever grateful for their patience and companionship, for precious breaks and for many wonderful moments. I would especially like to thank my parents. Your unconditional love and support has been and continues to be the foundation from which I set off on new challenges and adventures.

Last but not least, my thanks go to Hannah and Felix. Just getting to know you, Felix, has made this journey worthwhile. You accompanied this project from the very beginning and supported me with all the big and small problems without any hesitation. I am incredibly grateful to have you by my side. Without you, Hannah, the first draft of this work would certainly not have been finished until much later. Your infectious laugh, your curiosity and your enthusiasm for the world around you and the people in it remind me every day that the most important things can be found beyond my screen. The two of you are my greatest motivation and I love you both with all my heart.

Competing Interests The author has no competing interests to declare that are relevant to the content of this manuscript.

Contents

About the Author

Lisa Kriegmair worked as a researcher at Ludwig-Maximilians-Universität München (LMU) from 2017 to 2023, where she finished her PhD dissertation in 2023. Her research interests include European integration, Europeanisation and the processes of responsibility and blame attribution. Her work has been published in prominent journals such as *West European Politics*, the *European Journal of Political Research* and the *Journal of European Public Politics*. Her book *European Blame Games: Where does the Buck stop?* (with Tim Heinkelmann-Wild, Berthold Rittberger, Bernhard Zangl) was published by Oxford University Press in 2024. She currently works as a project coordinator for European and international affairs for the City of Munich (Germany).

List of Abbreviations

BE	Bloco de Esquerda (Left Block)
CDS	Centro Democrático e Social – Partido Popular (People's Party)
CEECs	Central and Easter European countries
CGTP	Confederação Geral dos Trabalhadores Portugueses-Intersindical Nacional (General Confederation of the Portuguese Workers)
CNOP	Conselho Nacional das Ordens Profissionais (National Council of Professional Associations)
CRAP	Comissão de Regulação do Acesso a Profissões (Commission for the Regulation of Access to Professions)
EU	European Union
ECB	European Central Bank
EDP	Excessive Deficit Procedure
EMU	European Monetary Union
ERO	Employment Protection Order
ICTU	Irish Congress of Trade Unions
IMF	International Monetary Fund
JLC	Joint Labour Committee
MP	Member of Parliament
MIP	Macroeconomic Imbalance Procedure
NGEU	Next Generation EU
OECD	Organisation for Economic Co-operation and Development
PASOK	Panellínio Sosialistikó Kínima (Panhellenic Socialist Movement)
PCP	Partido Comunista Português (Portuguese Communist Party)
PM	Prime Minister
PS	Partido Socialista (Socialist Party)
PSD	Partido Social Democrata (Social Democratic Party)
PSOE	Partido Socialista Obrero Español (Spanish Socialist Workers' Party)
REA	Registered Employment Agreements
SIPTU	Services, Industrial, Professional and Technical Union

SRAP	Sistema de Regulação de Acesso a Profissões (Regulation System for the Access to Professions)
SYRIZA	Sinaspismós Rizospastikís Aristerás – Proodeftikí Simachía (Coalition of the Radical Left – Progressive Alliance)
The Programme	Economic Adjustment Programme
UGT	União Geral de Trabalhadores (General Union of Workers)
WTO	World Trade Organization

List of Figures

List of Tables

Chapter 1
Introduction

In the European Union (EU), 'arguably the most ambitious international integration project in the world' (Schneider, 2020, p. 329), supranational influence has become a decisive factor in national policymaking. The introduction of the Six-Pack, Two-Pack, and the Fiscal Compact, enabled the Commission to formulate binding recommendations for member states' socio-economic policy that amount to an 'enforceable obligation' (Kreuder-Sonnen, 2016, p. 1356; see also La Porte & Heins, 2015; Savage & Verdun, 2016; Verdun & Zeitlin, 2018). Notably, conditionality has become a popular instrument to lever policy change in the EU. Most recently, Next Generation EU (NGEU), the 750-billion-euro stimulus package to support economic recovery after the COVID-19 pandemic, links the disbursal of funds to macroeconomic reforms. The Commission monitors member states' compliance with its country-specific recommendations and decides upon the payment of funds accordingly (La Porte & Jensen, 2021). EU member state governments thus frequently find themselves in situations where they have to introduce domestically unpopular policies to comply with EU requirements (Kriegmair et al., 2022).

While the EU has a long-standing record of using conditionality to induce policy changes in accession countries (Schimmelfennig & Sedelmeier, 2005; Smith, 2003), the use of formal and informal conditionality within the community did not start until the Euro crisis. Through the Economic Adjustment Programmes, member states in need of financial support formally exchanged extensive austerity measures for financial backing: Greece, Ireland, Portugal, and Cyprus introduced budgetary cutbacks, tax increases as well as large-scale transformations of their welfare systems and labour markets (Armingeon & Baccaro, 2012; Henning, 2017; Laffan, 2014). Similar EU pressures affected Italy and Spain. As remaining outside of official lending arrangements depended on EU support, specifically on bond purchases through the ECB (European Central Bank), EU institutions significantly influenced national reform trajectories through a more informal type of conditionality (Cioffi & Dubin, 2016; Pavolini et al., 2015; Sacchi, 2015).

L. Kriegmair, *Responsiveness and Responsibility in the Euro Crisis*,
Contributions to Political Science, https://doi.org/10.1007/978-3-031-84473-7_1

The EU conditionality in the Euro crisis epitomises the responsiveness-responsibility dilemma that comes with increasing supranational influence on national policymaking (Mair, 2009, 2011). Governments serve the dual functions of considering citizens' interests (*responsiveness*) and respecting procedural norms and pre-existing obligations (*responsibility*) in their policymaking. As supranational influence on national politics increases, governments find it increasingly difficult to act responsively to their public and at the same time fulfil their obligations vis-à-vis supranational institutions (Hagemann et al., 2017; Schneider, 2020). The EU conditionality in the Euro crisis illustrates this dilemma as if under a magnifying glass. If member state governments wanted to remain in the Eurozone, they had to introduce extensive reforms that had severe implications for the living standards and thus imposed considerable hardship on their electorate (Kreuder-Sonnen, 2016; Vasilopoulou et al., 2014). They thus faced a significant risk of being held responsible for acting against citizens' interests. Indeed, these governments seem to face the consequences of being made responsible for unpopular measures. Popular support for the governments at the receiving end of EU conditionality took a turn for the worse: the introduction of austerity politics was met with protests and uprising, many incumbent governments experienced electoral defeat, and levels of government trust decreased steeply (Armingeon & Baccaro, 2012; Laffan, 2014; Lewis-Beck & Lobo, 2017). In a nutshell, governments under EU conditionality faced the choice of leaving the Eurozone or leaving office.

How can governments mitigate such a severe dilemma? One route available to governments facing the responsibility-responsiveness dilemma is influencing responsibility attributions in the public. To mitigate the electoral repercussions of the responsibility-response dilemma, governments can accompany austerity politics with blame avoidance strategies (Green-Pedersen, 2002; Hering, 2008; Hinterleitner & Sager, 2017; Vis & Kersbergen, 2007; Wenzelburger, 2011). Indeed, studies show that governments under the spectre of EU conditionality employed various blame avoidance strategies.

On the one hand, Greek, Spanish, Portuguese, and Irish government representatives have shifted blame onto domestic opponents and EU institutions (Roose et al., 2017; Sommer, 2020; Vasilopoulou et al., 2014). On the other hand, there is evidence that Italian government representatives hardly ever engaged in blame shifting but rather blurred responsibility by highlighting cooperation among domestic policymakers (König, 2016a, 2016b). Moreover, in addition to blame shifting, the Portuguese government also emphasised the desirability of the reforms and counteracted the blame risk by emphasising the positive aspects of the measures (Moury & Standring, 2017). Thus, there is variation across countries and variation in the individual governments' choice of blame avoidance strategy.

This book aims to shed light on the variation in governments' choice of blame avoidance strategies in the Euro crisis. I investigate the constraints that EU conditionality imposes on governments' use of various blame avoidance strategies and how the latter chose specific strategies from the remaining blame avoidance toolkit. Specifically, I ask *what shapes governments' choice of blame avoidance strategy under EU conditionality*?

This chapter provides an overview of the book. The first section summarises existing scholarship on blame avoidance strategies. It shows that there are no ready-made answers as to how governments choose blame avoidance strategies under the constraint of EU conditionality. The second section advances the argument that while EU conditionality constrains the availability of blame avoidance strategies, governments' choice from the available presentational blame avoidance strategies depends on the policymaking context. The third section provides an overview of the research strategy and the empirical findings. Subsequently, I outline how the book contributes to EU scholarship. Finally, I provide the plan for the book.

1.1 The State of the Literature

Blame avoidance strategies denote all activities policymakers take to manipulate the perceived blameworthiness of policies or their perceived responsibility for policy decisions (Hood, 2011; Sulitzeanu-Kenan & Hood, 2005). There is elaborate literature on the different blame avoidance strategies available to policymakers (Hinterleitner & Sager, 2017; for overviews, see König & Wenzelburger, 2014). The most influential and widely used categorisation differentiates between agency, policy, and presentational strategies (Hood, 2011). While agency strategies aim at shifting the formal responsibility for potentially blameworthy policies onto other actors, policy strategies aim at designing processes to minimise the risk of blame by rendering policymakers' actions appear less blameworthy. Presentational strategies manipulate the public perception of both, responsibility and the potentially blameworthy policy. These strategies can help governments mitigate the responsibility-responsiveness dilemma by signalling that a policy does not run counter to citizens' interests or by denying that governments are responsible for unpopular policies.

Existing studies of blame avoidance in the Euro crisis predominantly focus on the occurrence of a specific presentational strategy, that is, blame shifting. Vasilopoulou et al. (2014) find that governing parties are more likely than policymakers from opposition parties to shift blame onto few, specific actors. Traber et al. (2020) find that governments' propensity to blame EU in general and troika institutions, the European Commission, the European Central Bank (ECB), and the IMF, rises under adverse domestic economic situations. Yet, governments vary regarding their blame shifting behaviour. Sommer (2020) finds that party ideology shapes governing parties' blame shifting behaviour. Left-wing parties such as the Spanish Socialist Party (PSOE) and Greek *SYRIZA* are more likely to shift blame to external actors such as EU institutions. In contrast, conservative parties, such as the Spanish *Partido Popular* and Greek *Néa Dimokratía*, are more reluctant to do so and engage in a favourable policy portrayal. An exception from the focus on blame shifting is König (2016a), who shows that government representatives during the Euro crisis aimed for communication strategies that blurred responsibility and underlined cooperation when political competition was low. In sum, scholarship suggests that governments, especially left-leaning ones, in the Euro crisis were more likely to employ blame shifting than other actors. This tendency further increased in times of political competition. Nevertheless, this literature falls short of providing clear expectations for which strategy governments choose when they engage in blame avoidance.

Extending the search for insights into policymakers' choice of blame avoidance strategy beyond this narrow focus of the Euro crisis shows that blame avoidance has garnered significant scholarly attention (for an overview, see Hinterleitner, 2017). First, scholars on welfare state reform have identified blame avoidance as vital for governments whose aim is to remain in office despite welfare retrenchment. This strand of literature has categorised the blame avoidance strategies available to governments and elaborated on the conditions for their effectiveness (Mortensen, 2012; Pierson, 1996; Vis, 2009; Vis & Kersbergen, 2007; Wenzelburger, 2011). Second, public policy scholars have studied policymakers' blame avoidance behaviour in the face of political crises and natural disasters and examined its effectiveness (Boin et al., 2009; Brändström & Kuipers, 2003; Hood et al., 2009). Third, scholarship on EU multilevel governance has pointed out the blame avoidance opportunities that the EU offers for member state governments. Whereas the previous strands of literature focus on mapping various blame avoidance strategies and exploring their effectiveness, EU scholars concentrate on blame shifting as one specific form of blame avoidance. They highlight that the complexity of the EU's multilevel system allows member state governments to shift blame to the EU and its institutions (Gerhards et al., 2009; Heinkelmann-Wild et al., 2020; Heinkelmann-Wild & Zangl, 2020; Hobolt & Tilley, 2014; Schlipphak & Treib, 2017). These strands of literature have identified several factors that impact policymakers' choice of blame avoidance strategy. However, they fall short of providing satisfactory answers to why governments employ various blame avoidance strategies under EU conditionality.

For one, the timing of blame avoidance activities matters. While agency and policy strategies are considered proactive strategies, which must be put into place well in advance of a potential blame generating event occurring, presentational strategies can be employed both proactively and reactively (Hinterleitner, 2020; Hinterleitner & Sager, 2017). What is more, policymakers' preference for risk aversion may lead them to employ a staged approach to blame avoidance, whereby they initially select defensive strategies that deny the blameworthiness of a policy and only move on to strategies that deny responsibility when pressure builds up (Hood et al., 2009). While the timing may play a role in the choice of blame avoidance strategy, these approaches are ill-equipped to explain why the use of blame avoidance strategies varies across governments.

Second, the institutional and political context in which policies are enacted shapes the plausibility of strategies that aim at manipulating the responsibility for and the perception of a policy. For one, the degree of political competition among parties shapes the availability of strategies that aim at blurring responsibility (König, 2016a). Moreover, complex decision-making structures lend themselves to strategies that aim at blurring or deflecting responsibility. This conjecture holds for government styles, where consensus democracies yield better chances for blurring or deflecting responsibility than majoritarian systems (König & Wenzelburger, 2014).

It also applies to multilevel systems, where the inclusion of different levels of government enables the manipulation of responsibility (Gerhards et al., 2009). While supranational decision-making processes enable governments to shift blame to EU institutions, intergovernmental and shared decision-making processes are more conducive to blurring responsibility (Heinkelmann-Wild et al., 2020; Heinkelmann-Wild & Zangl, 2020). These insights cannot answer the question of governments' choice of blame avoidance strategy in the Euro crisis. They neglect strategies that aim at reframing a policy and contesting its harmfulness in favour of strategies that shift or deflect blame. While they can thus develop expectations as to when blame shifting likely occurs, they have difficulties explaining how governments choose from a blame avoidance toolkit. Furthermore, these approaches cannot account for variation in a government's use of blame avoidance strategies in the context of EU conditionality, where the institutional context is constant for lending governments.

Third, policymakers' ideology shapes the plausibility of their blame avoidance strategies. While left-leaning parties can plausibly manipulate the perception of welfare state retrenchment by framing it necessary to save the welfare system, this possibility is not open to right-leaning parties (Green-Pedersen, 2002; Ross, 2000). Again, these insights focus on the factors that are conducive for a specific type of blame avoidance, namely the manipulation of the perception of harm that emanates from a policy while neglecting other strategies. Furthermore, these approaches cannot account for variation in a government's use of blame avoidance strategies.

In sum, existing approaches are too general to differentiate between specific blame avoidance strategies and to provide policy-specific expectations. First, most approaches focus on the context conducive to the use of a specific strategy rather than exploring which strategies governments choose from the blame avoidance toolbox in a potentially blameworthy situation. Second, existing scholarship has little to say as to why governments' choice of strategy varies in the context of EU conditionality. Thus, there are, as of yet, no ready-made answers. The question of why governments chose varying blame avoidance strategies under EU conditionality thus requires further analysis.

1.2 Blame Avoidance, Politicisation, and Government Reputation: The Argument in Brief

In this book, I demonstrate how governments navigate the responsibility-responsiveness dilemma under adverse circumstances. I explain systematically why governments employ specific blame avoidance strategies when introducing policies under the spectre of EU conditionality. The argument proceeds in four steps. First, I explain why blame avoidance considerations are highly relevant for governments interested in re-election. Second, I introduce EU conditionality as a scope condition for governments' choice of blame avoidance strategies. I demonstrate how the obligation to comply with EU lending conditionality constrains not only governments' policymaking but also their choice of blame avoidance strategies. Third, I develop a typology of the blame avoidance strategies governments have at their disposal under the spectre of EU conditionality. Fourth, I introduce two factors that explain why governments choose specific strategies from the blame avoidance toolkit.

Contested Responsibility and Incentives for Blame Avoidance

Governments, whose primary goal is to stay in office, must demonstrate to their electorate that they are responsive to public preferences and demands. Therefore, it is of utmost importance to them who is made responsible for unpopular policies and negatively perceived policy outcomes in the public. Attributions of responsibility are politically consequential, as they provide the public and individual voters with information that links governments to policy outcomes. They impact the perception of government responsiveness as well as trust, legitimacy beliefs, and electoral success (Anderson, 2000; Arceneaux, 2006; Atkeson & Partin, 1995; Hobolt & Tilley, 2014; Peffley, 1984; Powell, 2000; Rudolph, 2003).

Blame avoidance considerations rank high on governments' agenda because responsibility attributions are contested. On the one hand, the evaluation of an event or a policy is hardly ever straightforward but allows for different interpretations (Schumacher et al., 2013). On the other hand, limited clarity of responsibility hampers attribution processes (Anderson, 2000; Hobolt et al., 2013; Powell & Whitten, 1993; Rudolph, 2003). In complex policymaking contexts, and especially in the EU, it is not always clear who is responsible for a policy or policy outcome (Gerhards et al., 2009; Hobolt & Tilley, 2014). Consequently, governments have incentives and opportunities to engage in processes of responsibility attribution in the public and attempt to shape them in their favour.

To sway public responsibility judgements in their favour, governments draw on credit claiming and blame avoidance strategies (Mayhew, 1974; Weaver, 1986). Yet, voters and governments alike are not immune to negativity bias and thus weigh losses and adverse outcomes more heavily than positive events (Kahneman & Tversky, 1979; Rozin & Royzman, 2001; Tversky & Kahneman, 1986). Therefore, strategies of blame avoidance take precedence over credit claiming (Hood, 2011; Weaver, 1986).

The Constraining Effect of EU Conditionality

EU conditionality presents an important scope condition when analysing governments' choice of specific blame avoidance strategies. Generally, governments have at their disposal a toolkit of blame avoidance strategies. It includes agency strategies, which aim at shifting formal competencies, and consequently responsibility, onto other actors; policy strategies, which manipulate the evaluation of a policy and the responsibility judgement through policy design; and presentational strategies, which influence the evaluation of a policy and responsibility judgements in public discourse. Under EU conditionality, specific policy prescriptions, limited budgetary scope, and time pressure restrict governments' room for manoeuvre. As a consequence, agency and policy strategies are unavailable to governments that have to comply with EU requirements. Thus, even more than usual, governments must draw on presentational strategies to avoid blame for introducing unpopular policies, such as austerity, privatisation, and liberalisation measures dictated by EU conditionality.

More than Blame Shifting: A Typology of Blame Avoidance Strategies
Within the constraints of EU conditionality, governments still have different options available to them. I develop a typology of governments' blame avoidance toolkit under EU conditionality. Governments' presentational blame avoidance strategies can work on two dimensions of responsibility attributions: the harm dimension, where governments can either accept or deny the adverse effects of a policy, and the agency dimension, where governments choose to blur responsibility among actors or keep it centred (Hood, 2011; McGraw, 1991; Sulitzeanu-Kenan & Hood, 2005). Governments can also combine these dimensions in their strategies (König & Wenzelburger, 2014, pp. 409–410). Consequently, governments have at their disposal four different blame avoidance strategies when they have to comply with EU conditionality:

- First, governments can accept a policy's negative consequences, thus refraining from manipulating the harm dimension, and diffuse responsibility among actors. By employing a *circle the wagons* approach, governments do not deny that costs and hardship emerge due to reforms introduced in compliance with EU conditionality. Nor do they reject entirely the responsibility for the introduced policy. Instead, they reduce the amount of blame they incur by diffusing responsibility among several actors, highlighting their involvement in the policymaking process. When successful, this approach limits the amount of blame governments incur by spreading it among several political actors.
- Second, when governments accept that a policy has harmful consequences, adopting a *blame shifting* approach can help them avoid blame by centring blame on others. Governments can shift all the blame to specific and plausible targets, such as the preceding government or the EU and troika institutions, when they have to fulfil the requirements of EU conditionality. When successful, this approach helps governments evade blame by targeting another actor.
- Third, governments can refrain from manipulating the agency dimension and manipulate the harm dimension by denying a policy's negative consequences. When employing a *self-defence* approach, governments accept responsibility for reforms introduced in compliance with EU conditionality. They portray a respective policy positively and reduce the risk of being blamed by arguing that blame is not justified in the first place. When successful, this approach helps governments evade blame and opens the possibility to eventually gain credit for introduced policies.

- Fourth, governments can deny the cost and hardship emanating from the policy and diffuse responsibility. Governments who employ a *problem denial* approach portray an introduced policy in a positive light and, simultaneously, diffuse responsibility for the measure by highlighting the involvement of other actors in the policymaking process. They thus frame a policy as a measure whose positive effects are recognised not solely by the government but by a broader coalition of actors. When successful, this approach helps governments evade blame by showing that their policy choice is almost inevitable and without alternatives, as a broad coalition of actors sees it as the solution for current problems.

Explaining Governments' Strategy Choice

How do governments decide on which presentational blame avoidance strategy they focus? Building on existing literature on blame avoidance strategies (Green-Pedersen, 2002; Heinkelmann-Wild et al., 2020; Hinterleitner, 2020; Hinterleitner & Sager, 2017; Hood et al., 2009; Sommer, 2020; Traber et al., 2020), I introduce two factors that can account for policy-level variation as to whether policymakers aim at centring or blurring responsibility and whether they opt for acceptance or denial of harm emanating from a policy. I argue that when governments have to transpose measures required by EU conditionality, their choice of strategy depends on the context in which the policies are introduced, specifically the degree of politicisation of a measure and on their reputation for policy support.

First, the degree of a policy's politicisation influences governments' ability to diffuse responsibility. Governments are better positioned to blur responsibility when the policies they introduce face low politicisation. Politicisation denotes an expansion of political conflict: when issues are politicised, their salience in the public increases (1), the scope of actors in the public debate expands (2), and issue positions are polarised (3). These characteristics impede strategies that blur responsibility in highly politicised situations. The more attention a policy garners, the more numerous the actors that raise the issue and the more polarised the debate, the less viable strategies that blur responsibility. In these situations of high politicisation, governments find themselves at the centre of public blame attributions and pointing out shared responsibilities is not a sufficient means to avoid blame. Therefore, governments must forcefully enter the domestic blame game (Heinkelmann-Wild et al., 2020; Sommer, 2020) and draw on responsibility-centring strategies. Contrariwise, governments should be in a better position to blur responsibility when their policies show lower levels of politicisation.

Second, governing parties' reputation for policy support shapes the viability of blame avoidance strategies that manipulate the perception of harm. Under pressure to comply with EU conditionality, governments lack the time and means to initiate a time-consuming reframing process to contest the perception of a policy's harmful consequences. Instead, governments have to build on previous policy positions. If governing parties have an issue reputation because they publicly voiced support or even campaigned for policy reform in the past, this should facilitate reframing the policy in a positive light. Previous efforts lend plausibility to reframing efforts, as the public regards them as committed to a specific issue. Contrariwise, those without a reputation for policy support should have a much harder time denying a measure's harmfulness.

Combining these two factors, which constrain governments' choice of blame avoidance strategy, yields clear expectations for when governments are most likely to focus their blame avoidance efforts on a specific approach. Table 1.1 summarises these theoretical expectations.

- First, in cases of low politicisation, governments without a reputation for policy support will not deny the hardship imposed by a policy but avoid blame by blurring responsibility and thus diffusing it among several actors. In other words, they will predominantly opt for a *circle the wagons* approach rather than other blame avoidance strategies.
- Second, when governments face high politicisation of a policy and have no previous record of coming out in favour of this policy, they will primarily focus on *blame shifting* to redirect blame to another actor, such as the previous government, the EU in general or the troika institutions.
- Third, in cases of high politicisation, governments with a reputation for supporting a policy they are required to introduce under EU conditionality will tend to deny the harmfulness of the measures but refrain from manipulating the agency dimension so that responsibility remains centred on the government. In other words, they will adopt a *self-defence* approach more often than other blame avoidance strategies.
- Fourth, in cases of low politicisation, governments that have a reputation for policy support can deny the harmfulness of a policy and blur responsibility for the measure. They will tend to focus their blame avoidance efforts on a *problem denial* approach rather than other strategies.

In sum, blame avoidance is a highly relevant task for governments, as responsibility attributions are contested and have the potential to shape governments' public image and public perceptions of government responsiveness, trust, and legitimacy. I argue that while governments have an extensive toolkit of blame avoidance strategies at their disposal, the availability of specific strategies depends on the policy-making context. First, EU conditionality limits the availability of strategies and compels governments to use presentational blame avoidance strategies. It thus functions as an important scope condition. Second, two factors can explain governments' choice of specific strategies. The politicisation of a policy and a government's prior reputation for policy support determine whether governments opt for a circle the wagons, blame shifting, self-defence, or problem denial approach.

Table 1.1 Explanatory framework for governments' choice of blame avoidance strategy

	Low politicisation	**High politicisation**
No reputation for policy support	Circle the wagons	Blame shifting
Reputation for policy support	Problem denial	Self-defence

1.3 Analysing Blame Avoidance Strategies: Evidence from Ireland and Portugal

To evaluate the empirical fit of my explanatory framework, I conduct a co-variation analysis. This approach aims to establish that variation in the value of an independent variable yields the expected variation in the dependent variable (Blatter & Haverland, 2012, p. 33). To analyse the effect of the independent variables, politicisation of the policy and reputation for policy support, I conduct four pairwise comparisons. The qualitative content analysis of governments' blame avoidance statements in Parliamentary debates shows that the expected pattern of blame avoidance strategies was present in each case and across the cases.

The Research Strategy
For each pairwise comparison, cases were selected to approximate a most similar system design. I focus on five instances of policies introduced in Ireland and Portugal, which allow me to maximise contextual similarities, while providing the necessary variation on the independent variables:

- The reform of the wage setting system in Ireland.
- The introduction of a property tax in Ireland.
- The reform of the water supply system in Ireland.
- The reforms of regulated professions in Portugal.
- The labour market reforms in Portugal.

These cases lend themselves to comparison as they share contextual similarities. First, they all take place during the Euro crisis and deal with the introduction of reforms under EU conditionality as part of an Economic Assistance Programme (the Programme) with the EU and the IMF. Second, choosing cases from Ireland and Portugal, all reforms were introduced by governments with similar ideological backgrounds, who were elected after the negotiations of the Programme, exhibited medium to good compliance records and exited their respective financial assistance programmes on time and without precautionary credit lines (Henning, 2017, p. 126; Lütz et al., 2019, p. 1445; Pisani-Ferry et al., 2013, 85–98; Sapir et al., 2014, 35–43). Finally, all the selected policies come with a blame risk for governments, as they all imply losses in terms of rights or material resources for significant constituencies.

I conduct the analysis in a two-pronged manner. First, I provide in-case evidence for the policymaking context and governments' choice of blame avoidance strategies in each case. The close analysis of each case helps to ascertain that it indeed exhibits a specific combination of the independent variables. Moreover, the disaggregation of blame avoidance strategies by year and a closer look at the content of blame avoidance statements increase the confidence in the stability of the results on the dependent variable. These case studies thus establish a link between a combination of different values of the independent variables and a specific pattern of blame avoidance strategies in each case. Second, I compare within each case-pair that changes in the value of the independent variables indeed occur in concert with the expected changes in the patterns of blame avoidance strategies. The comparison across cases in a most similar systems design attempts to isolate the effect of the independent variable on the outcome. Figure 1.1 depicts how the cases help me assess the impact of each independent variable:

- First, I assess the impact of variation in politicisation in cases of governing parties' low reputation for policy support by comparing the reform of wage setting system and the introduction of a property tax in Ireland (I).
- Second, I analyse the impact of variation in politicisation in cases of governing parties' high reputation for policy support in a comparison of reforms of regulated professions and the labour market in Portugal (II).
- Third, I evaluate the impact of variation in governing parties' reputation for policy support in cases of low politicisation in a comparison of the reform of wage setting system in Ireland and reforms of regulated professions in Portugal (III).
- Fourth, I assess the impact of variation in governing parties' reputation for policy support in cases of high politicisation by comparing the introduction of a property tax with the reform of the water supply system in Ireland (IV).

I conduct a qualitative content analysis of Parliamentary debates to analyse governments' blame avoidance strategies. Previous studies have neglected this source in favour of newspaper reporting (König, 2016b; Roose et al., 2018; Sommer, 2020; Sommer et al., 2016) or the communication released by heads of government (König, 2016a; Traber et al., 2020). However, as Parliaments are essential arenas of accountability, where governments have to explain and justify their policy choices (Bovens, 2007; Rauh & De Wilde, 2018; Rauh et al., 2017), Parliamentary debates represent the ideal source to analyse governments' choice of blame avoidance strategy for varying policies. The qualitative content analysis of governments' blame

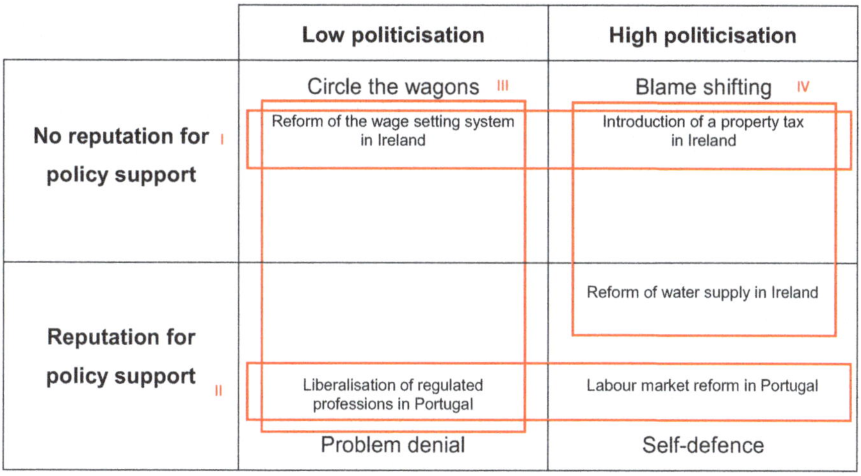

Fig. 1.1 Case selection for four pairwise comparisons

avoidance statements in Parliamentary debates shows that the expected pattern of blame avoidance strategies was present in each case and across the cases.

Blame Avoidance in Five Reform Instances Under EU Conditionality
First, the Irish government introduced a local property tax in Ireland to comply with EU's requirement to levy a recurring tax on residential property. The measure was highly politicised and came under considerable pressure both in- and outside Parliament, with several Members of Parliament (MPs) and activist organisations organising non-payment campaigns. The two governing parties had no reputation for supporting the measure, as neither actively promoted the introduction of a levy on residential properties before the Programme. Moreover, the larger coalition partner, Fine Gael, even denounced the measure during its 2011 election campaign as 'unfair'. In line with the theoretical expectations, the analysis of blame avoidance strategies shows that the Irish government employed blame shifting more frequently than any other blame avoidance strategy.

Second, the Irish government reformed Irish water services, which constituted compliance with the troika institution's requirement to establish a single utility responsible for water supply and introduce water charges covering the supply cost. The measures were highly politicised and led to the biggest anti-austerity protests in Ireland during the financial and Euro crises. The governing parties had a reputation for supporting the water services reform, with Fine Gael advocating for reform as early as 2009. In line with the theoretical expectations, the analysis shows that the Irish government primarily used a self-defence approach in this case.

Third, the Irish government reformed wage-setting mechanisms under the Programme requirement to review the existing wage-setting system and introduce necessary reforms to improve competitiveness. These reforms did not inspire significant levels of politicisation. Moreover, the Irish government did not have a reputation for policy support, as other parties had previously proposed most measures, and neither of the two coalition partners had campaigned to reform the wage-setting system before entering government in March 2011. In line with the theoretical expectations, the analysis shows that the Irish government employed circling the wagons rather than other strategies.

Fourth, the Portuguese government introduced labour market reforms to comply with the Programme conditionality. Politicisation of the policy was high, with the government facing considerable headwinds when introducing labour market reforms and the social partners increasingly contesting the measures. The governing parties had a reputation for policy support, having introduced far-reaching labour market reforms during their last term in office. In line with the theoretical expectations, the analysis of blame avoidance strategies shows that the Portuguese government primarily employed a self-defence approach.

Fifth, the Portuguese government introduced measures to liberalise regulated professions in compliance with the conditionality included in the Portuguese Programme. The liberalisation of contested professions faced low politicisation, with professional associations and opposition parties mounting little resistance to the reforms. The Portuguese government, or at least the larger coalition partner, the

Social Democratic Party (Partido Social Democrata, PSD), had a long-standing commitment to easing regulations of the goods and services markets and had voted in favour of liberalising regulated professions in the past. In line with the theoretical expectations, the analysis shows that the Portuguese government mainly focused on problem denial.

The disaggregation of blame avoidance strategies by year and a closer look at the content of blame avoidance statements show that governments' choice of strategy was predominantly consistent over time in the analysed cases, thus further strengthening the theoretical conjectures. Solely the Irish government's choice of blame avoidance strategies when talking about the reforms of the wage setting system changed over time due to an external event.

Patterns of Blame Avoidance Strategies Across Cases

The four pairwise comparisons show that the observed variance in governments' choice of strategy confirms the expectations derived from the theoretical framework. In a nutshell, governments engaged more in blame shifting and self-defence when policies were highly politicised, whereas the shares of circle the wagons and problem denial statements were higher when governments faced minor headwinds against the introduction of measures required by EU conditionality. Furthermore, governments systematically focus more on harm-denying strategies of self-defence and problem denial when they have a reputation for policy support and rely more heavily on harm-accepting strategies when they do not.

First, comparisons of cases that differ in the degree of politicisation show that governments consistently engage more in blame shifting and self-defence than in circle the wagons and problem denial when politicisation is high. First, in the cases of the reform of the wage-setting system and the introduction of a local property tax in Ireland, the government did not have a reputation for policy support. The Irish government should thus draw on strategies that accept the perceived harm that arises from the policies it introduced under EU conditionality in both cases. However, while the reform of the wage-setting system did not evoke high levels of politicisation, the introduction of a local property tax was highly politicised. Overall, the share of high-politicisation strategies was considerably lower in the first case than in the second. Zooming in on harm-accepting strategies, the share of circle the wagons statements was considerably larger in the former case, where politicisation was low, than in the latter case. Conversely, the share of blame shifting statements was larger in the latter case. Second, in the cases of the reforms of regulated professions and the labour market reforms in Portugal, the government has a reputation for policy support, so the government should opt for harm-denying strategies. Yet, the cases differ in the degree of politicisation. While the reforms of regulated professions were not politicised, the labour market reforms provoked high politicisation. Again, the share of high-politicisation strategies was considerably lower in the first case than the in latter. Zooming in on harm-denying strategies, the share of problem denial statements is much higher in the former case, where politicisation was low, than in the latter case. Conversely, the share of self-defence statements was higher in the latter case.

Second, comparisons of cases that differ in the reputation for policy support show that governments consistently choose strategies that vary in the evaluation of the policy while sticking to high-politicisation or low-politicisation strategies respectively. First, the comparison between the blame avoidance behaviour of the Irish and Portuguese governments in reforming wage setting in Ireland and regulated professions in Portugal confirms that both draw on low-politicisation strategies of circle the wagons and problem denial more than on high-politicisation strategies of blame shifting and self-defence. However, the share of circle the wagons statements is much higher in the former case, where the government had no reputation for policy support, than in the latter case. Conversely, the share of problem denial statements is higher in the latter case, where the government had a long-standing commitment to the policy. Second, the comparison of the Irish government's blame avoidance behaviour upon introducing the local property tax and reforming the Irish water services confirms that the Irish government draws on high-politicisation strategies more than on low-politicisation strategies in both cases. However, I observe a larger share of blame shifting statements in the former case, where the government had no reputation for policy support, than in the latter. Conversely, the Irish government's share of self-defence statements is higher in the latter case, where the government had a reputation for supporting the reform of Irish water services.

In sum, the theoretical framework thus fits well with the observed pattern of blame avoidance strategies in as well as across the cases. Furthermore, it exceeds the empirical fit of three alternative accounts: the sequential choice of strategies, the style of policymaking and the government's ideology, and the compliance record. The observed pattern of governments' choice of blame avoidance strategy only partially matched the three alternative explanations. Notably, all alternative accounts had difficulties explaining the Irish government's choice of strategy in the case of the introduction of the local property tax. Beyond the empirical fit of the alternative accounts, the sequential and compliance conjectures had difficulties accounting for variation between statements centring and blurring of responsibility and harm-accepting and -denying statements simultaneously, thus providing a coarser analysis of governments' blame avoiding behaviour.

1.4 Evaluating the Theoretical Framework: Contribution and Relevance

The book furthers our understanding of how governments navigate the responsibility-response dilemma incited by the intrusiveness of EU conditionality. As governments find themselves obliged to introduce the measures required by the EU, which impose costs on the public, signalling responsiveness to their electorate becomes difficult. To mitigate negative consequences, they thus attempt to influence responsibility judgements in the public. Their toolkit comprises presentational blame avoidance strategies that can challenge the policy's perception and that can manipulate the causal link between government action and the policy. Governments' strategy choice depends on the policymaking context. The politicisation of the policy and the government's reputation for policy support decide whether they opt for a circle the wagons, blame shifting, self-defence or problem denial approach. The three integral parts of the argument—EU conditionality as a scope condition, the typology of blame avoidance strategies, and the explanatory framework—contribute to the literatures on the limits of responsiveness in the EU, and blame avoidance and blame shifting in the EU. Furthermore, the insights of this book have implications for political accountability.

First, I theorise explicitly the constraints for governments' choice of blame avoidance strategy that emanate from EU conditionality. Highlighting the contextual specificities allows for the development of precise expectations about which blame avoidance strategies are available to governments under EU conditionality. More importantly, however, by spelling out how EU conditionality limits the availability of blame avoidance strategies, I show that the factors that constrain governments under the spectre of EU conditionality are by no means limited to the EU's lending activities. Rather, the specificity of policy prescriptions, limitations to the budget, and time pressure that restrict governments' room for manoeuvre are increasingly common in EU policymaking, for example, in the Stability and Growth Pact, the European Semester or NGEU. Theorising these constraints, the book adds to scholarship on the limits of government responsiveness in the EU (Hagemann et al., 2017; Mair, 2007, 2011; Schneider, 2020).

Second, I make visible important differences in governments' blame avoidance approaches under EU conditionality. Existing studies have focused either narrowly on blame shifting (Sommer, 2020; Traber et al., 2020; Vasilopoulou et al., 2014) or broadly on communication strategies (König, 2016a, 2016b; Moury & Standring, 2017; Roose et al., 2018; Sommer et al., 2016). I develop a typology and a methodological toolkit that allows for the systematic analysis of governments' varying blame avoidance approaches. In this way, I reveal differences in the blurring and centring responsibility and the policy evaluation that have so far gone unnoticed: Governments' attempts to signal responsiveness and avoid blame were not limited to shifting blame to the EU. Instead, they also engaged in strategies that blur responsibility and contest the perception of harm emanating from the policy.

Third, while existing studies have focused on governments' overall choices in blame avoidance, I provide a policy-specific explanation. This approach shows that the same governments opted for different strategies depending on the policy they talk about and highlights the importance of contextual factors for governments' strategy choice. While existing studies on blame avoidance in the EU have focused either on governments' preferences (Gerhards et al., 2009; Schlipphak & Treib, 2017; Traber et al., 2020; Vasilopoulou et al., 2014) or the institutional policymaking context (Heinkelmann-Wild et al., 2020; Heinkelmann-Wild & Zangl, 2020; Hobolt & Tilley, 2014), I show that governments' blame avoidance behaviour is solidly situated in the specific policymaking context. The governing parties' past behaviour and other political actors' behaviour during the introduction of a policy significantly shape governments' choice of strategy.

This focus on the policy-specific context helps explain why governments do not use the opportunities to shift blame to the EU that the intrusiveness of EU conditionality seemingly provides. Governments may have incentives to shift the blame for introducing unpopular policies to the EU level (Gerhards et al., 2009; Hobolt & Tilley, 2014; Schlipphak & Treib, 2017; Sommer, 2020; Traber et al., 2020; Vasilopoulou et al., 2014), and the requirements and monitoring activities of the troika institutions provide an institutional frame conducive for blame shifting (see, for instance, Moury & Standring, 2017). However, governments cannot always make use of the argument that their hands are tied by EU conditionality because the plausibility of this argument depends on governments' reputation for policy support. My theoretical framework thus offers clear expectations for when we observe blame shifting to the EU.

Furthermore, the book has implications beyond the blame avoidance nexus. Economic voting literature has long highlighted that diffuse responsibility and a lacking clarity of responsibility impede the link between unpopular policy outcomes and electoral outcomes (Anderson, 2000; Hobolt et al., 2013; Powell & Whitten, 1993). This casts a critical light on governments' efforts to blur responsibility. While such strategies may well be an effective means for blame avoidance, they constitute a problem for political accountability. My theoretical framework highlights the importance of politicisation for governments' ability to blur responsibility. This book thus underscores the positive effect of the politicisation of policies on accountability (De Wilde, 2011; Rauh & De Wilde, 2018).

In sum, the insights into the limitations to the use of blame shifting approaches and the impact of politicisation on responsibility blurring and, thus, accountability, which travel beyond the Euro crisis, should make this book a valuable read for a broader audience of scholars interested in the legitimacy and politicisation of international institutions in general and the EU specifically, as well as scholars interested in accountability in multilevel systems.

1.5 Plan of the Book

In this introduction, I gave an overview of this book's content. Before I elaborate on each point further in the following chapters, I will give a brief overview of the structure of the book.

In Chap. 2, I develop the theoretical framework of this book in four steps. First, I introduce the concept of responsibility attributions and explain how their effect on the public perception of government responsiveness and voting behaviour induces governments to engage in public attribution processes. Second, I present the blame avoidance strategies the literature has found governments have at their disposal and show how EU conditionality limits governments' strategy choice. Third, I develop a typology of the presentational blame avoidance strategies available to governments under EU conditionality. Finally, I explain when governments focus on each of the four strategies at their disposal, focusing on the degree of politicisation and governing parties' reputation for policy support.

Chapter 3 presents the research strategy and design I employ to evaluate the empirical fit of the theoretical framework developed in Chap. 2. My approach is best summarised as an x-centred, cross-sectional co-variation analysis. I conduct four most similar case comparisons that I complement with within-case evidence. I first present the case selection rationale before I provide a detailed account of the measurement of my independent and dependent variables. While I rely on secondary literature, media reporting and document analysis to establish the values of the independent variables, I conduct a content analysis of statements made by government representatives in Parliamentary debates to analyse my dependent variable, governments' blame avoidance strategies.

Chapters 4 and 5 consist of the analyses of the five cases: The reform of the wage setting system, the introduction of a property tax and the reform of the water supply system in Ireland, and the reforms of regulated professions and the labour market in Portugal. I establish in each case that the asserted values of the independent variables were indeed present and have led to the blame avoidance outcome predicted by the theoretical framework. To increase the confidence in the theoretical conjectures, I complement the analysis of blame avoidance strategies in each case with a disaggregation of strategies over time and provide insights into the content of governments' blame avoidance statements.

In Chap. 6, I compare governments' blame avoidance strategies across the examined cases in four pairwise comparisons. I evaluate the empirical fit of the theoretical expectations for all combinations of the independent variables, holding constant in each comparison one of the independent variables while varying the other. Furthermore, I evaluate the explanatory power of three alternative explanations—a sequential choice of blame avoidance strategies, policymaking style and government ideology, and governments' compliance records. I contrast the empirical fit of the theoretical framework with the alternative explanations.

Chapter 7 concludes by summarising the results of the book. I highlight the finding from the analysis of the five cases and the implications of the scholarship of the Euro crisis and blame avoidance.

References

Anderson, C. J. (2000). Economic voting and political context: A comparative perspective. *Electoral Studies, 19*(2–3), 151–170. https://doi.org/10.1016/S0261-3794(99)00045-1

Arceneaux, K. (2006). The federal face of voting: Are elected officials held accountable for the functions relevant to their office? *Political Psychology, 27*(5), 731–754. https://doi.org/10.1111/j.1467-9221.2006.00530.x

Armingeon, K., & Baccaro, L. (2012). Political economy of the sovereign debt crisis: The limits of internal devaluation. *Industrial Law Journal, 41*(3), 254–275.

Atkeson, L. R., & Partin, R. W. (1995). Economic and referendum voting: A comparison of gubernatorial and senatorial elections. *American Political Science Review, 89*(1), 99–107.

Blatter, J., & Haverland, M. (2012). *Designing case studies: Explanatory approaches in small-N research* (1. publ). *Research Methods Series*. Palgrave Macmillan.

Boin, A., Hart, P., & McConnell, A. (2009). Crisis exploitation: Political and policy impacts of framing contests. *Journal of European Public Policy, 16*(1), 81–106. https://doi.org/10.1080/13501760802453221

Bovens, M. (2007). Analysing and assessing accountability: A conceptual framework. *European Law Journal, 13*(4), 447–468. https://doi.org/10.1111/j.1468-0386.2007.00378.x

Brändström, A., & Kuipers, S. (2003). From 'normal incidents' to political crises: Understanding the selective politicization of policy failures. *Government and Opposition, 38*(3), 279–305. https://doi.org/10.1111/1477-7053.t01-1-00016

Cioffi, J. W., & Dubin, K. A. (2016). Commandeering crisis: Partisan labor repression in Spain under the guise of economic reform. *Politics and Society, 44*(3), 423–453.

de La Porte, C., & Heins, E. (2015). A new era of European integration? Governance of labour market and social policy since the sovereign debt crisis. *Comparative European Politics, 13*(1), 8–28.

de La Porte, C., & Jensen, M. D. (2021). The next generation EU: An analysis of the dimensions of conflict behind the deal. *Social Policy and Administration, 55*(2), 388–402.

De Wilde, P. (2011). No polity for old politics? A framework for analyzing the politicization of European Integration. *Journal of European Integration, 33*(5), 559–575. https://doi.org/10.1080/07036337.2010.546849

Gerhards, J., Offerhaus, A., & Roose, J. (2009). Wer ist verantwortlich? Die Europäische Union, ihre Nationalstaaten und die massenmediale Attribution von Verantwortung für Erfolge und Misserfolge. In F. Marcinkowski & B. Pfetsch (Eds.), *Politik in der Mediendemokratie* [Politics in the Media Democracy] (pp. 529–558). VS Verlag für Sozialwissenschaften. https://doi.org/10.1007/978-3-531-91728-3_22.

Green-Pedersen, C. (2002). *The Politics of Justification: Party Competition and Welfare-State Retrenchment in Denmark and The Netherlands from 1982 to 1998. Changing Welfare States*. Amsterdam University Press. https://doi.org/10.2307/j.ctt46n1h4

Hagemann, S., Hobolt, S. B., & Wratil, C. (2017). Government responsiveness in the European Union: Evidence from council voting. *Comparative Political Studies, 50*(6), 850–876. https://doi.org/10.1177/0010414015621077

Heinkelmann-Wild, T., & Zangl, B. (2020). Multilevel blame games: Blame-shifting in the European Union. *Governance, 33*(4), 953–969. https://doi.org/10.1111/gove.12459

Heinkelmann-Wild, T., Kriegmair, L., & Rittberger, B. (2020). The EU multi-level system and the Europeanization of domestic blame games. *Politics and Governance, 8*(1), 85–94.

Henning, C. R. (2017). *Tangled governance: International regime complexity, the Troika, and the Euro Crisis*. Oxford University Press.

Hering, M. (2008). Welfare state restructuring without grand coalitions: The role of informal cooperation in blame avoidance. *German Politics, 17*(2), 165–183. https://doi.org/10.1080/09644000802075757

Hinterleitner, M. (2017). Reconciling perspectives on blame avoidance behaviour. *Political Studies Review, 15*(2), 243–254.

Hinterleitner, M. (2020). *Policy controversies and political blame games*. Cambridge Studies in Comparative Public Policy. Cambridge University Press.

Hinterleitner, M., & Sager, F. (2017). Anticipatory and reactive forms of blame avoidance: Of foxes and lions. *European Political Science Review, 9*(4), 587–606.

Hobolt, S. B., & Tilley, J. (2014). *Blaming Europe? Responsibility without accountability in the European Union* (1st ed.). Oxford University Press.

Hobolt, S. B., Tilley, J., & Banducci, S. A. (2013). Clarity of responsibility: How government cohesion conditions performance voting. *European Journal of Political Research, 52*(2), 164–187.

Hood, C. (2011). *The blame game: Spin, bureaucracy, and self-preservation in government.* Princeton University Press.

Hood, C., Jennings, W., Dixon, R., Hogwood, B., & Beeston, C. (2009). Testing times: Exploring staged responses and the impact of blame management strategies in two examination fiasco cases. *European Journal of Political Research, 48*(6), 695–722.

Kahneman, D., & Tversky, A. (1979). Prospect theory: An analysis of decision under risk. *Econometrica, 47*(2), 263–292.

König, P. (2016a). Communicating austerity measures during times of crisis: A comparative empirical analysis of four heads of government. *The British Journal of Politics and International Relations, 18*(3), 538–558.

König, P. (2016b). Unpopular policies and the imperative of justification: Putting the Monti government's reform communication in a comparative perspective. *Journal of Comparative Policy Analysis: Research and Practice, 18*(2), 176–194.

König, P., & Wenzelburger, G. (2014). Toward a theory of political strategy in policy analysis. *Politics & Policy, 42*(3), 400–430. https://doi.org/10.1111/polp.12076

Kreuder-Sonnen, C. (2016). Beyond integration theory: The (anti-)constitutional dimension of European crisis governance. *Journal of Common Market Studies, 54*(6), 1350–1366.

Kriegmair, L., Rittberger, B., Zangl, B., & Heinkelmann-Wild, T. (2022). Dolce far niente? Non-compliance and blame avoidance in the EU. *West European Politics, 45*(5), 1153–1174.

Laffan, B. (2014). Testing times: The growing primacy of responsibility in the Euro Area. *West European Politics, 37*(2), 270–287.

Lewis-Beck, M. S., & Lobo, M. C. (2017). The economic vote: ordinary vs. extraordinary times. In K. Arzheimer, M. S. Lewis-Beck, & J. Evans (Eds.), *The Sage handbook of electoral behaviour* (2nd Volume, pp. 606–630). Sage. https://doi.org/10.4135/9781473957978.n26

Lütz, S., Hilgers, S., & Schneider, S. (2019). Games borrower governments play: The implementation of economic adjustment programmes in Cyprus and Portugal. *West European Politics, 42*(7), 1443–1463.

Mair, P. (2007). Political opposition and the European Union. *Government and Opposition, 42*(1), 1–17.

Mair, P. (2009). *Representative versus responsible government.* MPIfG Working Paper (09/8).

Mair, P. (2011). *Bini Smaghi vs. the parties: Representative government and institutional constraints.* EUI Working Papers (RSCAS 2011/22). https://cadmus.eui.eu/handle/1814/16354

Mayhew, D. R. (1974). *Congress: The electoral connection.* Yale University Press.

McGraw, K. M. (1991). Managing blame: An experimental test of the effects of political accounts. *American Political Science Review, 85*(4), 1133–1157.

Mortensen, P. B. (2012). "It's the Central Government's fault": Elected Regional Officials' use of blame-shifting rhetoric. *Governance, 25*(3), 439–461.

Moury, C., & Standring, A. (2017). 'Going Beyond the Troika': Power and discourse in Portuguese austerity politics. *European Journal of Political Research, 56*(3), 660–679.

Pavolini, E., León, M., Guillén, A. M., & Ascoli, U. (2015). From austerity to permanent strain? The EU and Welfare State Reform in Italy and Spain. *Comparative European Politics, 13*(1), 56–76.

Peffley, M. (1984). The voter as Juror: Attributing responsibility for economic conditions. *Political Behavior, 6*(3), 275–294.

Pierson, P. (1996). The new politics of the welfare state. *World Politics, 48*(2), 143–179.

Pisani-Ferry, J., Sapir, A., & Wolff, G. B. (2013). EU-IMF assistance to Euro-Area countries*: An Early Assessment* (Bruegel Blueprint).

Powell, G. B. (2000). *Elections as instruments of democracy: Majoritarian and proportional visions.* Yale University Press.

Powell, G. B., & Whitten, G. D. (1993). A cross-national analysis of economic voting: Taking account of the political context. *American Journal of Political Science, 37*(2), 391–414. https://doi.org/10.2307/2111378

Rauh, C., & De Wilde, P. (2018). The opposition deficit in EU accountability: Evidence from over 20 years of plenary debate in four Member States. *European Journal of Political Research, 57*(1), 194–216. https://doi.org/10.1111/1475-6765.12222

Rauh, C., De Wilde, P., & Schwalbach, J. (2017). *The ParlSpeech data set: Annotated full-text vectors of 3.9 million plenary speeches in the key legislative chambers of seven European States.* https://dataverse.harvard.edu/dataset.xhtml?persistentId=doi:10.7910/DVN/E4RSP9

Roose, J., Sommer, M., Scholl, F., Kousis, M., Kanellopoulos, K., & Loukakis, A. (2017). Debating responsibility on the Eurozone crisis in traditional media newspaper reporting in Greece and Germany under a social media lens. In M. Barisione & A. Michailidou (Eds.), *Palgrave studies in European political sociology. Social Media and European Politics: Rethinking power and legitimacy in the digital era* (Vol. 31, pp. 267–290). Palgrave Macmillan.

Roose, J., Sommer, M., & Scholl, F. (2018). Verantwortungszuschreibungen in der Eurozonen-Krise. In J. Roose, M. Sommer, & F. Scholl (Eds.), *Bürgergesellschaft und Demokratie. Europas Zivilgesellschaft in der Wirtschafts- und Finanzkrise: Protest, Resilienz und Kämpfe um Deutungshoheit* (Vol. 10, pp. 43–73). Springer VS.

Ross, F. (2000). Framing welfare reform in affluent societies: Rendering restructuring more palatable? *Journal of Public Policy, 20*(2), 169–193.

Rozin, P., & Royzman, E. B. (2001). Negativity bias, negativity dominance, and contagion. *Personality and Social Psychology Review, 5*(4), 296–320.

Rudolph, T. J. (2003). Institutional context and the assignment of political responsibility. *The Journal of Politics, 65*(1), 190–215.

Sacchi, S. (2015). Conditionality by other means: EU involvement in Italy's structural reforms in the sovereign debt crisis. *Comparative European Politics, 13*(1), 77–92.

Sapir, A., Wolff, G. B., Sousa, C. de, Terzi, & Alessio. (2014). *Committee Book on the Troika and Financial Assistance in the Euro Area: Successes and Failures* (Book on the request of the Economic and Monetary Affairs Committee).

Savage, J. D., & Verdun, A. (2016). Strengthening the European Commission's budgetary and economic surveillance capacity since Greece and the Euro area crisis: A book of five Directorates-General. *Journal of European Public Policy, 23*(1), 101–118.

Schimmelfennig, F., & Sedelmeier, U. (Eds.). (2005). Cornell paperbacks. *The Europeanization of Central and Eastern Europe*. Cornell University Press.

Schlipphak, B., & Treib, O. (2017). Playing the blame game on Brussels: The domestic political effects of EU interventions against democratic backsliding. *Journal of European Public Policy, 24*(3), 352–365. https://doi.org/10.1080/13501763.2016.1229359

Schneider, C. J. (2020). Public commitments as signals of responsiveness in the European Union. *The Journal of Politics, 82*(1), 329–344.

Schumacher, G., Vis, B., & van Kersbergen, K. (2013). Political parties' welfare image, electoral punishment and welfare state retrenchment. *Comparative European Politics, 11*(1), 1–21.

Smith, K. E. (2003). The evolution and application of EU membership conditionality. In M. Cremona (Ed.), *Collected courses of the academy of European Law: Vol. 12. The Enlargement of the European Union* (pp. 105–140). Oxford University Press.

Sommer, M. (2020). Blame-Shifting in times of permanent austerity: Evidence from Spain and Greece in the Eurozone crisis. *Journal of Common Market Studies, 58*(3), 562–579. https://doi.org/10.1111/jcms.12926

Sommer, M., Roose, J., Scholl, F., & Papanikolopoulos, D. (2016). The Eurozone crisis and party conflicts in Greece and Germany: Discursive struggles about responsibility. In T. Krieger, B. Neumärker, & D. Panke (Eds.), *Schriftenreihe des Arbeitskreises Europäische Integration e.V: Vol. 88, Europe's crisis: The conflict-theoretic perspective* (1. Aufl., pp. 87–112). Nomos. https://doi.org/10.5771/9783845262482-87

Sulitzeanu-Kenan, R., & Hood, C. (2005). *Blame avoidance with adjectives? Motivation, opportunity, activity and outcome.* Paper for the ECPR Joint Sessions, Blame Avoidance and Blame Management Workshop, 14th - 20th April 2005, Granada.

Traber, D., Schoonvelde, M., & Schumacher, G. (2020). Errors have been made, others will be blamed: Issue engagement and blame shifting in prime minister speeches during the economic crisis in Europe. *European Journal of Political Research, 59*(1), 45–67.

Tversky, A., & Kahneman, D. (1986). Rational choice and the framing of decisions. *The Journal of Business, 59*(4), 251–278.

Vasilopoulou, S., Halikiopoulou, D., & Exadaktylos, T. (2014). Greece in crisis: Austerity, populism and the politics of blame. *Journal of Common Market Studies, 52*(2), 388–402. https://doi.org/10.1111/jcms.12093

Verdun, A., & Zeitlin, J. (2018). Introduction: The European semester as a new architecture of EU socioeconomic governance in theory and practice. *Journal of European Public Policy, 25*(2), 137–148.

Vis, B. (2009). Governments and unpopular social policy reform: Biting the bullet or steering clear? *European Journal of Political Research, 48*(1), 31–57. https://doi.org/10.1111/j.1475-6765.2008.00783.x

Vis, B., & van Kersbergen, K. (2007). Why and how do political actors pursue risky reforms? *Journal of Theoretical Politics, 19*(2), 153–172. https://doi.org/10.1177/0951629807074268

Weaver, R. K. (1986). The politics of blame avoidance. *Journal of Public Policy, 6*(4), 371–398.

Wenzelburger, G. (2011). Political strategies and fiscal retrenchment: Evidence from four countries. *West European Politics, 34*(6), 1151–1184. https://doi.org/10.1080/01402382.2011.572385

Chapter 2
Explaining Governments' Blame Avoidance Strategies Under EU Conditionality

This chapter develops a theoretical framework to explain governments' blame avoidance behaviour under the spectre of EU conditionality. It consists of four parts. First, I demonstrate the relevance of blame avoidance strategies by locating them in the broader context of responsibility attribution and government responsiveness. Subsequently, I introduce EU conditionality as a scope condition for governments' choice of blame avoidance strategies. Third, I present the four blame avoidance strategies governments have at their disposal when facing EU conditionality. Finally, I develop specific expectations about when governments employ these four blame avoidance strategies.

Blame avoidance strategies have been studied in the broader context of responsibility attributions and government responsiveness. In the first section, I show that responsibility attributions are politically consequential constructs of public discourse and are thus subject to political contestation. Governments' need to signal responsiveness to the electorate means they have strong incentives to shape processes of responsibility attribution in their favour. As a result of negativity bias and their institutional position as blame takers, they focus more on blame avoidance than credit claiming strategies.

While governments have a toolkit of blame avoidance strategies at their disposal, section two explains how EU conditionality limits their availability. Governments can engage in prospective and retrospective blame avoidance and draw on agency, policy, and presentational strategies. I argue that specific characteristics of EU conditionality, namely specific policy prescriptions, limited budgetary scope, and time pressure, restrict governments' room for manoeuvre. Thus, governments must draw on presentational strategies to avoid blame for introducing unpopular policies required by EU conditionality.

Building on these insights, I present a typology of presentational blame avoidance strategies available to governments who must comply with EU conditionality in the third part of the chapter. I identify four strategies that aim to manipulate the

L. Kriegmair, *Responsiveness and Responsibility in the Euro Crisis*, Contributions to Political Science, https://doi.org/10.1007/978-3-031-84473-7_2

harm and agency dimensions of responsibility attributions: circle the wagons, blame shifting, self-defence, and problem denial.

The fourth section theorises when governments focus on each of the four strategies at their disposal. As boundedly rational actors, governments choose among the four presentational strategies the one that maximises their expected utility given the information they possess on the situation. This decision takes into account the contextual constraints regarding the plausibility of their statements and EU conditionality. Building on blame avoidance scholarship, I propose that governments' choice of blame avoidance strategy depends on the degree of politicisation of a policy and governing parties' reputation for policy support.

2.1 Contested Responsibility and Incentives for Blame Avoidance

A closer look at governments' blame avoidance strategies requires, in the first place, a clear understanding of the role of responsibility attributions in political processes. The practice of attributing responsibility is omnipresent in everyday life as well as politics. When something bad happens, we have an inherent need to explain this event and determine who caused it. When concerning political events and policy outcomes, these responsibility judgements are highly relevant for policymakers, as they are important signals of policymakers' responsiveness to citizens' preferences. I will show that governments have strong incentives to shape responsibility attributions, especially negative ones, in their favour.

In political science, responsibility judgements draw a direct connection between a specific issue and an actor who is claimed to have caused it. Attributions of responsibility are based on the perception that an actor's deliberate action has been instrumental to the occurrence of an outcome, such as a specific social or political event or condition, or a policy and its consequences (Arceneaux, 2006, p. 736; Gerhards et al., 2007; see also Iyengar, 1994). Furthermore, political actors are not only held responsible for what they do but also for what they do not do: '[v]oters need only believe that government policy could have done more to avert a problem even if it was caused by something else' (Arceneaux, 2006, p. 736; see also Bovens et al., 1999). This is the consequence of the social or institutional role that officeholders are assigned in society: they are obliged to fulfil specific tasks and are held responsible if they fail to do so (Arceneaux, 2006, p. 733; Hobolt & Tilley, 2014, pp. 9–10). Take, for instance, the Eurozone crisis: while economic and fiscal problems developed as a result of the collapse of US subprime mortgage markets and the ensuing global financial crisis, European governments were also made responsible for the crisis as they did not take precautions against fiscal imbalances and failed to introduce sufficient banking regulation before the financial crisis.

The attribution of responsibility has significant consequences for policymakers, whose reputation and electoral fate depends on whether they are perceived as responsive to citizens' preferences. The attribution of responsibility for positive and negative policy outcomes create the crucial link between policymakers and political outcomes and thus enable voters to hold policymakers accountable (Peffley, 1984). Economic voting scholars have shown succinctly that the electorate punishes the government in opinion polls and in elections for a bad economic situation or rewards it for a good economic outlook when it believes that the government is responsible for economic policy (Anderson, 2000; Arceneaux, 2006; Atkeson & Partin, 1995; Hobolt & Tilley, 2014; Peffley, 1984; Powell, 2000; Rudolph, 2003a).[1] The findings on the link between responsibility and electoral success apply beyond the realm of the economy. Voters retrospectively punish governments, whom they judge to be responsible for welfare retrenchment (Giger, 2010; Pierson, 1996),[2] corruption (Tavits, 2007), or EU policies (De Vries et al., 2011). Furthermore, terrorist attacks, natural disasters, and policy failures have electoral implications for the policymakers deemed responsible and can lead to resignations (Birkland, 2010; Boin et al., 2009; Bovens et al., 1999; Brändström & Kuipers, 2003; Malhotra & Kuo, 2008). Finally, responsibility attributions are not solely relevant for elected policymakers. Hobolt and Tilley (2014) point out that when voters identify non-elected policymakers as the responsible parties for adverse events, scandals or policy failures but cannot hold them accountable in elections, they lose trust in the institutions they represent, thus damaging institutional legitimacy in the long term (Hobolt & Tilley, 2014, 23–25, 136). Therefore, the attribution of responsibility for political decisions and outcomes is central to policymakers' reputation, legitimacy and, ultimately, electoral success (Hobolt & Tilley, 2014).

The process of attributing responsibility is by no means stating the obvious, as responsibility judgements are contested in the public. While the literature on economic voting underlines the link between institutional responsibility and responsibility attribution, both the scholarship on individual responsibility judgements and those scholars that focus on processes of responsibility attribution in the public, agree on one point: While institutional responsibilities are important for responsibility judgements, two factors tend to hamper clear responsibility attributions.

First, the evaluation of an event or a policy is hardly ever straightforward but allows for different interpretations (Schumacher et al., 2013). Framing processes in the mass media offer an interpretation of the consequences of an event or a policy that allows for its evaluation (Bovens et al., 1999; Brändström & Kuipers, 2003; Gerhards et al., 2007). Moreover, personal biases and motivated reasoning can influence evaluation of the economic outlook (Anderson et al., 2004; Wlezien et al., 1997). The evaluation of a policy and, consequently, the implications of

[1] Note that on the individual level, biases and motivated reasoning influence the direction of responsibility attributions and thus weaken the link between economic outlook and electoral outcomes. See, for example, Arceneaux (2006), Cutler (2004, 2008), Gomez and Wilson (2001), Rudolph (2003a, 2003b, 2006).

[2] Note that the results in the field of welfare retrenchment are mixed, however. Armingeon and Giger (2008) and Giger and Nelson (2011) do not find evidence that voters systematically punish governments for welfare retrenchment.

responsibility judgements are thus not objectively given but part of individual and public interpretation processes.

Second, institutional responsibilities are not always evident, and the link between actors and outcomes is conditioned by the clarity of responsibility (Anderson, 2000; Hobolt et al., 2013; Powell & Whitten, 1993; Rudolph, 2003a). The clarity of responsibility depends on institutional factors, such as bicameralism and the degree of legislative influence on decision making, as well as on characteristics of the government, such as majority status and the composition of the government (for an overview, see Hobolt et al., 2013). Moreover, vertical divisions of power impede the clarity of responsibility (Anderson, 2006; Cutler, 2004, 2008; León, 2011, 2012; León et al., 2018). Under low clarity of responsibility, individual biases and heuristics influence the attribution of responsibility (Arceneaux, 2006; Rudolph, 2003a, 2003b, 2006). The complexity of policymaking processes thus opens up room for varying responsibility judgements.

Scholarship on the EU's multilevel system further underlines the contested nature of responsibility judgements. EU policymaking introduces new actors, such as the Commission, the European Parliament and the European Council into the policymaking realm and broadens the range of policymaking arrangements. This complexity of policymaking processes in the EU makes it difficult for the general public to identify institutional responsibilities and assign responsibility accordingly (Gerhards et al., 2009; Moravcsik, 1994). The complexity in multilevel structures requires the public to draw on other heuristics to reach responsibility judgements (Heinkelmann-Wild et al., 2018; Hobolt & Tilley, 2014; Rittberger et al., 2017).

Consequently, the attribution of responsibility is a politically relevant and contested process, in which political actors have every incentive to become active and strategically influence responsibility judgements in their favour. The complexities of modern policymaking allow political actors to influence the formation of responsibility judgements in the mass media (Gerhards et al., 2007, 2009; Hansson, 2018a; Hood, 2011; Hood et al., 2009; Mortensen, 2012). This is especially true in the EU, where the multilevel system provides policymakers with ample opportunities to become actively involved in processes of responsibility attribution in the public (Heinkelmann-Wild et al., 2020; Heinkelmann-Wild & Zangl, 2020; Sommer, 2020).

The effects of responsibility attributions are not lost on governments, whose representatives thus have every incentive to attempt to manipulate attribution processes to evade blame for unpopular policies and to garner credit for popular ones (Iyengar, 1994, pp. 8–9; McGraw, 1991, p. 1133). Electoral pressures require governments to be responsive to their constituencies in the sense that they 'listen to and then respond to the demands of citizens and groups' (see also, Dahl, 1971; Hobolt & Klemmensen, 2008; Mair, 2009, p. 11; Schneider, 2020). As citizens often lack information to evaluate governments' responsiveness, governments need to signal their responsiveness (Schneider, 2020). Consequently, governments are concerned with being linked to popular policies while worrying about being made responsible for policies perceived negatively in the public (Leong & Howlett, 2017; McGraw, 1991, p. 1135).

The public policy literature highlights policymakers' efforts to shape public attribution processes. Policymakers engage in credit claiming to link themselves to popular measures, such as public spending (Grimmer et al., 2012; König & Siewert, 2020; Mayhew, 1974). At the same time, they attempt to avoid blame for unpopular policies (see, e.g., Vis, 2016). In his seminal work on blame avoidance, Weaver (1986) argues that while governments are interested in both credit claiming and blame avoidance, the latter takes precedence due to voters' cognitive biases. Individuals are not indifferent between choices with the same payoff when one is framed in terms of gains and one in terms of losses. Instead, real and potential losses weigh more heavily than gains (Kahneman & Tversky, 1979; Tversky & Kahneman, 1986). Furthermore, individuals pay more attention to negative evaluations than to positive ones, and negative evaluations increase in their negativity more quickly than positive ones. These phenomena are summarised under the label negativity bias (Rozin & Royzman, 2001). As boundedly rational actors, governments may fall victim to negativity bias as well. According to prospect theory, they give more weight to the risk of losses or blame than to the opportunity to gain credit. Consequently, governments who want to stay in office should be more concerned with avoiding blame than claiming credit and employ a distinct set of strategies to this end (Hood, 2011; Weaver, 1986).[3]

What is more, their institutional position puts governments in a central place in public discourses on responsibility and further increases their interest in engaging in blame avoidance. Scholarship on the interactions of policymakers contesting responsibility judgements mostly focus on attributions for controversial events and policy outcomes in so-called blame games (Hansson, 2018b; Hinterleitner, 2020; Hood, 2011). These games, which are played between blame makers and blame takers (Hood, 2011, p. 7), put policymakers in government centre-stage, as natural blame takers (Hinterleitner, 2020, p. 18). This further increases governments' need to engage in the process of responsibility attribution.

In sum, this section elucidated the relevance of blame avoidance strategies by locating the phenomenon in the broader context of responsibility attributions and government responsiveness. I showed that responsibility attributions in the political sphere are judgements based on a causal link between an actor's actions or omissions and a specific outcome. Responsibility judgements can impact policymakers' reputations and electoral fate. As constructs of public discourse, responsibility attributions are subject to political contestation. This applies especially in the realm of the EU, where the complexities of the multilevel system open opportunities for political actors to shift responsibility. Therefore, governments have strong incentives to engage in processes of responsibility attribution in the public. As a result of negativity bias and their institutional position as blame takers, they focus more on blame avoidance than credit claiming strategies. In the next section, I elaborate on

[3] This argument does not require assumptions on governments' bounded rationality. Instead, assuming voters' cognitive biases would also be in line with the assumption of perfectly rational governments: If voters tend to give more attention to losses than gains, governments should take this bias into account in their decision-making process.

the blame avoidance strategies governments draw on to engage in processes of responsibility attribution and how EU conditionality constrains the available toolkit of blame avoidance strategies.

2.2 The Impact of EU Conditionality on the Blame Avoidance Toolkit

The effects of responsibility attributions are not lost on governments, who need to signal responsiveness to their public and thus have every incentive to evade blame for unpopular policies. In the following section, I provide an overview of governments' blame avoidance toolkit and introduce EU conditionality as an important scope condition. I explain that specific characteristics of EU conditionality limit the availability of blame avoidance strategies.

The strategies governments employ to avoid blame have been studied in the context of welfare retrenchment (Hinterleitner, 2017; for overviews, see, for instance, König & Wenzelburger, 2014; Vis, 2016), in the aftermath of political crisis and natural disasters (Boin et al., 2009; Brändström & Kuipers, 2003; Hinterleitner & Sager, 2015; Hood et al., 2009), and—albeit to a lesser extent—in the context of the EU (Heinkelmann-Wild et al., 2020; Heinkelmann-Wild & Zangl, 2020; Hobolt & Tilley, 2014; Schimmelfennig, 2020; Sommer, 2020). These strands of literature show that blame avoidance is a common behaviour in the political sphere that appears in different guises (Hinterleitner, 2017, 2020; Hood, 2011; Vis, 2016).

In a seminal categorisation, Hood (2011) sorts different forms of blame avoidance into three categories, which work on the evaluation of a policy or event and the question of responsibility.[4] First, agency strategies aim at shifting formal competencies, and consequently responsibility, onto other actors. Governments can manipulate responsibility judgements, for example, by delegating tasks to other levels of government, agencies, or private actors. Second, policy strategies manipulate both the evaluation and the responsibility judgement through policy design. Via policy design, governments can influence the evaluation of a policy, for instance, by choosing a policy that distributes harm evenly, or they can work on responsibility judgements by drawing on generally shared best practices. Third, policymakers can use presentational strategies to manipulate either the policy evaluation or responsibility judgements, for instance, by verbally shifting blame onto other actors or reframing the issue so that governments' policies are perceived more favourably.[5]

Presentational strategies play a prominent role in the tool kit of blame avoidance strategies. First, governments in democratic systems are constantly obliged to

[4] See König and Wenzelburger (2014) for an overview and a critique of different attempts to structure strategies of blame avoidance.

[5] Vis (2016) develops similar types of blame avoidance strategies in the realm of welfare retrenchment, differentiating between manipulating procedures, manipulating perceptions and manipulating payoffs.

explain and justify their conduct and thus engage in communication strategies to win legitimacy for their policies and themselves (Fonseca & Ferreira, 2015; Grimmer et al., 2012; König, 2016a; König & Siewert, 2020; Leong & Howlett, 2017). As the evaluation of a policy is hardly ever straightforward, communication strategies can be assumed to play an essential part in any blame avoidance attempt (König, 2016a, p. 540; Ross, 2000, p. 170). Second, the availability of different strategies hinges on contextual factors. Specifically, '[t]he strategies that governing elites employ to prepare for blameworthy events are very different to those that they apply in the midst of a "blame game"' (Hinterleitner & Sager, 2020, p. 116). The literature distinguishes between prospective and retrospective blame avoidance. While presentational strategies can be used both prospectively and retrospectively, agency and policy strategies are decidedly prospective approaches. To be successful, they need to be put in place well before questions of responsibility arise (Hinterleitner, 2020; Hinterleitner & Sager, 2020). In consequence, different contexts give rise to the use of different blame avoidance strategies. Agency and policy strategies are often employed in the context of welfare retrenchment, whereas governments cannot rely on these strategies amid a political controversy (Hinterleitner, 2020, pp. 20–23; Hinterleitner & Sager, 2017; Hood et al., 2009; see also McGraw, 1991).

How does EU conditionality impact governments' blame avoidance toolbox? Conditionality denotes the practice of linking benefits to the fulfilment of conditions (Smith, 2003, p. 108). As a foreign policy tool, it is employed by states and international institutions in the context of development aid (Stokke, 1995), EU enlargement (Schimmelfennig & Sedelmeier, 2005), and lending by International Financial Institutions, such as the IMF (Babb & Carruthers, 2008; Copelovitch, 2010; Dreher, 2009). For those at the receiving end, conditionality impacts policy decisions, as it changes governments' cost-benefit calculations. The impact of conditionality is probably strongest for lending conditionality, where financial assistance, which is often the only option available to states with difficulties to refinance public debt, depends on the prior fulfilment of policy requirements (Greer, 2014; Steinwand & Stone, 2008). EU conditionality in Euro crisis exercised similarly intense pressure on receiving governments. States which required financial assistance to evade the risk of sovereign default and of leaving the Eurozone were forced to comply with requirements for fiscal consolidation, financial sector regulation, and structural reforms (Greer, 2014; Laffan, 2014; Lütz & Kranke, 2013). EU conditionality exhibits characteristics, namely the prescription of specific policy goals, limited budgetary scope and time constraints, that limit the availability of some blame avoidance strategies.

First, conditionality forces governments to fulfil specific policy goals. EU conditionality was especially strict as it detailed the means to reach policy goals (Ioannidis, 2014; Theodoropoulou, 2015). Therefore, many scholars share the view that in the Euro crisis, the borrowing countries lost the ability to choose among policy alternatives (Afonso et al., 2014; Armingeon & Baccaro, 2012; Moreira et al., 2015; Petmesidou & Glatzer, 2015). Consequently, under EU conditionality, governments have little leeway in the introduction of austerity policies that impose significant hardship on the public and thus come with a high blame risk.[6]

Second, lending conditionality typically includes fiscal policy provisions, which limit governments' budgetary freedom (Greer, 2014). As EU Programmes target member states with high and unsustainable debt, conditionality prescribes severe budgetary cuts to help consolidate national finances. Programme conditionality includes specific targets for budgetary cutbacks and areas, where savings are to be effected. These include, for instance, cuts to the public sector wage bill, welfare retrenchment, and increasing the pension age (Greer, 2014; La Porte & Heins, 2015; Laffan, 2014; Pisani-Ferry et al., 2013). Consequently, governments under EU conditionality are severely restricted in allocating financial resources.

Third, governments under conditionality face time constraints. To ensure compliance, lenders monitor the implementation of the required measures and link implementation to credit disbursal (Babb & Carruthers, 2008; Greer, 2014). In the Euro crisis, the troika institutions regularly visited the countries which received financial assistance to verify compliance records and decided upon the disbursal of credit tranches accordingly. To facilitate monitoring, the Programmes include specific timeframes to introduce the required measures. In some cases, the disbursal of credit tranches was even specifically linked to important reforms (Featherstone, 2014; Henning, 2017; Sacchi, 2015). Consequently, under EU conditionality, governments have to adhere to strict reform schedules.

This setup of EU conditionality limits the blame avoidance strategies governments have at their disposal. The constraints of conditionality preclude the use of agency and policy strategies. For one, to be credible, the reallocation of formal policymaking responsibilities via agency strategies, such as delegation, requires governments to change institutional settings well before policymaking (Hinterleitner, 2020, p. 22). Under the spectre of conditionality, governments are forced to implement the required policies within a short timeframe and sometimes even face specific implementation deadlines. They thus lack time to introduce agency strategies to help them avoid blame for the policies introduced in compliance with EU conditionality.

What is more, policy strategies that aim to manipulate the evaluation of policies require governments to choose among different policy alternatives, compensate those who stand to lose from a policy, or delay negative consequences (Vis, 2016, p. 130). In the face of EU conditionality, governments find their room for manoeuvre severely constrained. Again, they face short time frames for the transposition of policies required by EU conditionality. Furthermore, Programme requirements limit the budgetary freedom of governments and prescribe specific policies. Consequently, governments lack the freedom of choice among policy options to employ policy strategies successfully when implementing Programme conditionality.[7]

[6] As I explained in Chap. 1, this holds for both formal and informal conditionality.

[7] See Traber et al. (2020) for a similar argument on blame avoidance in times of economic crisis.

Finally, the implementation of Programme conditionality requires governments to employ blame avoidance strategies both in anticipation of the blame generating event, that is, the implementation of Programme conditionality, and after implementation has taken place.[8] The need for retrospective blame avoidance thus additionally inhibits governments' use of agency and policy strategies. Consequently, governments that have to comply with Programme conditionality have to rely on presentational strategies of blame avoidance.

In sum, governments have a toolbox of various blame avoidance strategies at their disposal. Yet, they are limited in their choice of strategy under the spectre of EU conditionality. Budgetary constraints, the specificity of the conditions and the short timeframe under which conditional measures have to be introduced constrain governments' strategy choice. To retain public support, I thus argue that governments that have to introduce specific policies to comply with EU conditionality have to rely on presentational strategies of blame avoidance. The subsequent section develops my typology of presentational blame avoidance strategies.

2.3 Blame Avoidance Under EU Conditionality: A Typology

In their efforts to evade the blame that comes with introducing unpopular policies, such as austerity, privatisation and liberalisation measures required by EU conditionality, governments are limited to presentational strategies. Nevertheless, within this constraint, they have different options available. In the following, I develop a typology of governments' blame avoidance strategies under EU conditionality. To do so, I focus on the two contested parts of responsibility attributions—the evaluation of the policy and the target to whom responsibility is attributed.

When choosing a suitable presentational strategy, governments have different options. The first decision is whether to talk about unpopular policies that come with a blame risk in the first place. A commonly cited strategy is to avoid blame by staying silent and drawing the public attention to another policy issue. Policymakers tend to publicly highlight those issues on which they can claim credit and downplay others, which favour their competitors (Petrocik, 1996; Traber et al., 2020). In this vein, Hood points out that one way for officeholders to avoid blame is by changing the subject or 'burying bad news' (see also Hinterleitner, 2020, p. 22; Hood, 2011, p. 56). However, governments are often unable to avoid policy issues that carry a blame risk because those issues are salient in the public (Green-Pedersen, 2002; Klüver & Sagarzazu, 2016; Traber et al., 2020). What is more, obfuscation does not necessarily pay off. Elmelund-Præstekær et al. (2015) show that governments who

[8] As governments employ presentational strategies to avoid blame for transposing the requirements of EU conditionality both pro- and retrospectively, I stick to the label of blame avoidance strategies rather than the more specific label of blame management strategies, which refers to those strategies that are employed retrospectively (see, McGraw (1991)).

try to hide unpopular measures from the public are punished by voters when their obfuscation attempts fail.

When governments have to implement policies required by EU conditionality, obfuscation is unlikely to pay off for policymakers (Lefkofridi & Nezi, 2020). The public is likely well informed about the content of the conditionality required by the troika institutions, especially since the latter regularly monitor the reform process (Greer, 2014; Henning, 2017; Sacchi, 2015). Governments should thus have little chance to obfuscate unpopular reforms. For them, the conventional wisdom 'it is better "to do something than to do nothing"' (Hood et al., 2009, p. 699) applies.

Under the spectre of conditionality, governments' presentational blame avoidance strategies build on the two contested elements of responsibility attributions: the evaluation of the policy for which responsibility is attributed and the target to whom causal responsibility is attributed. For blame to be attributed, there needs to be a perceived loss, harm or cost (*harm dimension*). Additionally, the responsibility for the experience of this loss must be attributed to one actor or several actors (*agency dimension*) (Bovens et al., 1999; Brändström & Kuipers, 2003; Hood, 2011; Iyengar, 1989; Sulitzeanu-Kenan & Hood, 2005).

First, governments can choose to manipulate the perceived loss that the public or a specific constituency observes due to a policy. According to Hood (2011), a perceived loss exists when 'something is seen as being worse for some person or group than it could have been if matters had been handled differently' (Hood, 2011, p. 6). Yet, the evaluation of a policy is not straightforward (Bovens et al., 1999; Brändström & Kuipers, 2003; Schumacher et al., 2013). The popularity of a policy depends not solely on its political content but also on the way it is presented by decision-makers (Elmelund-Præstekær et al., 2015; Elmelund-Præstekær & Emmenegger, 2013, p. 24). Governments can thus deny or downplay the harm or costs that emerged as consequences of a policy and highlight its positive effects instead.

This approach 'focuses on the outcome and claims that contrary to accusations, the consequences are not so undesirable and therefore that less or no blame is warranted' (McGraw, 1991, p. 1136). In this way, unpopular policies can gain public support when policymakers employ a 'vice into virtue' approach (Levy, 1999; see also Ross, 2000, 170) that justifies reforms by stressing current policy failures. Similarly, Ringe (2005) points out that the provision of focal points, highlighting certain normative or political consequences of a policy over others, can help garner support for a legislative proposal without changing actor preferences. As strategies that work on the harm dimension give reasons why the policy is actually beneficial either immediately or in the foreseeable future, they can help governments reach credit claiming as well as blame avoidance goals (Hood, 2011, p. 53; König, 2016b, p. 188).

Second, governments can manipulate to whom responsibility is attributed. The manipulation of the agency dimension has to be differentiated from agency strategies. Whereas the latter are concerned with organisational design and intend to deflect blame by 'achieving disconnection among different units and disconnection from past structures' (Hood, 2011, p. 69), the manipulation of the agency dimension takes place via communicative acts. This approach focuses on the public perception of the 'causal link between actor and outcome and involves a denial of partial or full responsibility' (McGraw, 1991, p. 1136). Governments can alleviate the blame attributed to them by either blurring the responsibility among several actors or redirecting it to other actors.

On the one hand, Sulitzeanu-Kenan and Hood (2005) argue that the amount of blame directed at a given actor depends on the coherence of attributions. When responsibility is directed at several actors and thus blurred, the amount of blame targeted at an individual actor is lower compared to cases where responsibility, and thus blame, is centred on only one actor. Thompson (1980) called the difficulty of deciding who is responsible for policy outcomes in cases where many policymakers are involved in a decision-making process the 'problem of many hands'. Under these circumstances, policymakers can use excuses to qualify their culpability for policy outcomes, and, while they do not evade blame altogether, they lessen the amount of blame they incur. The literature on clarity of responsibility discussed above supports this conjecture as well. König and Wenzelburger (2014) argue that the clarity of responsibility is low when stakeholders, such as trade unions, employer associations and other interest groups, are involved in welfare state policy, which then makes it hard for voters to judge governments' responsibility for retrenchment policies (König & Wenzelburger, 2014, p. 409). Similarly, Brädström and Kuipers remark that invoking complex causal chains can help governments avoid blame as 'blame dispersed is sanctions avoided' (Brändström & Kuipers, 2003, p. 298). Taken together, governments can avoid blame for unpopular policies by blurring responsibility among actors.

On the other hand, governments can centre responsibility for policies and policy outcomes—either on themselves or other actors. In favourable circumstances, governments centring responsibility on themselves engage in credit claiming (Mayhew, 1974; Weaver, 2018). In potentially blame-generating situations, it is unreasonable to expect governments, as blame avoiders, to accept responsibility for themselves.[9] Instead, governments should aim to shift blame onto another specific actor, who then serves as a lightning rod (Brändström & Kuipers, 2003; Hood, 2011; Sulitzeanu-Kenan & Hood, 2005; Weaver, 1986). In government-opposition blame games, attributing responsibility for harmful policy outcomes to a specific actor is generally the home turf of opposition parties, who act as blame generators (Hansson, 2018a, 2018b; Hinterleitner, 2020; Hinterleitner & Sager, 2015). Nevertheless, governments can deny their responsibility and shift it to others to avoid blame. Performance evaluations in the public are generally adjusted in a zero-sum manner so that more

[9] The literature focusing on blame management strategies in political scandals or policy fiascos, names excuses as one strategy that centres responsibility. By making excuses, policymakers accept both harm and responsibility, offer apologies, and even resign sometimes (see Hood et al. 2009; Capelos and Wurzer 2009; Hood 2011). However, this work does not focus on policymaking (König and Wenzelburger 2014, 405–406). It is not plausible to expect governments to draw on this approach when they are in the process of policymaking or implementation (for a similar argument, see König 2016a, 540–541). After all, for their apologies to be credible, they would have to stop implementing the unpopular policies. Therefore, centring responsibility on themselves should be restricted to situations in which governments deny the harmfulness of a policy they introduce.

blame for other actors directly leads to less blame for the government itself (Kumlin, 2011). By shifting blame onto other actors, governments thus avoid blame themselves.

Governments are not entirely free to shift responsibility onto other actors. Many scholars assume—either implicitly or explicitly—that actors involved in the process of attributing responsibility have to remain plausible in their public commutation strategies (Gerhards et al., 2009; Heinkelmann-Wild et al., 2020; Heinkelmann-Wild & Zangl, 2020; Hinterleitner, 2019; Mayhew, 1974; McGraw, 1991; Weaver, 1986). While partisan bias has been found to influence citizens' openness to information that fits their preferred worldview (Lodge & Taber, 2013; Taber & Lodge, 2006), they 'will come to believe what they want to believe only to the extent that reason permits' (see also Bisgaard, 2015; Kunda, 1990, p. 483). Therefore, citizens reject statements that obviously contradict reality to keep up the 'illusion of objectivity' (Pyszczynski & Greenberg, 1987, cited in Kunda, 1990, 498). Consequently, governments' choice of strategy is limited by what they can plausibly claim in the public.

In this context, the literature on blame games in the national sphere has highlighted the predecessor government as a suitable target for governments' blame-shifting activities (Hinterleitner, 2020, p. 148; Hobolt & Tilley, 2014, pp. 116–117). Moreover, in the context of the EU's multilevel system, EU institutions involved in policymaking processes become a plausible target for responsibility shifting (Gerhards et al., 2009; Heinkelmann-Wild, Kriegmair, & Rittberger, 2020; Heinkelmann-Wild & Zangl, 2020; Hobolt & Tilley, 2014). This option is especially relevant for governments, who have to comply with EU conditionality. The troika institutions, which monitor the transposition of conditionality and enforce compliance, present plausible blame targets. Governments can thus shift blame to their predecessor or EU and troika institutions to avoid becoming the target of blame attributions themselves.

Summing up, governments' presentational blame avoidance strategies can work on two dimensions of responsibility attributions: the harm dimension, where governments can either deny or accept the adverse effects of a policy, and the agency dimension, where governments choose to blur responsibility among actors or keep it centred. Governments can also combine these dimensions in their strategies (König & Wenzelburger, 2014, pp. 409–410). This leaves governments with four different blame avoidance strategies at their disposal when they have to comply with EU conditionality. These strategies are summarised in Table 2.1.

First, governments can diffuse responsibility among actors, but accept the negative consequences of a policy, thus refraining from manipulating the harm

Table 2.1 Governments' blame avoidance strategies in the face of EU conditionality

	Blurred responsibility	Centred responsibility
Accept perceived harm	**Circle the wagons**	**Blame shifting**
Deny perceived harm	**Problem denial**	**Self-defence**

dimension. When employing a *circle the wagons* approach, governments do not deny that costs emerge due to reforms introduced to comply with EU conditionality, nor do they entirely deny their own responsibility. Instead, they close ranks with other policymakers and reduce the amount of blame they incur by diffusing responsibility among actors. This can involve, for instance, highlighting the role of domestic interest groups or the involvement of courts (König & Wenzelburger, 2014, p. 409), the consensus among policymakers (Weaver, 1986, p. 389), and joint interests and activities of the government and international actors. When successful, this approach limits the amount of blame governments incur by spreading it among several political actors.

An example of a circle the wagons approach can be found in the account of local health care retrenchment in Sweden by Fredriksson et al. (2019), who show that regional politicians diffused responsibility by including civil servants and clinic managers in their communication of cuts in local health care provisions. Moreover, during the Euro crisis, the Portuguese government blurred responsibility by highlighting that their fiscal consolidation policies corresponded to the requirements of EU conditionality (Moury & Standring, 2017).

Second, governments can refrain from diffusing responsibility and accept that a policy has harmful consequences. When they have to comply with EU conditionality, it is unreasonable to expect that governments, as blame avoiders, accept responsibility themselves. Governments should thus opt for *blame shifting*, a strategy that helps governments avoid blame by centring blame on others (Weaver, 1986, p. 386). Governments can shift blame to plausible targets, such as the preceding government or the EU and troika institutions, when they have to fulfil the requirements of EU conditionality. This strategy does not blur responsibility for a policy but keeps it centred and aims at changing the target. When successful, this approach helps governments evade blame by targeting another actor.

An example of a government employing a blame shifting approach is the Belgian government of Jean Luc Dehaene, which justified its social policy reform in 1993 by pointing to EU pressure for convergence (Wenzelburger, 2011, p. 1168). Similarly, Greek governments actively engaged in blame shifting to their predecessors and the troika institutions during the Financial Assistance Programmes for Greece (Sommer, 2020; Vasilopoulou et al., 2014).

Third, governments can refrain from manipulating the agency dimension and manipulate the harm dimension by denying the negative consequences of a policy. They accept responsibility for reforms introduced in compliance with EU conditionality, and their statements focus on their own actions rather than those of external actors. By employing a *self-defence* approach, governments portray a respective policy positively and reduce the risk of being blamed by arguing that blame is not justified in the first place (Hood, 2011, p. 50).[10] This blame avoidance strategy is closely linked to the concept of credit claiming and, when successful, offers

[10] I diverge in this categorisation from Hood (2011), who subsumes all approaches that deny harmful policies or events under the label 'problem denial'.

governments the opportunity to go beyond the avoidance of blame and claim credit instead (Hood, 2011, p. 53).

An example of a government employing a self-defence approach is the Danish Prime Minister, Helle Thorning-Schmidt, who announced a retrenchment of Danish early retirement benefits in 2011. The Prime Minister argued that the reduction would target two pressing problems: a rising public deficit and the unsustainability of the pension system in the face of demographic change, and defended the government's policy as economically responsible (Elmelund-Præstekær et al., 2015). Similarly, the incumbent Greek Panhellenic Socialist Movement (PASOK) highlighted the positive aspects of its policies during the Euro crisis (Roose et al., 2018; Sommer et al., 2016).

Fourth, governments can aim at diffusing responsibility and, at the same time, deny the negative consequences of the policy. Governments who employ a *problem denial* approach portray a policy introduced in compliance with EU conditionality in a positive light and diffuse responsibility for the measure among actors, similar to a circle the wagons approach. This approach helps a government avoid blame by framing a policy as a measure whose positive effects are recognised not solely by the government but by a broader coalition of actors. In this way, governments can invoke the perception that a measure is almost inevitable or without any tangible alternatives. When successful, this approach helps governments evade blame by showing that their policy choice is almost inevitable and without alternatives, as a broad coalition of actors sees it as the only solution for current problems.

An example of a government employing a problem denial strategy is the technocratic Italian government under Prime Minister Prodi, which in 1995 introduced a pension reform. The government framed the measure as a necessary step given Italy's deficit, which would Italy help fulfil conditions for Italy's accession to the European Monetary Union (EMU), a goal generally supported by the public (Bonoli, 2012; Dyson & Featherstone, 1996). Likewise, when introducing the pension reform under the implicit conditionality of the ECB (Sacchi, 2015), the Italian government of PM Monti engaged in a negative portrayal of the status quo and underlined consensual policymaking and the importance of national unity (König, 2016b).

In sum, under the spectre of EU conditionality, governments have at their disposal four strategies of blame avoidance, which focus on the harm and the agency dimension: circle the wagons, blame shifting, self-defence, and problem denial. The examples illustrating these strategies show that governments have employed all four strategies when introducing policies in compliance with EU prescriptions. In the next section, I develop the conditions which explain policymakers' focus on one strategy rather than the others.

2.4 Explaining Governments' Strategy Choice

I assume governments to be boundedly rational actors who are risk-averse and choose among alternatives the one that maximises their expected utility given the information they possess on the situation. Yet, they do not always make optimal choices due to their own cognitive limitations and the complexity of their environment (Jones, 1999; Simon, 1990). While governments have different preferences that can be subsumed under the labels of vote-seeking, office-seeking, and policy-seeking (Strom, 1990), I assume that their ultimate goal is to stay in office. To do so, governing parties require electoral support (Green-Pedersen, 2002, p. 31). This does not preclude governing parties from having specific policy goals. However, they must stay in office to make binding policy decisions. Moreover, if government policies do not gain citizens' support, these policies are likely to fail (Wenzelburger, 2011).[11]

As boundedly rational actors, governments chose from the blame avoidance toolkit the strategy that maximises their expected utility given the information they possess on the situation. This decision takes into account the contextual constraints highlighted in the previous sections. First, they must consider that budgetary constraints, the specificity of the conditions and the short timeframe under which conditional measures have to be introduced limit the availability of blame avoidance strategies. Second, as governments want their blame avoidance strategies to succeed, their claims need to resonate with broader audiences in the public. As pointed out in the previous section, blame avoidance efforts need to be plausible and reflect the policymaking context to be accepted in the public (Bisgaard, 2015; see also Kunda, 1990; McGraw et al., 1993, p. 292).

How, then, do governments decide on which presentational blame avoidance strategy they focus? The literature on blame avoidance so far falls short of providing convincing explanations for governments' choice of blame avoidance strategy under EU conditionality. One proposition in the literature on blame avoidance is that governments employ blame avoidance strategies sequentially, depending on their effectiveness and potential for blame avoidance and credit claiming (Hood et al., 2009). Following this reasoning, every government should follow the same order that starts with addressing the harm dimension before moving on to strategies that aim to manipulate the agency dimension when the former fail to work effectively. This approach cannot explain why governments follow different blame avoidance approaches. In contrast to this approach, I argue that just as governments consider their statements' plausibility and the constraints conditionality imposes on the use of agency and policy strategies, they do not freely choose among presentational strategies. Instead, they employ a calculus approach to evaluate the potential to manipulate the harm and agency dimensions.

---

[11] Hinterleitner and Sager (2017) point out that blame endangers governments' goals regardless of whether they are office-, vote-, or policy-seeking, or whether they aim at increasing their institutional power.

Second, structural constraints of the European multilevel system, such as the formal decision-making and implementing structures, impact the direction of individual responsibility judgements and public attributions and thus constrain the possibilities available to policymakers (Hobolt & Tilley, 2014; Rittberger et al., 2017). The features of the political system influence not solely the use of blame avoidance strategies in general but also the propensity towards different presentational strategies (Heinkelmann-Wild et al., 2020; König, 2016b). However, the policymaking structures are similar for all EU member states who came under EU conditionality in the financial and Euro crisis (Henning, 2017; Ioannidis, 2014; Lütz & Kranke, 2010; Pisani-Ferry et al., 2013; Sacchi, 2015), so they cannot account for differences in governments' choice of blame avoidance strategy.

Third, scholars have identified two characteristics of political systems and governments that constrain governments' choice of strategy. For one, the political ideology of governing parties impacts governments' blame-shifting activities (Green-Pedersen, 2002; Sommer, 2020). As voters associate certain politics with some parties rather than others, governing parties have different capabilities regarding blame avoidance. While left-wing parties can, for instance, plausibly justify that welfare retrenchment is necessary to remedy past policy failures and employ a 'Nixon goes to China logic', this approach is not feasible for right-wing parties, who will come under suspicion to follow hidden, ideological motives (Green-Pedersen, 2002; Ross, 2000). Furthermore, the system of party competition has been found to influence governments' blame avoidance opportunities. The availability of blame avoidance strategies depends on the strength of opposition that governing parties face. For instance, centre parties in pivot systems are less likely to face stiff opposition from either the left or the right, as neither side wants to be isolated and thus excluded from office in the long run (Green-Pedersen, 2002, pp. 37–38). While these factors can explain differences among political systems and governments, they are not suited to account for variances between different reform instances.

Nevertheless, the literature highlights two important constraints governments generally face in their decision-making processes: their reputation and the political conflict surrounding an issue. Building on these insights, I derive two factors that can account for policy-level variation in policymakers' aim at centring or blurring responsibility and whether they opt for acceptance or denial of harm emanating from a policy. When governments have to transpose measures required by EU conditionality, their choice of strategy depends on the context in which the policies are introduced, specifically the degree of politicisation of a policy, and on their past position, namely their reputation for policy support.

The Effect of Politicisation on Governments' Propensity for Blurring Responsibility

Governments must decide whether they blur responsibility among actors or keep it centred—either on themselves or other actors. Blurring responsibility among actors comes with certain advantages for governments. When the responsibility is dispersed among several actors, the government's blame risk is reduced in two ways. First, reducing the blame attributed to the government in this way should be less costly than entirely shifting blame to another actor. Second, when attempts at disputing the harm imposed by a policy fails, the government incurs less blame when responsibility is blurred. Beyond reducing the blame risk, responsibility blurring comes with an additional advantage. When governments disperse responsibility rather than shifting it entirely to another actor, they still retain the chance of (some) claiming credit later on, should the mood on the policy shift. Approaches that blur responsibility should thus be the preferred choice of risk-averse blame avoiders. Their viability varies, however. I argue that whether strategies that blur responsibility for a policy are available hinges on the degree of politicisation of the policy.

Competition over policies varies. While some policies are hardly discussed outside of elite circles and register little interest in the public, others enter public discourse and provoke heavy criticism and large-scale protests. In European integration studies, the processes of rendering a political issue contentious are denoted as politicisation. While the term is used in a variety of ways, there is a convergence towards three aspects of politicisation that describe an expansion of political conflict: when issues are politicised, their salience in the public increases (1), the scope of actors in the public debate expands (2), and issue positions are polarised (3) (De Wilde, 2011; De Wilde & Zürn, 2012; Green-Pedersen, 2012; Hutter & Grande, 2014). All three characteristics of politicisation impede the use of strategies that blur responsibility.

First, salience refers to the public interest in a policy. When an issue is high on the agenda of political parties and the public, it garners more attention from the respective actors and is thus more salient (Green-Pedersen, 2012, p. 117). When governments' policy decisions are high on the agenda of other parties, it likely witnesses an increase in blame. In their function as policymakers, governments are always prime blame targets and at risk of attack by blame makers (Hansson, 2018a, 2018b; Hinterleitner, 2020, p. 18). Opposition parties function as prominent blame makers in the national arena (Hinterleitner, 2020, p. 18). While unpopular policies, such as those required by EU conditionality, should always garner some criticism from opposition parties, these potential blame makers' activities vary as they have to decide on where to allocate their resources, such as media access or speaking time in Parliament (Hinterleitner & Sager, 2017, p. 597). Their decision to increase the salience of an issue and engage in blame games depends, among other things, on whether they expect issue engagement to be beneficial (Traber et al., 2020; Weaver,

2018).[12] Some policies thus become more salient than others. At times, blame makers target the government more fiercely so that the latter's risk of being involved in a public blame game or a blame 'firestorm' increases (Hinterleitner, 2020, p. 20; Hood et al., 2009). When an issue is high on blame makers' agenda and they decide to contest a policy and actively engage in a blame game or in 'attack politics', governments face higher blame pressure (Weaver, 2018). In these situations, when governments can expect to find themselves at the centre of blame attributions, pointing out shared responsibilities is neither a plausible nor a sufficient means to avoid blame. Therefore, they should enter the domestic blame game forcefully (Heinkelmann-Wild et al., 2020; Sommer, 2020)—either attempting to shift blame at another actor or accepting responsibility and reclaiming the policy as a success. Contrariwise, when an issue is comparatively low on potential blame makers' agenda, and they are reluctant to attack the government, the blame pressure the government experiences is lower, and it can more easily blur responsibility so that blame is dispersed among several actors.

Second, an expansion of actors in the public debate denotes the involvement of actors beyond political elites. In the European Integration literature, this often refers to involvement of political actors beyond political elites in executive and government functions, such as opposition parties, but also interest groups, social movements and the wider public (Hutter & Grande, 2014, p. 1004). I argue that an expansion to actors outside of Parliament furthers the dynamic that renders governments focal in blame games over salient policies described in the previous paragraph. When constituents rally against a policy, governments' blame risk increases. For instance, this occurs when important interest groups publicly oppose government policy or when public protests occur. As the number of actors that debate a policy increases, so does the number of potential blame makers who target the government for its policy choice. Consequently, governments should find themselves once more facing heavy blame pressure, so strategies that blur responsibility are not sufficient as a means of blame avoidance. Instead, the more debates over a policy remain limited to discussions among political party elites, and the fewer actors take part, the easier it should be for governments to evade blame by blurring responsibility.

Third, in a polarised political conflict, the actors involved put forward differing positions and, in the most extreme case, belong to opposing camps (De Wilde et al., 2016, p. 7; Hutter & Grande, 2014, p. 1004). The support of other political actors, such as interest groups and political parties, is important for governments as it favourably impacts policy formation processes (Armingeon & Baccaro, 2012, p. 268; Moravcsik, 1994, p. 61). Beyond policy formation, support for its policy can also impact the government's choice of blame avoidance strategy. De Wilde (2011) points out that a salient public debate among a large group of actors does not necessarily go hand in hand with discord. When a broad alliance of actors agrees on (large

[12] Blame makers thus face the decision of whether attributing blame to the government improves their own position, which, among other factors, depends on their own involvement in policymaking processes.

parts of) the government's policy, not only is policy formation a consensual process but highlighting broad support for its policy also makes it more plausible for governments to blur responsibility. This insight is supported by other scholarship that finds that a consensual style of politics is more amenable to blame dispersion than more conflictual politics (Green-Pedersen, 2002), that the formation of coalition governments can reduce the blame risk (Hering, 2008; Vis & Kersbergen, 2007), and that cross-partisan consensus can limit interparty attacks (Ross, 2000). When polarisation is low, governments are thus more likely to highlight consensus and shared responsibilities (König, 2016a). Instead, when polarisation is high and actors face each other from opposing camps, it is more difficult for governments to highlight shared responsibility for the policy formation process and disperse blame. Governments must expect actors from the opposing camp to enter into a blame game and highlight the government's responsibility for polarised issues. In these cases, governments face high blame pressure and strategies that blur responsibility are not sufficient to evade blame.

In sum, blurring responsibility has benefits that should make it the first choice for risk-averse governments. However, it is infeasible in situations of high politicisation. The more attention a policy garners, the more numerous the actors that raise the issue and the more polarised the debate, the less viable strategies that blur responsibility. In these situations of high politicisation, governments find themselves at the centre of public blame attributions and thus have few options to blur responsibility. They should thus opt for strategies that either attempt to shift blame at another actor or accept responsibility and attempt to reclaim the policy as a success. Instead, governments should be in a better position to blur responsibility when the policies they introduce show lower levels of politicisation.

The Effect of a Reputation for Policy Support on Governments' Acceptance of Harm

Governments decide whether to accept or deny the harmfulness of a policy they introduce under EU conditionality. The dominant position in the literature is that the manipulation of the harm component of a policy is preferable to manipulating the agency dimension. First, the denial of harmful consequences means that the issue of blame does not arise in the first place (Hood, 2011; Hood et al., 2009). Therefore, it should be the preferred route for risk-averse blame avoiders. Moreover, it allows not only the evasion of blame, but policymakers can even gain credit for policies (Elmelund-Præstekær & Emmenegger, 2013, p. 24; König, 2016a, p. 178). Consequently, all governments should dispute the harmful consequences of a policy in their communication before moving to strategies that manipulate the agency dimension (Hood et al., 2009).

I argue that governments are not free to decide how to communicate an unpopular policy. Instead, policymakers' need to remain plausible in their communication strategy means that the viability of disputing the harmfulness of a policy varies (Mayhew, 1974, pp. 52–61). Under pressure to comply with EU conditionality, governments' room for manoeuvre is limited. Just as they lack the time and means to put into place agency and policy strategies to avoid blame, they are not in a position to initiate a time-consuming reframing process to contest the perceived harmful consequences of a policy. Instead, governments have to build on their previous reputations.

Parties have reputations for owning certain issues, which the public regards them as being better able to handle than their opponents (Budge & Farlie, 1977; Budge et al., 1987; Petrocik, 1996). These reputations are established over time by a 'history of attention, initiative, and innovation towards these problems which leads voters to believe that one of the parties [...] is more sincere and committed to doing something about them' (Petrocik, 1996, p. 826). Issue reputation influences voters' decisions: they are more likely to vote in favour of the party they consider competent to solve salient policy problems. What is more, issue reputation also influences parties' legislative agendas once they are in office: governing parties use their time in office to focus on issues for which they have ownership (Egan, 2013; Green & Jennings, 2019; Green-Pedersen & Mortensen, 2010).

Just as issue reputation impacts governing parties' legislative behaviour, it also impacts their use of blame avoidance strategies. Indeed, scholars have linked the plausibility of policymakers' blame avoidance strategies to parties' public image. Ross (2000) argues that actors from left-leaning parties command more authority to reframe retrenchment than representatives of conservative or liberal parties because they are believed to be more credible and trustworthy regarding welfare policy (Ross, 2000, p. 174). Similarly, Green-Pedersen (2002) argues that left-wing parties' issue ownership for welfare state issues allows them to employ a credible justification strategy and argue for the necessity of reforms (Green-Pedersen, 2002, p. 36). Contrasting these insights, Sommer (2020) finds that left-wing governing parties have an increased propensity for blame shifting, as they are likely punished for acting against their traditional party position and cannot plausibly reframe reforms in a positive way as this would contradict traditional party positions (Sommer, 2020, p. 565).

I argue that beyond party ideology, governing parties' reputation for supporting specific policies shapes their choice of blame avoidance strategy. If governing parties have an issue reputation because they publically voiced support or even campaigned for policy reform in the past, this should facilitate reframing the policy in a positive light because it builds on previous framing efforts. The public regards them as committed to a specific issue, and their previous support for the policy lends plausibility to reframing efforts. Contrariwise, governing parties who have previously refrained from supporting policy reform or even opposed a policy should have a much harder time denying a measure's harmfulness. Highlighting positive effects would represent a complete reversal of their previous position. As issue reputations are slowly established over time (Petrocik, 1996, p. 827), they cannot be changed in the short term. EU conditionality requires the swift adoption of the required policies. Thus, governing parties who cannot build on previous reframing efforts should opt for strategies that accept the harmfulness of required reforms and seek to avoid blame by manipulating the agency dimension. In sum, governing parties' reputation for policy support shapes the viability of blame avoidance strategies that manipulate the perception of harm.

To summarise, the availability of presentational blame avoidance strategies at governments' disposal is limited. First, governments' ability to diffuse responsibility is constrained by the degree of politicisation of a policy: Governments should be in a better position to blur responsibility when the policies they introduce face low levels of politicisation than in situations of high politicisation. Second, governments' issue reputation constrains the viability of strategies that aim at manipulating the perception of harm: While governing parties' reputation for policy support facilitates reframing the policy in a positive light, those without a reputation for policy support should have a much harder time denying the harmfulness of a measure. Combining these two factors, which constrain governments' choice of blame avoidance strategy, yields clear expectations for when governments are most likely to focus their blame avoidance efforts on a specific approach. Table 2.2 summarises the theoretical framework.

- First, in cases of low politicisation—and thus low blame pressure—governments, who have no reputation for policy support, will not spend available resources on denying a policy's harmfulness. Instead, they will focus on avoiding blame by blurring responsibility and thus diffusing blame among several actors. In other words, they will predominantly opt for a *circle the wagons* approach rather than other blame avoidance strategies.
- Second, when governments face high politicisation and have no previous record of coming out in favour of a policy, they will not focus on denying the harmful consequences of a policy. As blurring responsibility is insufficient in the face of high blame pressure, they mainly focus on *blame shifting* to redirect blame to another actor, such as the previous government, the EU or the troika institutions.
- Third, in cases of high politicisation, governments with a reputation for supporting a policy that they are required to introduce under EU conditionality will concentrate their blame avoidance efforts on denying the harmfulness of the measures, but refrain from manipulating the agency dimension, so that responsibility remains centred on the government. In other words, they will adopt a *self-defence* approach more often than other blame avoidance strategies.
- Fourth, in cases of low politicisation, governments with a reputation for policy support can deny the harmfulness of a policy and blur responsibility for the measure. They will focus their blame avoidance efforts on a *problem denial* approach rather than other strategies.

In sum, this chapter showed that responsibility attributions are politically consequential, so policymakers have every incentive to influence contested attribution processes. In doing so, negativity bias makes them especially susceptible to responsibility being attributed to them for unpopular policies, thus making them primarily

Table 2.2 Explanatory framework for governments' choice of blame avoidance strategy

	Low politicisation	**High politicisation**
No reputation for policy support	Circle the wagons	Blame shifting
Reputation for policy support	Problem denial	Self-defence

blame avoiders. While governments can draw on an extensive toolbox comprising agency, policy, and presentational strategies, I showed that governments' choice of blame avoidance strategy is limited under the requirements of EU conditionality. Budgetary constraints, the specificity of the conditions and the short timeframe under which conditional measures have to be introduced constrain governments' strategy choices. They have at their disposal four strategies of presentational blame avoidance that influence the harm and the agency dimension of responsibility attributions: circle the wagons, blame shifting, self-defence, and problem denial.

As boundedly rational actors, governments choose among these four presentational strategies the one that maximises their expected utility given the information they possess on the situation at a time. This decision considers the contextual constraints regarding EU conditionality and the plausibility of their statements. The need to remain plausible means that the policymaking context constrains governments in their strategy choice. Specifically, their choice of blame avoidance strategy depends on the degree of politicisation and their reputation for policy support.

When politicisation is low, governments will predominantly focus on low-politicisation strategies that blur responsibility. When they have no record of previous support for the measure required by EU conditionality, they will focus on a circle the wagons approach. When they have a reputation for policy support, they will predominantly employ problem denial instead. Contrariwise, governments will primarily employ high-politicisation strategies that centre responsibility when politicisation is high. When they have no record of policy support, governments will predominantly engage in blame shifting, whereas they will focus on self-defence in those cases where they have a reputation for supporting a policy. To evaluate the fit of these conjectures, I will test this theoretical framework empirically in Chaps. 4–6. Beforehand, I lay out the research design in the next chapter.

References

Afonso, A., Zartaloudis, S., & Papadopoulos, Y. (2014). How party linkages shape austerity politics: Clientelism and fiscal adjustment in Greece and Portugal during the Eurozone crisis. *Journal of European Public Policy, 22*(3), 315–334.

Anderson, C. J. (2000). Economic voting and political context: A comparative perspective. *Electoral Studies, 19*(2–3), 151–170. https://doi.org/10.1016/S0261-3794(99)00045-1

Anderson, C. D. (2006). Economic voting and multilevel governance: A comparative individual-level analysis. *American Journal of Political Science, 50*(2), 449–463. https://doi.org/10.1111/j.1540-5907.2006.00194.x

Anderson, C. J., Mendes, S. M., & Tverdova, Y. V. (2004). Endogenous economic voting: Evidence from the 1997 British election. *Electoral Studies, 23*(4), 683–708. https://doi.org/10.1016/j.electstud.2003.10.001

Arceneaux, K. (2006). The Federal Face of voting: Are elected officials held accountable for the functions relevant to their office? *Political Psychology, 27*(5), 731–754. https://doi.org/10.1111/j.1467-9221.2006.00530.x

Armingeon, K., & Baccaro, L. (2012). Political economy of the sovereign debt crisis: The limits of internal devaluation. *Industrial Law Journal, 41*(3), 254–275.

Armingeon, K., & Giger, N. (2008). Conditional punishment: A comparative analysis of the electoral consequences of welfare state retrenchment in OECD nations, 1980-2003. *West European Politics, 31*(3), 558–580. https://doi.org/10.1080/01402380801939834

Atkeson, L. R., & Partin, R. W. (1995). Economic and referendum voting: A comparison of gubernatorial and senatorial elections. *American Political Science Review, 89*(1), 99–107.

Babb, S. L., & Carruthers, B. G. (2008). Conditionality: Forms, function, and history. *Annual Review of Law and Social Science, 4*(1), 13–29.

Birkland, T. A. (2010). *After disaster: Agenda setting, public policy, and focusing events*. American Governance and Public Policy. Georgetown University Press. http://search.ebscohost.com/login.aspx?direct=true&scope=site&db=nlebk&db=nlabk&AN=21644

Bisgaard, M. (2015). Bias will find a way: Economic perceptions, attributions of blame, and partisan-motivated reasoning during crisis. *The Journal of Politics, 77*(3), 849–860. https://doi.org/10.1086/681591

Boin, A., Hart, P., & McConnell, A. (2009). Crisis exploitation: Political and policy impacts of framing contests. *Journal of European Public Policy, 16*(1), 81–106. https://doi.org/10.1080/13501760802453221

Bonoli, G. (2012). Blame avoidance and cedit claiming revisited. In G. Bonoli & D. Natali (Eds.), *The politics of the new welfare state* (pp. 93–110). Oxford University Press.

Bovens, M., Hart, P., Dekker, S., & Verheuvel, G. (1999). The politics of blame avoidance: Defensive tactics in a Dutch crime-fighting fiasco. In H. K. Anheier (Ed.), *When things go wrong: Organizational failures and breakdowns* (pp. 123–148). Sage. https://doi.org/10.4135/9781452231457.n8

Brändström, A., & Kuipers, S. (2003). From 'normal incidents' to political crises: Understanding the selective politicization of policy failures. *Government and Opposition, 38*(3), 279–305. https://doi.org/10.1111/1477-7053.t01-1-00016

Budge, I., & Farlie, D. (1977). *Voting and party competition: A theoretical critique and synthesis applied to surveys from ten democracies* (1st ed.). Wiley.

Budge, I., Robertson, D., & Hearl, D. (1987). *Ideology, strategy and party change: Spatial analyses of post-war election programmes in 19 democracies*. Cambridge University Press.

Capelos, T., & Wurzer, J. (2009). United front: Blame management and scandal response tactics of the United Nations. *Journal of Contingencies and Crisis Management, 17*(2), 75–94. https://doi.org/10.1111/j.1468-5973.2009.00567.x

Copelovitch, M. S. (2010). *The International Monetary Fund in the global economy: Banks, bonds, and bailouts*. Cambridge University Press.

Cutler, F. (2004). Government responsibility and electoral accountability in federations. *Publius: The Journal of Federalism, 34*(2), 19–38. https://doi.org/10.1093/oxfordjournals.pubjof.a005028

Cutler, F. (2008). Whodunnit? Voters and responsibility in Canadian federalism. *Canadian Journal of Political Science, 41*(3), 627–654. https://doi.org/10.1017/S0008423908080761

Dahl, R. A. (1971). *Polyarchy: Participation and opposition*. Yale University Press.

de La Porte, C., & Heins, E. (2015). A new era of European integration? Governance of labour market and social policy since the sovereign debt crisis. *Comparative European Politics, 13*(1), 8–28.

De Vries, C. E., Edwards, E. E., & Tillman, E. R. (2011). Clarity of responsibility beyond the pocketbook: How political institutions condition EU issue voting. *Comparative Political Studies, 44*(3), 339–363. https://doi.org/10.1177/0010414010384373

De Wilde, P. (2011). No polity for old politics? A framework for analyzing the politicization of European integration. *Journal of European Integration, 33*(5), 559–575. https://doi.org/10.1080/07036337.2010.546849

De Wilde, P., & Zürn, M. (2012). Can the politicization of European integration be reversed? *Journal of Common Market Studies, 50*(S1), 137–153. https://doi.org/10.1111/j.1468-5965.2011.02232.x

De Wilde, P., Leupold, A., & Schmidtke, H. (2016). Introduction: The differentiated politicisation of European governance. *West European Politics, 39*(1), 3–22. https://doi.org/10.1080/01402382.2015.1081505

Dreher, A. (2009). IMF conditionality: Theory and evidence. *Public Choice, 141*(1–2), 233–267. https://doi.org/10.1007/s11127-009-9486-z

Dyson, K., & Featherstone, K. (1996). Italy and EMU as a 'Vincolo Esterno': Empowering the technocrats, transforming the state. *South European Society and Politics, 1*(2), 272–299.

Egan, P. J. (2013). *Partisan priorities: How issue ownership drives and distorts American politics*. Cambridge University Press. https://doi.org/10.1017/CBO9781107337138

Elmelund-Præstekær, C., & Emmenegger, P. (2013). Strategic re-framing as a vote winner: Why vote-seeking governments pursue unpopular reforms. *Scandinavian Political Studies, 36*(1), 23–42. https://doi.org/10.1111/j.1467-9477.2012.00295.x

Elmelund-Præstekær, C., Klitgaard, M. B., & Schumacher, G. (2015). What wins popular support? Communicating or obfuscating welfare state retrenchment. *European Political Science Review, 7*(3), 427–450. https://doi.org/10.1017/S1755773914000253

Featherstone, K. (2014). External conditionality and the debt crisis: The 'troika' and public administration reform in Greece. *Journal of European Public Policy, 22*(3), 295–314.

Fonseca, P., & Ferreira, M. J. (2015). Through 'seas never before sailed': Portuguese government discursive legitimation strategies in a context of financial crisis. *Discourse and Society, 26*(6), 682–711. https://doi.org/10.1177/0957926515592780

Fredriksson, M., Gustafsson, I.-B., & Winblad, U. (2019). Cuts without conflict: The use of political strategy in local health system retrenchment in Sweden. *Social Science & Medicine, 237*, 112464. https://doi.org/10.1016/j.socscimed.2019.112464

Gerhards, J., Offerhaus, A., & Roose, J. (2007). Die Öffentliche Zuschreibung von Verantwortung: Zur Entwicklung eines inhaltsanalytischen Instrumentariums. *Kölner Zeitschrift Für Soziologie Und Sozialpsychologie, 59*(105–124), 105.

Gerhards, J., Offerhaus, A., & Roose, J. (2009). Wer ist verantwortlich? Die Europäische Union, ihre Nationalstaaten und die massenmediale Attribution von Verantwortung für Erfolge und Misserfolge. In F. Marcinkowski & B. Pfetsch (Eds.), *Politik in der Mediendemokratie: [Politics in the media democracy]* (pp. 529–558). VS Verlag für Sozialwissenschaften. https://doi.org/10.1007/978-3-531-91728-3_22

Giger, N. (2010). Do voters punish the government for welfare state retrenchment? A comparative study of electoral costs associated with social policy. *Comparative European Politics, 8*(4), 415–443. https://doi.org/10.1057/cep.2009.4

Giger, N., & Nelson, M. (2011). The electoral consequences of welfare state retrenchment: Blame avoidance or credit claiming in the era of permanent austerity? *European Journal of Political Research, 50*(1), 1–23. https://doi.org/10.1111/j.1475-6765.2010.01922.x

Gomez, B. T., & Wilson, J. M. (2001). Political sophistication and economic voting in the American electorate: A theory of heterogeneous attribution. *American Journal of Political Science, 45*(4), 899. https://doi.org/10.2307/2669331

Green, J., & Jennings, W. (2019). Party reputations and policy priorities: How issue ownership shapes executive and legislative agendas. *British Journal of Political Science, 49*(2), 443–466. https://doi.org/10.1017/S0007123416000636

Green-Pedersen, C. (2002). *The politics of justification: Party competition and welfare-state retrenchment in Denmark and The Netherlands from 1982 to 1998. Changing Welfare States*. Amsterdam University Press. https://doi.org/10.2307/j.ctt46n1h4.

Green-Pedersen, C. (2012). A Giant fast asleep? Party incentives and the politicisation of European integration. *Political Studies, 60*(1), 115–130. https://doi.org/10.1111/j.1467-9248.2011.00895.x

Green-Pedersen, C., & Mortensen, P. B. (2010). Who sets the agenda and who responds to it in the Danish parliament? A new model of issue competition and agenda-setting. *European Journal of Political Research, 49*(2), 257–281. https://doi.org/10.1111/j.1475-6765.2009.01897.x

Greer, S. (2014). Structural adjustment comes to Europe: Lessons for the Eurozone from the conditionality debates. *Global Social Policy, 14*(1), 51–71.

Grimmer, J., Messing, S., & Westwood, S. J. (2012). How words and money cultivate a personal vote: The effect of legislator credit claiming on constituent credit allocation. *American Political Science Review, 106*(4), 703–719. https://doi.org/10.1017/S0003055412000457

Hansson, S. (2018a). Defensive semiotic strategies in government: A multimodal study of blame avoidance. *Social Semiotics, 28*(4), 472–493. https://doi.org/10.1080/10350330.2017.1334358

Hansson, S. (2018b). The discursive micro-politics of blame avoidance: Unpacking the language of government blame games. *Policy Sciences, 51*(4), 545–564. https://doi.org/10.1007/s11077-018-9335-3

Heinkelmann-Wild, T., & Zangl, B. (2020). Multilevel blame games: Blame-shifting in the European Union. *Governance, 33*(4), 953–969. https://doi.org/10.1111/gove.12459

Heinkelmann-Wild, T., Rittberger, B., & Zangl, B. (2018). The European blame game: Explaining public responsibility attributions in the European Union. In A. Kruck, K. Oppermann, & A. Spencer (Eds.), *Political mistakes and policy failures in international relations* (pp. 171–189). Palgrave Macmillan. https://doi.org/10.1007/978-3-319-68173-3_8

Heinkelmann-Wild, T., Kriegmair, L., & Rittberger, B. (2020). The EU multi-level system and the Europeanization of domestic blame games. *Politics and Governance, 8*(1), 85–94.

Henning, C. R. (2017). *Tangled governance: International regime complexity, the troika, and the euro crisis*. Oxford University Press.

Hering, M. (2008). Welfare state restructuring without grand coalitions: The role of informal cooperation in blame avoidance. *German Politics, 17*(2), 165–183. https://doi.org/10.1080/09644000802075757

Hinterleitner, M. (2017). Reconciling perspectives on blame avoidance behaviour. *Political Studies Review, 15*(2), 243–254.

Hinterleitner, M. (2019). Salami tactics and the implementation of large-scale public projects. *Journal of European Public Policy, 26*(11), 1696–1714.

Hinterleitner, M. (2020). *Policy controversies and political blame games. Cambridge Studies in Comparative Public Policy*. Cambridge University Press.

Hinterleitner, M., & Sager, F. (2015). Avoiding blame: A comprehensive framework and the Australian home insulation program fiasco. *Policy Studies Journal, 43*(1), 139–161.

Hinterleitner, M., & Sager, F. (2017). Anticipatory and reactive forms of blame avoidance: Of foxes and lions. *European Political Science Review, 9*(4), 587–606.

Hinterleitner, M., & Sager, F. (2020). Governing elites under pressure: Blame avoidance strategies and welfare state retrenchment. In R. Careja, P. Emmenegger, & N. Giger (Eds.), *The European social model under pressure: Liber Amicorum in honour of Klaus Armingeon* (1st ed., pp. 109–122). Springer Fachmedien Wiesbaden.

Hobolt, S. B., & Klemmensen, R. (2008). Government responsiveness and political competition in comparative perspective. *Comparative Political Studies, 41*(3), 309–337.

Hobolt, S. B., & Tilley, J. (2014). *Blaming Europe? Responsibility without accountability in the European Union* (1st ed.). Oxford University Press.

Hobolt, S. B., Tilley, J., & Banducci, S. A. (2013). Clarity of responsibility: How government cohesion conditions performance voting. *European Journal of Political Research, 52*(2), 164–187.

Hood, C. (2011). *The blame game: Spin, bureaucracy, and self-preservation in government*. Princeton University Press.

Hood, C., Jennings, W., Dixon, R., Hogwood, B., & Beeston, C. (2009). Testing times: Exploring staged responses and the impact of blame management strategies in two examination fiasco cases. *European Journal of Political Research, 48*(6), 695–722.

Hutter, S., & Grande, E. (2014). Politicizing Europe in the National Electoral Arena: A comparative analysis of five west European countries, 1970-2010. *Journal of Common Market Studies, 52*(5), 1002–1018.

Ioannidis, M. (2014). EU financial assistance conditionality after 'Two Pack'. *Zeitschrift Für Ausländisches Öffentliches Recht Und Völkerrecht, 74*, 61–104.

Iyengar, S. (1989). How citizens think about national issues: A matter of responsibility. *American Journal of Political Science, 33*(4), 878–900.

Iyengar, S. (1994). *Is anyone responsible? How television frames political issues*. American Politics and Political Economy Series. University of Chicago Press.

Jones, B. D. (1999). Bounded rationality. *Annual Review of Political Science, 2*(1), 297–321. https://doi.org/10.1146/annurev.polisci.2.1.297

Kahneman, D., & Tversky, A. (1979). Prospect theory: An analysis of decision under risk. *Econometrica, 47*(2), 263–292.

Klüver, H., & Sagarzazu, I. (2016). Setting the agenda or responding to voters? Political parties, voters and issue attention. *West European Politics, 39*(2), 380–398.

König, P. (2016a). Communicating austerity measures during times of crisis: A comparative empirical analysis of four heads of government. *The British Journal of Politics and International Relations, 18*(3), 538–558.

König, P. (2016b). Unpopular policies and the imperative of justification: Putting the Monti Government's reform communication in a comparative perspective. *Journal of Comparative Policy Analysis: Research and Practice, 18*(2), 176–194.

König, P., & Siewert, M. B. (2020). Why don't citizens give governments credit when they deliver on electoral pledges? *Policy & Politics, 48*(3), 503–519.

König, P., & Wenzelburger, G. (2014). Toward a theory of political strategy in policy analysis. *Politics & Policy, 42*(3), 400–430. https://doi.org/10.1111/polp.12076

Kumlin, S. (2011). Claiming blame and giving credit? Unintended effects of how government and opposition frame the Europeanization of welfare. *European Union Politics, 12*(4), 575–595. https://doi.org/10.1177/1465116511417296

Kunda, Z. (1990). The case for motivated reasoning. *Psychological Bulletin, 108*(3), 480–498.

Laffan, B. (2014). Testing times: The growing primacy of responsibility in the euro area. *West European Politics, 37*(2), 270–287.

Lefkofridi, Z., & Nezi, R. (2020). Responsibility versus responsiveness… to whom? A theory of party behavior. *Party Politics, 26*(3), 334–346.

León, S. (2011). Who is responsible for what? Clarity of responsibilities in multilevel states: The case of Spain. *European Journal of Political Research, 50*(1), 80–109.

León, S. (2012). How do citizens attribute responsibility in multilevel states? Learning, biases and asymmetric federalism. Evidence from Spain. *Electoral Studies, 31*(1), 120–130.

León, S., Jurado, I., & Garmendia Madariaga, A. (2018). Passing the buck? Responsibility attribution and cognitive bias in multilevel democracies. *West European Politics, 41*(3), 660–682.

Leong, C., & Howlett, M. (2017). On credit and blame: Disentangling the motivations of public policy decision-making behaviour. *Policy Sciences, 50*(4), 599–618.

Levy, J. (1999). Vice into virtue? Progressive politics and welfare reform in continental Europe. *Politics and Society, 27*, 239–273.

Lodge, M., & Taber, C. S. (2013). *The rationalizing voter. Cambridge Studies in Public Opinion and Political Psychology*. Cambridge University Press.

Lütz, S., & Kranke, M. (2010). *The European Rescue of the Washington Consensus?* EU and IMF lending to central and eastern European countries (LEQS Paper 22/2010). London School of Economics and Political Science.

Lütz, S., & Kranke, M. (2013). The European Rescue of the Washington Consensus? EU and IMF lending to central and eastern European countries. *Review of International Political Economy, 21*(2), 310–338.

Mair, P. (2009). *Representative versus responsible government*. MPIfG working paper (09/8).

Malhotra, N., & Kuo, A. G. (2008). Attributing blame: The public's response to hurricane Katrina. *The Journal of Politics, 70*(1), 120–135.

Mayhew, D. R. (1974). *Congress: The electoral connection*. Yale University Press.

McGraw, K. M. (1991). Managing blame: An experimental test of the effects of political accounts. *American Political Science Review, 85*(4), 1133–1157.

McGraw, K. M., Timpone, R., & Bruck, G. (1993). Justifying controversial political decisions: Home style in the laboratory. *Political Behavior, 15*(3), 289–308.

Moravcsik, A. (1994). *Why the European Union strengthens the state: Domestic politics and international cooperation*. CES Working Paper(52). Harvard University.

Moreira, A., Alonso Domínguez, Á., Antunes, C., Karamessini, M., Raitano, M., & Glatzer, M. (2015). Austerity-driven labour market reforms in southern Europe: Eroding the security of labour market insiders. *European Journal of Social Security, 17*(2), 202–226.

Mortensen, P. B. (2012). "It's the central government's fault": Elected regional Officials' use of blame-shifting rhetoric. *Governance, 25*(3), 439–461.

Moury, C., & Standring, A. (2017). 'Going beyond the troika': Power and discourse in Portuguese austerity politics. *European Journal of Political Research, 56*(3), 660–679.

Peffley, M. (1984). The voter as juror: Attributing responsibility for economic conditions. *Political Behavior, 6*(3), 275–294.

Petmesidou, M., & Glatzer, M. (2015). The crisis imperative, reform dynamics and rescaling in Greece and Portugal. *European Journal of Social Security, 17*(2), 158–182.

Petrocik, J. R. (1996). Issue ownership in presidential elections, with a 1980 case study. *American Journal of Political Science, 40*(3), 825–850.

Pierson, P. (1996). The new politics of the welfare state. *World Politics, 48*(2), 143–179.

Pisani-Ferry, J., Sapir, A., & Wolff, G. B. (2013). *EU-IMF assistance to euro-area countries: An Early Assessment* (Bruegel Blueprint).

Powell, G. B. (2000). *Elections as instruments of democracy: Majoritarian and proportional visions*. Yale University Press.

Powell, G. B., & Whitten, G. D. (1993). A cross-national analysis of economic voting: Taking account of the political context. *American Journal of Political Science, 37*(2), 391–414. https://doi.org/10.2307/2111378

Ringe, N. (2005). Policy preference formation in legislative politics. *American Journal of Political Science, 49*(4), 731–745.

Rittberger, B., Schwarzenbeck, H., & Zangl, B. (2017). Where does the Buck stop? Explaining public responsibility attributions in complex international institutions. *Journal of Common Market Studies, 55*(4), 909–924.

Roose, J., Sommer, M., & Scholl, F. (2018). Verantwortungszuschreibungen in der Eurozonen-Krise. In J. Roose, M. Sommer, & F. Scholl (Eds.), *Bürgergesellschaft und Demokratie. Europas Zivilgesellschaft in der Wirtschafts- und Finanzkrise: Protest, Resilienz und Kämpfe um Deutungshoheit* (Vol. 10, pp. 43–73). Springer VS.

Ross, F. (2000). Framing welfare reform in affluent societies: Rendering restructuring more palatable? *Journal of Public Policy, 20*(2), 169–193.

Rozin, P., & Royzman, E. B. (2001). Negativity bias, negativity dominance, and contagion. *Personality and Social Psychology Review, 5*(4), 296–320.

Rudolph, T. J. (2003a). Institutional context and the assignment of political responsibility. *The Journal of Politics, 65*(1), 190–215.

Rudolph, T. J. (2003b). Who's responsible for the economy? The formation and consequences of responsibility attributions. *American Journal of Political Science, 47*(4), 698–713.

Rudolph, T. J. (2006). Triangulating political responsibility: The motivated formation of responsibility judgments. *Political Psychology, 27*(1), 99–122. https://doi.org/10.1111/j.1467-9221.2006.00451.x

Sacchi, S. (2015). Conditionality by other means: EU involvement in Italy's structural reforms in the sovereign debt crisis. *Comparative European Politics, 13*(1), 77–92.

Schimmelfennig, F. (2020). Politicisation management in the European Union. *Journal of European Public Policy, 27*(3), 342–361. https://doi.org/10.1080/13501763.2020.1712458

Schimmelfennig, F., & Sedelmeier, U. (Eds.). (2005). *Cornell paperbacks. The Europeanization of Central and Eastern Europe*. Cornell University Press.

Schneider, C. J. (2020). Public commitments as signals of responsiveness in the European Union. *The Journal of Politics, 82*(1), 329–344.

Schumacher, G., Vis, B., & van Kersbergen, K. (2013). Political parties' welfare image, electoral punishment and welfare state retrenchment. *Comparative European Politics, 11*(1), 1–21.

Simon, H. A. (1990). Bounded rationality. In J. Eatwell, M. Milgate, & P. Newman (Eds.), *The new Palgrave. Utility and probability* (pp. 15–18). Palgrave Macmillan UK.

Smith, K. E. (2003). The evolution and application of EU membership conditionality. In M. Cremona (Ed.), *Collected courses of the Academy of European Law: Vol. 12. The enlargement of the European Union* (pp. 105–140). Oxford University Press.

Sommer, M. (2020). Blame-shifting in times of permanent austerity: Evidence from Spain and Greece in the Eurozone crisis. *Journal of Common Market Studies, 58*(3), 562–579. https://doi.org/10.1111/jcms.12926

Sommer, M., Roose, J., Scholl, F., & Papanikolopoulos, D. (2016). The Eurozone crisis and party conflicts in Greece and Germany: Discursive struggles about responsibility. In T. Krieger, B. Neumärker, & D. Panke (Eds.), *Schriftenreihe des Arbeitskreises Europäische integration e.V: Vol. 88, Europe's crisis: The conflict-theoretic perspective* (1. Aufl., pp. 87–112). Nomos. https://doi.org/10.5771/9783845262482-87

Steinwand, M. C., & Stone, R. W. (2008). The International Monetary Fund: A review of the recent evidence. *The Review of International Organizations, 3*(2), 123–149.

Stokke, O. (Ed.). (1995). *Norwegian foreign policy studies: Vol. 82. Aid and political conditionality*. Frank Cass.

Strom, K. (1990). A behavioral theory of competitive political parties. *American Journal of Political Science, 34*(2), 565. https://doi.org/10.2307/2111461

Sulitzeanu-Kenan, R., & Hood, C. (2005). *Blame avoidance with adjectives? Motivation, opportunity, activity and outcome* [Paper for the ECPR joint sessions, blame avoidance and blame management workshop, 14th–20th April 2005, Granada].

Taber, C. S., & Lodge, M. (2006). Motivated skepticism in the evaluation of political beliefs. *American Journal of Political Science, 50*(3), 755–769.

Tavits, M. (2007). Clarity of responsibility and corruption. *American Journal of Political Science, 51*(1), 218–229. https://doi.org/10.1111/j.1540-5907.2007.00246.x

Theodoropoulou, S. (2015). National social and labour market policy reforms in the shadow of EU bail-out conditionality: The cases of Greece and Portugal. *Comparative European Politics, 13*(1), 29–55.

Thompson, D. F. (1980). Moral responsibility of public officials: The problem of many hands. *The American Political Science Review, 74*(4), 905–916. https://doi.org/10.2307/1954312

Traber, D., Schoonvelde, M., & Schumacher, G. (2020). Errors have been made, others will be blamed: Issue engagement and blame shifting in prime minister speeches during the economic crisis in Europe. *European Journal of Political Research, 59*(1), 45–67.

Tversky, A., & Kahneman, D. (1986). Rational choice and the framing of decisions. *The Journal of Business, 59*(4), 251–278.

Vasilopoulou, S., Halikiopoulou, D., & Exadaktylos, T. (2014). Greece in crisis: Austerity, populism and the politics of blame. *Journal of Common Market Studies, 52*(2), 388–402. https://doi.org/10.1111/jcms.12093

Vis, B. (2016). Taking stock of the comparative literature on the role of blame avoidance strategies in social policy reform. *Journal of Comparative Policy Analysis: Research and Practice, 18*(2), 122–137. https://doi.org/10.1080/13876988.2015.1005955

Vis, B., & van Kersbergen, K. (2007). Why and how do political actors pursue risky reforms? *Journal of Theoretical Politics, 19*(2), 153–172. https://doi.org/10.1177/0951629807074268

Weaver, R. K. (1986). The politics of blame avoidance. *Journal of Public Policy, 6*(4), 371–398.

Weaver, R. K. (2018). The nays have it: How rampant blame generating distorts American policy and politics. *Political Science Quarterly, 133*(2), 259–289. https://doi.org/10.1002/polq.12771

Wenzelburger, G. (2011). Political strategies and fiscal retrenchment: Evidence from four countries. *West European Politics, 34*(6), 1151–1184. https://doi.org/10.1080/01402382.2011.572385

Wlezien, C., Franklin, M., & Twiggs, D. (1997). Economic perceptions and vote choice: Disentangling the endogeneity. *Political Behavior, 19*(1), 7–17. https://doi.org/10.1023/A:1024841605168

Chapter 3
Research Design

This chapter presents the research strategy and research design, which I employ to evaluate the theoretical framework developed in Chap. 2 in the subsequent chapters. My approach is best summarised as an x-centred co-variation analysis of four most similar case comparisons that I complement with in-case evidence. In each case, I analyse governments' blame avoidance strategies by conducting a qualitative content analysis of Parliamentary debates.

In the first section, I present in detail the co-variation analysis, which analyses four pairwise comparisons of most similar cases, that exhibit clear variation in the independent variables. My two-pronged approach combines detailed accounts of each case, which ascertain the presence of the respective values of the independent variables and the expected patterns of blame avoidance strategies with the comparison of cases in four pairwise comparisons, which help establish that the presence or absence of each independent variable indeed has the hypothesised effect by controlling for alternative variables. I introduce the universe of cases, which focuses on instances of EU conditionality in the context of the financial and Euro crisis, and explain my strategy for selecting suitable cases for the analysis. I focus on five instances of policies introduced in Ireland and Portugal while these countries were subject to Economic Adjustment Programmes—the reform of the wage setting system, the introduction of a property tax and the reform of the water supply system in Ireland, and the reforms of regulated professions and the labour market in Portugal. The universe of cases and the case selection contribute to the internal validity of the inferences, which can be drawn from the empirical analysis.

In the second part of this chapter, I then provide a detailed account of the measurement of the two independent variables, the politicisation of the analysed policy and governing parties' reputation for policy support. I argue that the level of politicisation depends on whether government policies come under pressure both in- and outside Parliament. Moreover, governing parties' reputation for policy support

L. Kriegmair, *Responsiveness and Responsibility in the Euro Crisis*, Contributions to Political Science, https://doi.org/10.1007/978-3-031-84473-7_3

hinges on prior records of attempting to introduce similar measures or campaigning in favour of the respective measures and on the content of coalition agreements. While the proposed operationalisation admittedly falls short of defining absolute cut-off points for the values of the variables, the benefit of the setup of four most similar pairwise comparisons is that the value of the independent variable in each case is not solely determined on the basis of in-case evidence, but also made plausible relative to the compared case.

The third and final section concerns the measurement of the dependent variable, governments' blame avoidance strategies. I use Parliamentary debates to conduct a qualitative content analysis of statements made by government representatives on the policies of interest in each case, as these debates are the best place to observe governments' communication strategies on a vast number of policies. My coding rules build on existing coding schemes for analysing of responsibility attributions and extend them by differentiating between different evaluations of the attribution object and different properties of the attribution target. Using this coding scheme, I identify 663 blame avoidance statements in 273 Parliamentary debates in the five cases.

3.1 Method and Case Selection

The aim of this dissertation is to explain under what conditions governments choose a specific blame avoidance strategy over others. In Chap. 2, I proposed that governments' choice of strategy depends on the degree of politicisation of a policy and the governing parties' reputation for policy support. The empirical analysis must thus evaluate whether x-centred variation leads to the expected variation in the outcome (Blatter & Haverland, 2012, p. 36; Mahoney & Goertz, 2006, p. 230). This research goal is best achieved in a co-variation analysis. Unlike causal process tracing approaches, which aim to establish the existence of a causal mechanism between condition and outcome (Beach & Pedersen, 2016, p. 304), this approach refrains from showing empirically that a causal pathway is present in a case (Blatter & Haverland, 2012, p. 52). Instead, it builds on the comparison between similar cases that vary in the value of the independent variable to establish 'whether a certain factor has an effect' (Blatter & Haverland, 2012, p. 33). This approach fits well with the theoretical argument developed in Chap. 2.

To analyse the effect of the independent variables, I conduct four pairwise comparisons. In each case, I follow a two-pronged approach, whereby the respective values of the independent variables and the expected value of the dependent variable are first established in each case before I verify that varying the value of the independent variables indeed leads to the expected differences in governments' blame avoidance strategies. For this purpose, I select five cases of policies introduced in countries subject to Economic Adjustment Programmes in the Euro crisis. The restricted universe of cases and the case selection contribute to the internal validity of the inferences, which can be drawn from the empirical analysis.

Co-variation Analysis and Pairwise Comparisons

The co-variational approach aims to approximate the conditions of an experiment, whereby researchers estimate the effect of an explanatory factor by controlling for alternative factors that impact the outcome. While experimental control is impossible to achieve when working with case studies, the careful selection of cases according to a most similar system design allows for drawing inferences based on co-variation of the independent and the dependent variable (Blatter & Haverland, 2012, pp. 37–42). This approach assumes a deterministic relationship between the independent and the dependent variable (Blatter & Haverland, 2012, pp. 39–40). This assumption is consistent with the hypotheses I formulated in Chap. 2. While I do not argue that governments will commit to one strategy of blame avoidance entirely, I expect a clear pattern that consistently shows their preference for one strategy over the rest. This pattern should be observable in each case study and depend on the variation in the two theorised independent variables.

The empirical analysis follows a two-pronged approach. In the first step, the intensive analysis of each case helps to ascertain that the case indeed exhibits a specific combination of the independent variables (Blatter & Haverland, 2012, pp. 63–64). Furthermore, these case studies establish that the expected pattern of blame avoidance strategies was present in each case. Specifically, the disaggregation of blame avoidance strategies by year and a closer look at the content of blame avoidance statements increase the confidence in the stability of the results. These case studies thus establish a link between a combination of different values of the independent variables and a specific pattern of blame avoidance strategies in each case. In a second step, I then compare the results across cases to show that changes in the value of the independent variables indeed occur in concert with the expected changes in the patterns of blame avoidance strategies in a series of pairwise comparisons. The comparison across cases in a most similar systems design attempts to isolate the effect of the independent variable on the outcome.

Selecting cases in line with a most similar systems design requires the comparison of cases that, first, exhibit variation on the value of the independent variable and, second, are as similar as possible concerning other control variables (Przeworski & Teune, 1970, pp. 32–34; Seawright & Gerring, 2008, p. 304). This setup allows the researcher to draw causal inferences based on Mill's method of difference, whereby similarities cannot explain differences in the outcome, but only differences can do so (Beach & Pedersen, 2016, p. 237; Blatter & Haverland, 2012, pp. 42–43). This approach assumes that independent variables 'have an autonomous causal power' (Blatter & Haverland, 2012, p. 41) and can thus not test whether the combination of factors leads to a specific outcome (Beach & Pedersen, 2016, p. 240). Therefore, I test the theoretical framework developed in Chap. 2 in case pairs that differ in the value of one independent variable while holding the other constant.

This setup yields four pairwise comparisons, which, together, evaluate the explanatory value of the theoretical framework. Specifically, I asses:

- The impact of variation in politicisation in cases of governing parties' low reputation for policy support (I).
- The impact of variation in politicisation in cases of governing parties' high reputation for policy support (II).
- The impact of variation in governing parties' reputation for policy support in cases of low politicisation (III).
- The impact of variation in governing parties' reputation for policy support in cases of high politicisation (IV).

Case Selection

The four pairwise comparisons exploit spatial variations between countries, which entered Economic Assistance Programmes with the EU and the IMF after the financial crisis, and differences between the policies introduced in these countries in compliance with EU conditionality. Specifically, I selected five cases that lend themselves to comparison in a most similar system design. Figure 3.1 depicts the cases and how they help me assess the impact of each independent variable.

- First, by comparing the reform of the wage setting system and the introduction of a property tax in Ireland, I assess the impact of variation in politicisation in cases of governing parties' low reputation for policy support (I).
- Second, in the comparison of reforms of regulated professions and the labour market in Portugal, I analyse the impact of variation in politicisation in cases of governing parties' high reputation for policy support (II).
- Third, in a comparison of reforms of regulated professions in Portugal and the reform of the wage setting system in Ireland, I evaluate the impact of variation in governing parties' reputation for policy support in cases of low politicisation (III).
- Fourth, by comparing the introduction of a property tax with the reform of the water supply system in Ireland, I assess the impact of variation in governing parties' reputation for policy support in cases of high politicisation (IV).

The case selection summarised in Fig. 3.1 requires two steps of justification—on the choice of countries and the choice of policies (see Green-Pedersen, 2002 for a similar approach). The universe of cases this dissertation focuses on are instances of reforms introduced under formal or informal EU conditionality during the financial and Euro crisis.[1] Since 2008, the EU has provided financial assistance linked to conditionality to seven of its member states: Hungary, Romania, Latvia, Greece, Ireland, Portugal, and Cyprus. In addition, Spain and Italy had to introduce severe austerity measures and reforms to avoid entering a full-fledged Programme with the EU. As their remaining outside of such conditional lending arrangements was dependent on support from the EU, specifically on bond purchases through the

[1] This excludes, for instance, instances of accession conditionality, which the EU used in the context of the accession of Central and Eastern European countries (CEECs), see, for instance, Schimmelfennig and Sedelmeier (2005). It also precludes instances of IMF lending conditionality, see, for instance, Dreher (2009)

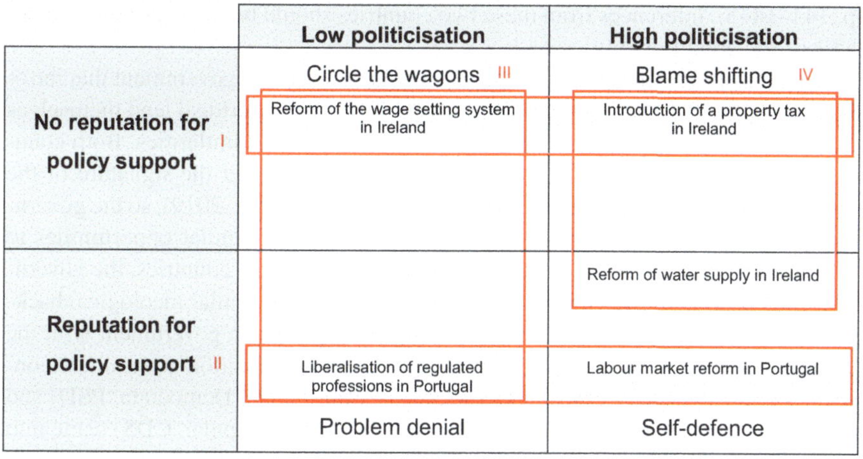

Fig. 3.1 Case selection for four pairwise comparisons

ECB, EU institutions and the IMF had considerable influence on national reform trajectories through informal conditionality that went beyond the formal influence through EU procedures around the EMU (Cioffi & Dubin, 2016; Henning, 2017; Pavolini et al., 2015; Sacchi, 2015).

These cases share important contextual similarities,[2] as they all occur in the period after the onset of the financial crisis in 2007. Moreover, the procedures and the content of EU conditionality exhibit similarities. First, the EU institutions, the Commission and the European Central Bank (ECB) worked with the IMF to provide financial assistance linked to conditionality. The European Commission and the IMF undertook similar monitoring tasks in all cases of EU conditionality (Greer, 2014; Henning, 2017; Pisani-Ferry et al., 2013). Second, in all cases, the outlined conditionality followed a similar neoliberal logic and went beyond the *acquis communautaire* in that they included specific requirements for budgetary cuts as well as long-term structural reform requirements, such as reforms of employment regulation, the organisation of the public administration, or the service sector and professional regulations (Greer, 2014; La Porte & Heins, 2015; Lütz & Kranke, 2013; Sacchi, 2015; Theodoropoulou, 2015).

Drawing on this universe of cases, I focus on two Programme countries—Ireland and Portugal. Both the Irish and the Portuguese government were committed to the Programme, exhibited medium to good compliance records and exited their respective financial assistance programmes on time and without precautionary credit lines (Henning, 2017, p. 126; Lütz et al., 2019, p. 1445; Pisani-Ferry et al., 2013, 85–98; Sapir et al., 2014, 35–43). Thus, whereas Greece, for instance, is often considered an outlier in terms of programme compliance and success (Lütz et al., 2019,

[2] For an overview of similarities between the cases, see Table A1 in the Appendix.

pp. 144–1445), inferences from these two countries should be generalisable to other cases of EU conditionality.

While most of my pairwise comparisons hold constant the government that introduced reforms, as I will show in the next step, Ireland and Portugal lend themselves to cross-country comparison as they share some additional similarities. Both countries experienced elections and a change in government after the signature of the Economic Assistance Programme (Dukelow, 2015; Lütz et al., 2019), so the governments tasked with the transposition of conditionality had similar opportunities to shift responsibility to their predecessor. Furthermore, in both countries, the governments responsible for transposing EU conditionality had a similar ideological background. While the conservative Fine Gael formed a coalition government with the Labour Party in Ireland after elections in March 2011, a coalition government consisting of the conservative Social Democrats (Partido Social Democrata, PSD) and the Popular Party (Centro Democrático e Social—Partido Popular, CDS) came into office in Portugal after elections in June 2011. Therefore, at least the larger coalition partners in both countries are located right to the centre of the political spectrum (Dukelow, 2015; Lütz et al., 2019).

Second, I select instances of policies introduced to comply with EU conditionality from these two countries that vary concerning the two independent variables, policy politicisation and governing parties' reputation for policy support, while displaying similarities in other dimensions (Blatter & Haverland, 2012, p. 42; Seawright & Gerring, 2008, p. 304). As I will describe in detail in Chaps. 4 and 5, the reforms of the wage setting system and the water supply system and the introduction of the local property tax in Ireland, as well as the labour market reforms and the liberalisation of regulated professions in Portugal were measures introduced by the respective governments to comply with EU conditionality. Furthermore, these measures come with a blame risk for governments, as they all imply losses of rights or material resources for significant constituencies. In this way, these policies meet the scope conditions of the theoretical framework.

The cases exhibit additional similarities. They all belong to the realm of structural conditionality and follow the neoliberal logic of limiting government expenditure and strengthening competition exemplified in the Washington consensus (Bini Smaghi, 2015; Greer, 2014). Structural reforms play a central role in adjustment efforts in the EMU, where monetary adjustment is impossible due to the single currency, and fiscal adjustment comes with the risk of high multiplier effects. Furthermore, structural reforms are especially intrusive as they aim at changing national legislation (Babb & Carruthers, 2008) and thus have long-term effects that persist after the end of the Programmes. Finally, Fig. 3.1 shows that the cases I selected for each of the four pairwise comparisons vary with regard to one of the independent variables. In the subsequent chapters, I will portray each of the cases in detail with regard to the value of the independent variables.

In sum, the two-step selection procedure for the four pairwise comparisons allows me to select for each comparison cases that are similar in many dimensions and exhibit clear variation in the independent variables. While the confirmatory power of comparisons based on the logic of differences is often considered limited due to the complexity of cases (Beach & Pedersen, 2016, pp. 239–240), three factors support the internal validity of this research design.

First, as case-specific knowledge of the cases reduces false inferences, the subsequent chapters provide detailed accounts of each case. These determine whether a combination of specific values of the independent variables and the expected pattern of blame avoidance strategies was indeed present in each case.

Second, the analyses of four pairwise comparisons help ascertain that the presence or absence of each independent variable has the hypothesised effect by controlling for alternative variables that may influence governments' choice of blame avoidance strategy.

Third, limiting the universe of cases temporarily and spatially allows me to limit the number of variables I have to control. While this undoubtedly limits the potential for generalisation (Blatter & Haverland, 2012, p. 74; Meur & Berg-Schlosser, 1994, pp. 195–196), it strengthens the internal validity of the research design. This focus on internal validity is adequate because this project builds a novel framework to account for governments' varying choice of blame avoidance strategy. The following subsections of this chapter provide detailed information on the measurement of the independent and dependent variables.

3.2 Measuring Politicisation and Issue Reputation

The analysis of pairwise comparisons according to a most similar system design requires, in the next step, a clear operationalisation of the independent variables on which cases are selected. Blatter and Haverland highlight the necessity to define clear thresholds to decide whether a case exhibits the 'correct' values of the independent variable (Blatter & Haverland, 2012, p. 66). I argue that the level of politicisation depends on whether government policies face outright rejection both in- and outside Parliament. Moreover, governing parties' reputation for policy support hinges on prior records of attempting to introduce similar measures or campaigning in favour of the respective measures and on coalition agreements.

Politicisation

In Chap. 2, I argued that while governments prefer blame avoidance strategies that blur responsibility, these are not always available to governments. The viability depends on the degree of politicisation of a policy. Policies are politicised when (1) their salience in the public increases, (2) the scope of involved actors expands, and (3) issue positions are polarised (De Wilde, 2011; De Wilde et al., 2016; De Wilde & Zürn, 2012; Green-Pedersen, 2012; Hutter & Grande, 2014). The more attention a policy garners, the more numerous the actors that raise the issue and the more polarised the debate, the less viable strategies that blur responsibility. How is the degree of politicisation best measured for each policy?

When it comes to policies introduced under EU conditionality, I argue that the degree of politicisation is best captured by focusing on the scope of actors and issue polarisation. While policies may exhibit varying degrees of salience, it is hard to define a threshold. As I pointed out in the previous chapter, all policies required by the troika institutions have garnered at least some public attention. The public was well informed about the content of the conditionality, and measures attracted attention as their implementation is regularly monitored by the troika institutions (Greer, 2014; Henning, 2017; Sacchi, 2015). In the following, I will thus focus on differences between policies concerning the scope of actors involved in public debates about the policies and the polarisation of issue positions.

First, some policies mobilise a larger number of actors in- and outside Parliament to engage in public debates than others. Opposition parties function as prominent blame makers in the national arena (Hinterleitner, 2020, p. 18) so their engagement with the government's policy can be considered an important hurdle for an issue to be politicised. If all or most parties in a political system remain silent on the issue, the policy is unlikely to be politicised. Opposition in Parliament is, however, not sufficient. Governments' policies need to mobilise actors outside Parliament for a policy to become politicised. This occurs, for instance, when important interest groups and social movements publicly engage with government policy or when public protests take place. If a policy does not mobilise political actors outside Parliament to engage with the policy, it is not considered politicised.

Second, some policies may attract more intensive conflict than others. Some policies face fundamental criticism from an opposing camp. When political actors outright reject the government's policy, debates are likely heated and conflict intense, thus contributing to the issue's politicisation. When policy debates mostly centre on criticism concerning specific details instead, they are less heated and the policy less politicised.

In sum, I argue that the degree of politicisation is best captured by focusing on whether the policy faces fundamental rejection by a significant coalition of actors both in- and outside Parliament. For each case, I draw on media reporting, documents issued by parties and interest groups, and secondary literature to assess whether policies introduced to comply with EU conditionality were highly politicised. This approach admittedly falls short of defining absolute values for actor scope and polarisation, which are sufficient for high politicisation. However, the benefit of setting up four most similar pairwise comparisons is that the value of the independent variable in each case is not solely determined based on in-case evidence but is also made plausible relative to the compared case.

Reputation for Policy Support

In Chap. 2, I argued that governments, who have to transpose conditionality, are not in a position to initiate a time-consuming reframing process to contest the perceived harmful consequences of a policy but, instead, have to build on previous policy positions. Therefore, their issue reputation can constrain governments' choice in blame avoidance strategy. On the one hand, if governing parties have a reputation for support because they publically backed or even campaigned for policy reform in the past, this should facilitate reframing the policy in a positive light because it builds on previous framing efforts. Contrariwise, governing parties who have previously refrained from supporting policy reform or even opposed a policy should have a much harder time denying a measure's harmfulness.

To determine governments' reputation for policy support, I look at three factors—governing parties' prior reform efforts, previous electoral campaigns and coalition agreements. First, when governing parties introduced similar reforms in past terms in office or attempted to introduce similar measures, they likely have a public reputation for a specific issue position. Second, the presence of the measures in the previous electoral programme indicates long-term support for a policy. Third, when governing parties make specific reference to a policy in their coalition agreement, this should signal the importance of the measure to the public. These factors should make it easier for a governing party to portray a policy positively, as it can draw on previous framing efforts. Conversely, when a governing party has no prior connections to an issue or even argued against a measure before the Programme, it does not have a reputation for policy support. It should, therefore, be more challenging to reframe the policy positively, whereas admissions of the negative consequences of a policy should be more plausible coming from a party without a prior record of policy support. In coalition governments, it suffices if one governing party has a reputation for policy support.

For each case, I draw on party programmes, media reporting, and secondary literature to assess whether governing parties have a record of supporting the respective policies. Again, this approach falls short of defining a specific cut-off point between cases of a high and low reputation for policy support. Instead, I rely on differences between the cases to make plausible the determined value of the independent variable relative to the compared case.

In sum, I draw on a diverse set of sources to determine the values of my independent variables, politicisation, and reputation for issue ownership. For politicisation to be high, measures transposed in compliance with EU conditionality need to face outright rejection by actors both in- and outside Parliament. For governing parties to have a reputation for policy support, they need to have prior records of attempting to introduce similar measures or campaigning in favour of the respective measures. Additionally, including a policy in governing parties' coalition agreements signals policy support.

3.3 Measuring Blame Avoidance Strategies

In the final subsection of this chapter, I present my strategy for measuring the dependent variable, that is, governments' blame avoidance strategies. In a nutshell, I use Parliamentary debates to conduct a qualitative content analysis of statements made by government representatives on the policies of interest in each case. My coding rules build on existing coding schemes to analyse responsibility attributions and extend them by differentiating between different evaluations of the attribution object and different properties of the attribution target. Using these coding rules, I identify

663 blame avoidance statements in 273 Parliamentary debates coded in the five cases.

Government Statements in Parliamentary Debates

The analysis of governments' choice of presentational blame avoidance strategies necessitates a look at governments' speech acts. Different sources are available for this task, such as press releases and publications on policymakers' websites, media reporting, and Parliamentary debates. Each source has advantages and drawbacks, which I will discuss to explain my focus on Parliamentary debates. I subsequently give details on the data collection strategy.

First, researchers can draw on statements publically available on policymakers' websites. These usually include press releases and statements, as well as speeches in- and outside Parliament (König, 2016a; Schumacher et al., 2016; Traber et al., 2020). This source gives a continuous measure of governments' strategy choices and has the advantage of covering statements from diverse contexts. However, policymakers have considerable freedom of choice regarding the content of these publications, including which topics they focus on and on which they prefer to remain silent. While this makes press releases and other material published by policymakers themselves an excellent source for studies on issue salience (Klüver & Sagarzazu, 2016; Sagarzazu & Klüver, 2017), it makes this source less suitable for the analysis of government's blame avoidance strategies because this data source is limited to those topics that governments choose to talk about.

Second, a prominent approach in the literature is the analysis of government strategies in media reporting (Heinkelmann-Wild & Zangl, 2020; König, 2016a; Roose et al., 2018; Sommer, 2020). Mass media plays a 'central role of intermediation between citizens and the state' (Hutter et al., 2016, p. 42) and provides extensive information on policymaking and conflicts among political actors. What is more, Gerhards et al. (2009) point out that 'in modern societies, the process of attribution of political responsibility is taking place primarily in the mass media public' (Gerhards et al., 2009, p. 106; see also Roose et al., 2017, p. 47). A such, media reporting is a suitable and frequently employed source for the study of public responsibility attributions (Gerhards et al., 2009; König, 2016b; Kriegmair et al., 2022; Rittberger et al., 2017). However, this approach can only measure those government statements that are replicated in the media.[3] Furthermore, media reporting may be biased by editors selecting topics on criteria, such as negativity and conflict (Wenzelburger, 2014, pp. 81–82), which favour some blame avoidance strategies over others. In this way, the analysis of media reporting does not yield a complete picture of governments' use of blame avoidance strategies, as these statements already took the first hurdle of getting public exposure.

Third, governments' blame avoidance strategies can be measured in Parliamentary debates (Heinkelmann-Wild et al., 2020a; Vasilopoulou et al., 2014). Parliaments

[3] Heinkelmann-Wild and Zangl (2020) refer to statements that 'made it to the general public' in this context. See Heinkelmann-Wild and Zangl (2020), 959 FN 10.

are important arenas of accountability, where governments have to explain and justify their policy choices (Bovens, 2007; Rauh & De Wilde, 2018; Rauh et al., 2017). Opposition parties play a central role in holding governments accountable because they are important generators of blame (Hansson, 2018; Hinterleitner, 2020; Weaver, 2018). Consequently, governments cannot evade topics and are forced to take a position in Parliamentary debates. Therefore, Parliamentary debates are the ideal source to analyse governments' choice of blame avoidance strategy for varying policies.

I collected relevant debates from the national repositories for Parliamentary debates in Ireland[4] and Portugal.[5] In the first step, I selected all debates that contained keywords pertaining to the selected policies. The selection of keywords was based on the information collected in the process of case selection. Furthermore, I used reiterative searches to identify those keywords that yield the best coverage of the respective policy.[6] In a second step, I then identified those debates relevant for the analysis, that is, those in which government representatives made statements regarding the respective policies. As summarised in Table 3.1, this process yielded a total of 273 Parliamentary debates for the analysis of governments' blame avoidance strategies.

Table 3.1 shows significant discrepancies between the collected and the relevant debates. These differences result from of collected debates, where no statements by government representatives were found. This was the case, i.e. when the transcripts solely recorded votes on the respective policies, when future debates on the policies were announced, or when MPs mentioned the respective policies, but government representatives did not. The table further shows significant differences between the relevant debates in the five cases. These differences may result from differences in Parliamentary traditions (Rauh & De Wilde, 2018) or the varying salience of the policies for opposition parties. However, as I am not comparing the frequency of government statements across the cases, these differences do not influence the validity of the findings.

Coding Governments' Blame Avoidance Strategies

The 273 Parliamentary debates constitute my sample for the analysis of governments' blame avoidance strategies. I conduct a qualitative content analysis of the relevant debates. Specifically, my approach is a frequency analysis (Mayring, 2015). The analysis structures the textual basis with the help of predefined categories (Mayring, 2015, p. 67) and quantifies the relative occurrence of these categories in the analysed text (for a similar approach, see König, 2016b; Mayring, 2015, 13, 65).

---

[4] Irish Parliamentary debates can be found and browsed at https://www.oireachtas.ie/en/debates/find/?debateType=dail (last accessed 16 November 2020).

[5] Portuguese Parliamentary debates can be found and browsed at http://debates.parlamento.pt/pesquisa (last accessed 27 November 2020).

[6] Keywords were added until searches for the names of specific laws that were introduced to comply with EU conditionality did not yield any additional hits. A list of all collected debates can be found in Appendix A 4 (separate Excel file).

Table 3.1 Collection of Parliamentary debates for the analysis of blame avoidance strategies

Case	Keywords	Collected debates	Relevant debates	Blame avoidance statements
Reform of the wage setting system in Ireland	'registered employment agreement' 'employment regulation order' 'JCL'	109	61	113
Introduction of property tax in Ireland	'local property tax' 'site valuation'	152	40	150
Reform of the water supply system in Ireland	'water utility' 'water charges'	248	112	304
Reforms of regulated professions in Portugal	'exercício da profissão' 'associação pública profissional' 'acesso a profissões'	99	18	44
Labour market reform in Portugal	'código do trabalho' 'contratação coletiva' 'despedimento AND critério'	165	42	106
Total		773	273	663

Most studies interested in responsibility attributions and communication strategies employ a qualitative approach (i.e. Gerhards et al., 2009; Hobolt & Tilley, 2014; König, 2016a, 2016b; Rittberger et al., 2017), as the identification of complex statements that include the evaluation of an issue and responsibility judgements is difficult to code in an automated fashion (Gerhards et al., 2007, p. 107).[7]

Conducting a frequency analysis requires the development of a coding scheme to identify and categorise blame avoidance strategies (Mayring, 2015, p. 15). My coding scheme draws on existing approaches to code responsibility attributions (Gerhards et al., 2007; Heinkelmann-Wild et al., 2020a, 2020b; Heinkelmann-Wild & Zangl, 2020; Kriegmair et al., 2022; Rittberger et al., 2017; Roose et al., 2018; Roose et al., 2017; Sommer, 2020). These approaches have in common that they code responsibility attributions, which contain the following three elements:

- An *attribution sender* who attributes responsibility for a policy and its effects.
- An *attribution object* for which responsibility is attributed.
- An *attribution target* to whom responsibility is attributed.

[7] To my knowledge, Traber et al. (2020) present the first attempt at an automated coding of governments' communication strategies. The authors combine predefined targets of blame statements with a sentiment analysis of the keywords surrounding each mentioned target. Yet, this approach cannot account for differences in centring and blurring of responsibility, and, as the subsequent operationalisation of the four strategies will show, would have difficulties in differentiating between different types of justification, which influence the evaluation of a policy.

In the analysis of governments' blame avoidance strategies, the sender of attributions remains constant and is limited to representatives of the relevant government. Furthermore, the attribution object is limited to the specific policy under analysis. These two attributes, government membership of the sender and reference to the relevant policy, define all statements coded for the analysis.

The categorisation developed in Chap. 2 distinguishes the four different blame avoidance strategies by differentiating between different evaluations of the attribution object and different properties of the attribution target. To operationalise the four strategies, once more summarised in Table 3.2, I draw on McGraw's differentiation between justifications, which deny the harmful consequences of a political outcome, and excuses, which deny a senders' responsibility for adverse outcomes (McGraw, 1991; McGraw et al., 1995) and complement these categories with further reflections on the differences between centred and blurred responsibility. A detailed account of the coding rules can be found in the Appendix.

First, statements that follow a *circle the wagons* approach do little to challenge negative perceptions of a policy. Therefore, senders do not reframe the policy positively, even when a previous speaker criticised the policy. When using a circle the wagons approach, senders do not deny that they had some responsibility for a specific policy outcome but close the ranks with other policymakers and blur responsibility by emphasising the role of others in the policymaking process.

In this project, senders, for instance, underline the government's cooperation with different national-level actors, such as parties, interest groups, or social partners, to develop the policy. Senders can also diffuse responsibility vertically by emphasising that the government and international and EU-level actors work hand in hand and have similar goals. Furthermore, they can emphasise the role of the government as the actor to whom the public delegated the task of fulfilling public interests.[8] Table 3.3 gives an example of a government sender employing a circle the wagons approach. Additional coding examples and explanations for coding decisions can be found in Table A2 in the Appendix.

Second, statements that employ a *blame shifting* logic acknowledge, or at least do not deny, the negative consequences of a policy choice. This means that the sender of the statement does not aim at positively reframing the policy, even if a previous speaker criticised the policy. When engaging in blame shifting, senders deny all responsibility for a policy and shift blame onto others. Blame shifting statements thus differ from a circle the wagons approach by negating the government's role in policymaking.

For the purpose of this project, senders employing blame shifting statements can emphasise that the government's hands regarding a policy are tied by decisions

[8] While McGraw et al. (1993) characterises so-called communitarian appeals, which portray senders as a delegate of their constituents as a type of principled justification, I argue that policymakers limit their own responsibility for policy outcomes by underlining their role as representatives of their electorate.

Table 3.2 Governments' blame avoidance strategies in the face of EU conditionality

	Blurred responsibility	Centred responsibility
Accept perceived harm	**Circle the wagons**	**Blame shifting**
Deny perceived harm	**Problem denial**	**Self-defence**

made at the EU level—either via EU legislation or troika commitments—or, alternatively, the predecessor government. It is typical for blame shifting statements that the sender emphasises government commitments that restrict the government's room for manoeuvre or make a specific government decision necessary. A particular case of blame shifting behaviour are those statements which shift blame to both the previous government and the troika institutions. These statements still count as blame shifting rather than circling the wagons, as the government denies all responsibility for the measures. Table 3.3 gives examples of government senders employing a blame avoidance approach. Additional coding examples for blame avoidance statements and explanations for coding decisions can be found in Table A3 in the Appendix.

Third, *self-defence statements* differ from the aforementioned types of statements in that they do not deny the government's responsibility for a policy. Instead, they challenge negative perceptions of a policy by reframing it more positively (Bovens et al., 1999). These statements underline the government's agency and give justifications for the policy choice. Self-defence statements thus differ from blame shifting statements in that they underline positive aspects of a policy and underline the government's responsibility.

In this project, senders employing self-defence statements emphasise the government's commitment to a measure or the existence of choice. To obstruct blame from the government, senders engage in the reframing of the unpopular policies. For instance, senders highlight the fairness of measures. What is more, they make an effort to show that the policies remedy existing policy failures and underline improvements by comparing the consequences of the policy to a negatively depicted past (McGraw, 1991, p. 1152). Moreover, they point out that the policies will bring additional benefits now or in the foreseeable future that have so far been overlooked by the actors criticising it. Table 3.3 gives an example of a government sender employing a self-defence approach. Additional coding examples and explanations for coding decisions can be found in Table A4 in the Appendix.

Fourth, senders use a *problem denial* strategy to pre-empt blame by making a policy option appear as common sense or a technical issue. They simultaneously aim to reframe the contested policy and blur responsibility for the measure. Unlike statements that follow a circle the wagons approach, senders engaging in problem denial underline that these necessary measures will yield positive results in the future or at least prevent future negative consequences.

In this project, senders engage in problem denial in two different ways. On the one hand, senders underline positive aspects of a policy as they do when engaging in self-defence, while simultaneously aiming at blurring responsibility. By

Table 3.3 Coding examples for each blame avoidance strategy

Blame avoidance strategy	Statement	Explanation
Circle the wagons	I would like to say that the government considers that the issue of the national minimum wage should be discussed, in the first instance, in the proper forum, with the social partners in social dialogue. […] In the original Memorandum of Understanding signed by the previous government, as you know, there was a clause saying that this matter had to be subject to prior consultation with the troika. […] there is no obligation on companies to pay the minimum wage. Today, any businessman who wants to pay more than the minimum wage can do so. (Diário da Assembleia da República, 2014a, p. 20)	In this statement, the Portuguese Employment Minister, Pedro Mota Soares, does not contradict criticism that the current minimum wage is too low. Instead, he argues that the government alone was not to blame for the failure to raise the national minimum wage by underlining the role of national-level actors, such as social partners, employers, and the predecessor government, as well as the troika institutions. He does not deny the government's involvement but blurs responsibility
Blame shifting	In addressing this matter we should begin with first principles. Ireland is committed, under the EU-IMF programme, to the introduction of a property tax. […] It was considered, in light of the complex issues involved, that a local property tax would take time to introduce and accordingly to meet the requirements of the EU-IMF programme, the Government decided to introduce a household charge in 2012 as an interim measure. (Dáil Éireann, 2012, p. 55)	The Environment Minister Phil Hogan does not deny previous criticism that the administration of the household charge was problematic. Instead, he underlines that the commitments arising from Ireland's Economic Assistance Programme necessitate the introduction of a property tax and as an intermediate measure, the introduction of a household charge. By highlighting Ireland's international commitments, he signals that the government's hands are bound, thus shifting blame to Ireland's international lenders
Self-defence	We want to ensure that if people want to create employment, the right quality water will be there. That is what this Bill is about. It is about ensuring our environment is protected, health is protected and that we have a proper supply everywhere. Therefore, we must ensure we get everybody on board. (Dáil Éireann, 2013, p. 780)	In a debate about the Water Services Bill, the Irish Minister of State, Fergus O'Dowd, highlights that the government's reforms of the water supply system have tangible benefits for the environment, water quality and the economy. He does not deny the government's role in policymaking and refrains from talking about the introduction of water charges but highlights positive aspects of the policy

(continued)

Table 3.3 (continued)

Blame avoidance strategy	Statement	Explanation
Problem denial	The bill we are presenting today follows the first stage of the legislative process that transposed Directive 2008/96/EC on road safety management […] Several entities collaborated in this diploma, in a working group constituted for the revision of the regulatory model of the road sector, which included, besides a vast set of entities, the Orders of Engineers and Technical Engineers. I would also like to emphasize that international experience in this matter has shown the efficiency and benefits that unequivocally result from the performance of these audits to reduce the occurrence of accidents […] I would like to point out the vital importance of this draft law in establishing road safety audits as a technical instrument that is absolutely fundamental to the pursuit of an interest that belongs to all and is certainly shared by all: the safety and reduction of accidents on our roads. (Diário da Assembleia da República, 2014b, p. 14)	The Portuguese Secretary of State for Transport, Sérgio Monteiro, portrays the introduction of regulations regarding professions managing road safety management as a technical matter of transposing an EU Directive. He pre-empts criticism of the measures by portraying the reforms as safety measures, which technical experts nationally and internationally agree save lives. He does not underline the government's role in policymaking, but highlights the close cooperation with experts, thus blurring responsibility among several actors

underlining the involvement of other domestic and international actors in the policymaking process, they portray the policy as a collaborative endeavour. On the other hand, they can frame the policy in a way that raises them above political controversy by making it hard to disagree with. Senders can, for instance, portray a policy as a technical issue or as a logical modernisation in the eye of current developments, such as globalisation (Watson & Hay, 2003). Moreover, they can underline the necessity of the policy, appeal to common sense, or use comparisons to other countries which employ similar policies. Typically, problem denial statements present a policy as a collaborative effort developed by a wide range of actors. They refrain from pointing out the responsibility of a particular actor, such as the government, but instead are formulated in a passive way or highlight the cooperation of several actors that cooperated on an issue. Table 3.3 gives an example of a government sender employing a problem denial approach. Additional coding examples and explanations for coding decisions can be found in Table A5 in the Appendix.

I coded the 273 Parliamentary speeches in accordance with the coding rules.[9] I used the automatic translation to translate Portuguese Parliamentary debates into English. This approach is reasonable as recent studies have shown that automated translations can be used for quantitative 'bag-of-words' topic modelling (Traber

[9] Coding rules are given in detail in the Appendix.

et al., 2020; Vries et al., 2018). While coding blame avoidance strategies is admittedly more complex than 'bag of words' approaches, the coder serves as a check of the quality of the translations, which means that the confidence in the results should be even higher than in unsupervised, quantitative analyses. All in all, Table 3.1 shows that the frequency analysis of Parliamentary speeches yielded 663 blame avoidance statements.

In sum, this chapter presented the research strategy I employ to evaluate the theoretical framework developed in Chap. 2. I conduct a co-variation analysis of four most similar case comparisons and focus on five instances of policies introduced in Ireland and Portugal while these countries were subject to Economic Adjustment Programmes. The universe of cases and the case selection contribute to the internal validity of the inferences, which can be drawn from the empirical analysis. I then introduced the measurement of the two independent variables, politicisation and governing parties' reputation for policy support. I argued that the level of politicisation depends on whether government policies come under pressure both in- and outside Parliament. Moreover, governing parties' reputation for policy support hinges on prior records of attempting to introduce similar measures or campaigning in favour of the respective measures and on the content of coalition agreements. While the proposed operationalisation admittedly falls short of defining absolute cut-off points for the values of the variables, the benefit of the setup of four most similar pairwise comparisons is that the value of the independent variable in each case is not solely determined on the basis of in-case evidence, but also made plausible relative to the compared case. In this way, I exploit the benefits of the comparative research design. In the third and final section, I delved into the measurement of the dependent variable, governments' blame avoidance strategies. Using Parliamentary debates to conduct a qualitative content analysis of government representatives' statements, I identify 663 blame avoidance statements in 273 Parliamentary debates in the five cases.

In the following two chapters, I analyse governments' choice of blame avoidance strategy in the five selected cases. Each case study provides detailed information on the values of the dependent variables and examines whether the observed use of blame avoidance strategies is in line with the theoretical framework. These case studies then form the basis for the four pairwise comparisons in Chap. 6.

References

Babb, S. L., & Carruthers, B. G. (2008). Conditionality: Forms, function, and history. *Annual Review of Law and Social Science, 4*(1), 13–29.

Beach, D., & Pedersen, R. (2016). *Causal case study methods: Foundations and guidelines for comparing, matching, and tracing*. University of Michigan Press. https://doi.org/10.3998/mpub.6576809

Bini Smaghi, L. (2015). Governance and conditionality: Toward a Sustainable Framework? *Journal of European Integration, 37*(7), 755–768. https://doi.org/10.1080/07036337.2015.1079372

Blatter, J., & Haverland, M. (2012). *Designing case studies: Explanatory approaches in small-N research* (1. publ). *Research Methods Series*. Palgrave Macmillan.

Bovens, M. (2007). Analysing and assessing accountability: A conceptual framework. *European Law Journal, 13*(4), 447–468. https://doi.org/10.1111/j.1468-0386.2007.00378.x

Bovens, M., Hart, P., Dekker, S., & Verheuvel, G. (1999). The politics of blame avoidance: Defensive tactics in a Dutch crime-fighting fiasco. In H. K. Anheier (Ed.), *When things go wrong: Organizational failures and breakdowns* (pp. 123–148). Sage. https://doi.org/10.4135/9781452231457.n8

Cioffi, J. W., & Dubin, K. A. (2016). Commandeering crisis: Partisan labor repression in Spain under the Guise of Economic Reform. *Politics and Society, 44*(3), 423–453.

Dáil Éireann. (2012). *6 November 2012: Official Report - unrevised* (Parliamentary Debates), *781 (1)*.

Dáil Éireann. (2013). *14 February 2013: Official Report - unrevised* (Parliamentary Debates), *792 (3)*.

de La Porte, C., & Heins, E. (2015). A new era of European integration? Governance of labour market and social policy since the sovereign debt crisis. *Comparative European Politics, 13*(1), 8–28.

de Meur, G., & Berg-Schlosser, D. (1994). Comparing political systems: Establishing similarities and dissimilarities. *European Journal of Political Research, 26*(2), 193–219.

de Vries, E., Schoonvelde, M., & Schumacher, G. (2018). No longer lost in translation: Evidence that Google Translate works for comparative bag-of-words text applications. *Political Analysis, 26*(4), 417–430. https://doi.org/10.1017/pan.2018.26

De Wilde, P. (2011). No polity for old politics? A framework for analyzing the politicization of European Integration. *Journal of European Integration, 33*(5), 559–575. https://doi.org/10.1080/07036337.2010.546849

De Wilde, P., & Zürn, M. (2012). Can the politicization of European integration be reversed? *Journal of Common Market Studies, 50*(S1), 137–153. https://doi.org/10.1111/j.1468-5965.2011.02232.x

De Wilde, P., Leupold, A., & Schmidtke, H. (2016). Introduction: The differentiated politicisation of European Governance. *West European Politics, 39*(1), 3–22. https://doi.org/10.1080/01402382.2015.1081505

Diário da Assembleia da República. (2014a). *Reunião Plenária de 26 de Fevereiro de 2014* (I Série - Número 53).

Diário da Assembleia da República. (2014b). *Reunião Plenária de 13 de Março de 2014* (I Série - Número 60).

Dreher, A. (2009). IMF conditionality: Theory and evidence. *Public Choice, 141*(1–2), 233–267. https://doi.org/10.1007/s11127-009-9486-z

Dukelow, F. (2015). Pushing against an open door': Reinforcing the neo-liberal policy paradigm in Ireland and the impact of EU intrusion. *Comparative European Politics, 13*(1), 93–111.

Gerhards, J., Offerhaus, A., & Roose, J. (2007). Die Öffentliche Zuschreibung von Verantwortung: Zur Entwicklung eines inhaltsanalytischen Instrumentariums. *Kölner Zeitschrift Für Soziologie Und Sozialpsychologie, 59*(105–124), 105.

Gerhards, J., Offerhaus, A., & Roose, J. (2009). Wer ist verantwortlich? Die Europäische Union, ihre Nationalstaaten und die massenmediale Attribution von Verantwortung für Erfolge und Misserfolge. In F. Marcinkowski & B. Pfetsch (Eds.), *Politik in der Mediendemokratie: [Politics in the Media Democracy]* (pp. 529–558). VS Verlag für Sozialwissenschaften. https://doi.org/10.1007/978-3-531-91728-3_22

Green-Pedersen, C. (2002). *The politics of justification: Party competition and welfare-state retrenchment in Denmark and The Netherlands from 1982 to 1998*. Changing Welfare States. Amsterdam University Press. https://doi.org/10.2307/j.ctt46n1h4
Green-Pedersen, C. (2012). A giant fast asleep? Party incentives and the politicisation of European Integration. *Political Studies, 60*(1), 115–130. https://doi.org/10.1111/j.1467-9248.2011.00895.x
Greer, S. (2014). Structural adjustment comes to Europe: Lessons for the Eurozone from the conditionality debates. *Global Social Policy, 14*(1), 51–71.
Hansson, S. (2018). The discursive micro-politics of blame avoidance: Unpacking the language of government blame games. *Policy Sciences, 51*(4), 545–564. https://doi.org/10.1007/s11077-018-9335-3
Heinkelmann-Wild, T., & Zangl, B. (2020). Multilevel blame games: Blame-shifting in the European Union. *Governance, 33*(4), 953–969. https://doi.org/10.1111/gove.12459
Heinkelmann-Wild, T., Kriegmair, L., & Rittberger, B. (2020a). The EU multi-level system and the Europeanization of domestic blame games. *Politics and Governance, 8*(1), 85–94.
Heinkelmann-Wild, T., Kriegmair, L., Rittberger, B., & Zangl, B. (2020b). Divided they fail: The politics of wedge issues and Brexit. *Journal of European Public Policy, 27*(5), 723–741. https://doi.org/10.1080/13501763.2019.1683058
Henning, C. R. (2017). *Tangled governance: International regime complexity, the Troika, and the Euro crisis*. Oxford University Press.
Hinterleitner, M. (2020). Policy controversies and political blame games. Cambridge studies in comparative public policy. .
Hobolt, S. B., & Tilley, J. (2014). *Blaming Europe? Responsibility without accountability in the European Union* (1st ed.). Oxford University Press.
Hutter, S., & Grande, E. (2014). Politicizing Europe in the national electoral arena: A comparative analysis of five west European countries, 1970-2010. *Journal of Common Market Studies, 52*(5), 1002–1018.
Hutter, S., Grande, E., & Kriesi, H. (Eds.). (2016). *Politicising Europe: Integration and mass politics* (1st ed.). Cambridge University Press.
Klüver, H., & Sagarzazu, I. (2016). Setting the agenda or responding to voters? Political parties, voters and issue attention. *West European Politics, 39*(2), 380–398.
König, P. (2016a). Communicating austerity measures during times of crisis: A comparative empirical analysis of four heads of government. *The British Journal of Politics and International Relations, 18*(3), 538–558.
König, P. (2016b). Unpopular policies and the imperative of justification: Putting the Monti Government's Reform Communication in a comparative perspective. *Journal of Comparative Policy Analysis: Research and Practice, 18*(2), 176–194.
Kriegmair, L., Rittberger, B., Zangl, B., & Heinkelmann-Wild, T. (2022). Dolce far niente? Non-compliance and blame avoidance in the EU. *West European Politics, 45*(5), 1153–1174.
Lütz, S., & Kranke, M. (2013). The European Rescue of the Washington Consensus? EU and IMF Lending to Central and Eastern European Countries. *Review of International Political Economy, 21*(2), 310–338.
Lütz, S., Hilgers, S., & Schneider, S. (2019). Games borrower governments play: The implementation of economic adjustment programmes in Cyprus and Portugal. *West European Politics, 42*(7), 1443–1463.
Mahoney, J., & Goertz, G. (2006). A tale of two cultures: Contrasting quantitative and qualitative research. *International Journal of Public Opinion Research, 14*(3), 227–249.
Mayring, P. (2015). *Qualitative Inhaltsanalyse: Grundlagen und Techniken* (12., überarb. Aufl.). *Beltz Pädagogik*. Beltz.
McGraw, K. M. (1991). Managing blame: An experimental test of the effects of political accounts. *American Political Science Review, 85*(4), 1133–1157.
McGraw, K. M., Timpone, R., & Bruck, G. (1993). Justifying controversial political decisions: Home style in the laboratory. *Political Behavior, 15*(3), 289–308.

McGraw, K. M., Best, S., & Timpone, R. (1995). "What they say or what they do?": The impact of elite explanation and policy outcomes on public opinion. *American Journal of Political Science, 39*(1), 53–74.

Pavolini, E., León, M., Guillén, A. M., & Ascoli, U. (2015). From austerity to permanent strain? The EU and Welfare State Reform in Italy and Spain. *Comparative European Politics, 13*(1), 56–76.

Pisani-Ferry, J., Sapir, A., & Wolff, G. B. (2013). *EU-IMF assistance to euro-area countries: An early assessment* (Bruegel Blueprint).

Przeworski, A., & Teune, H. (1970). *The logic of comparative social inquiry*. Wiley-Interscience.

Rauh, C., & De Wilde, P. (2018). The opposition deficit in EU accountability: Evidence from over 20 years of plenary debate in four Member States. *European Journal of Political Research, 57*(1), 194–216. https://doi.org/10.1111/1475-6765.12222

Rauh, C., De Wilde, P., & Schwalbach, J. (2017). *The ParlSpeech data set: Annotated full-text vectors of 3.9 million plenary speeches in the key legislative chambers of seven European States*. https://doi.org/10.7910/DVN/E4RSP9

Rittberger, B., Schwarzenbeck, H., & Zangl, B. (2017). Where does the buck stop? Explaining public responsibility attributions in complex international institutions. *Journal of Common Market Studies, 55*(4), 909–924.

Roose, J., Sommer, M., Scholl, F., Kousis, M., Kanellopoulos, K., & Loukakis, A. (2017). Debating responsibility on the eurozone crisis in traditional media newspaper reporting in Greece and Germany under a social media lens. In M. Barisione & A. Michailidou (Eds.), *Palgrave studies in European political sociology. Social Media and European Politics: Rethinking Power and Legitimacy in the Digital Era* (Vol. 31, pp. 267–290). Palgrave Macmillan.

Roose, J., Sommer, M., & Scholl, F. (2018). Verantwortungszuschreibungen in der Eurozonen-Krise. In J. Roose, M. Sommer, & F. Scholl (Eds.), *Bürgergesellschaft und Demokratie. Europas Zivilgesellschaft in der Wirtschafts- und Finanzkrise: Protest, Resilienz und Kämpfe um Deutungshoheit* (Vol. 10, pp. 43–73). Springer VS.

Sacchi, S. (2015). Conditionality by other means: EU involvement in Italy's structural reforms in the sovereign debt crisis. *Comparative European Politics, 13*(1), 77–92.

Sagarzazu, I., & Klüver, H. (2017). Coalition governments and party competition: Political communication strategies of coalition parties. *Political Science Research and Methods, 5*(2), 333–349. https://doi.org/10.1017/psrm.2015.56

Sapir, A., Wolff, G. B., Sousa, C. de, Terzi, & Alessio. (2014). *Committee study on the Troika and financial assistance in the Euro Area: Successes and failures* (Study on the request of the Economic and Monetary Affairs Committee).

Schimmelfennig, F., & Sedelmeier, U. (Eds.). (2005). *Cornell paperbacks. The Europeanization of Central and Eastern Europe*. Cornell University Press.

Schumacher, G., Martijn Schoonvelde, Tanushree Dahiya, & Vries, E. de. (2016). *EUSpeech: A new dataset of EU elite speeches*. https://doi.org/10.7910/DVN/XPCVEI

Seawright, J., & Gerring, J. (2008). Case selection techniques in case study research. *Political Research Quarterly, 61*(2), 294–308.

Sommer, M. (2020). Blame-shifting in times of permanent austerity: Evidence from Spain and Greece in the Eurozone crisis. *Journal of Common Market Studies, 58*(3), 562–579. https://doi.org/10.1111/jcms.12926

Theodoropoulou, S. (2015). National social and labour market policy reforms in the shadow of eu bail-out conditionality: The cases of Greece and Portugal. *Comparative European Politics, 13*(1), 29–55.

Traber, D., Schoonvelde, M., & Schumacher, G. (2020). Errors have been made, others will be blamed: Issue engagement and blame shifting in prime minister speeches during the economic crisis in Europe. *European Journal of Political Research, 59*(1), 45–67.

Vasilopoulou, S., Halikiopoulou, D., & Exadaktylos, T. (2014). Greece in crisis: Austerity, populism and the politics of blame. *Journal of Common Market Studies, 52*(2), 388–402. https://doi.org/10.1111/jcms.12093

Watson, M., & Hay, C. (2003). The discourse of globalisation and the logic of no alternative: Rendering the contingent necessary in the political economy of new labour. *Policy & Politics, 31*(3), 289–305. https://doi.org/10.1332/030557303322034956
Weaver, R. K. (2018). The nays have it: How Rampant blame generating distorts American policy and politics. *Political Science Quarterly, 133*(2), 259–289. https://doi.org/10.1002/polq.12771
Wenzelburger, G. (2014). Blame avoidance, electoral punishment and the perceptions of risk. *Journal of European Social Policy, 24*(1), 80–91. https://doi.org/10.1177/0958928713511282

Chapter 4
Blame Avoidance Strategies in Ireland: Three Cases of Reforms

When Ireland became the second country after Greece to request financial assistance from the EU in November 2010, it looked back on two decades of economic growth. However, the financial crisis put a severe strain on the Irish banking system, which had profited from low financial regulation and had significant exposure to the global financial markets. What is more, it halted the real estate boom that had fostered Irish economic growth. Between 2008 and 2010, the Irish government was forced to issue several rounds of far-reaching guarantees for Irish banks to prevent a complete collapse of the banking system (Henning, 2017; Pisani-Ferry et al., 2013). Consequently, the national debt doubled between 2008 and 2010 and the collapse of the Irish property bubble led to a sharp increase in unemployment, thus further pressuring government finances (MacCarthaigh & Hardiman, 2020).

As fiscal debt became increasingly unsustainable despite several rounds of austerity measures in late 2010, the then-governing coalition government, consisting of Fianna Fáil and the Green Party, negotiated a loan agreement with the troika institutions that required significant fiscal adjustment, a reform of the Irish banking sector and structural reforms. The Programme ran for 3 years, from December 2010 to December 2013. It was predominantly implemented by the successive government, consisting of Fine Gael and the Labour Party, which came into office after March 2011 (Dukelow, 2015; Hick, 2018). While the Programme focused heavily on a reform of the Irish banking sector, it also contained provisions to consolidate public finances and encourage economic growth.

This chapter analyses the blame avoidance strategies the Irish government used in three cases of reform required under the Programme conditionality. The cases vary with regard to the politicisation of the measures and the government's reputation for policy support. Specifically, while two cases display high politicisation of policies but vary in the government's reputation for policy support, the third case was less politicised and exhibits little government reputation for policy support. Following the theoretical framework, I, therefore, expect to find a different pattern

L. Kriegmair, *Responsiveness and Responsibility in the Euro Crisis*, Contributions to Political Science, https://doi.org/10.1007/978-3-031-84473-7_4

of blame avoidance strategies in the analysis of each case. While I do not argue that governments will commit consistently to one strategy of blame avoidance, I expect a clear pattern that shows their preference for the predominant strategy.

First, I study the introduction of a local property tax in Ireland, which the Irish government introduced to comply with the troika institution's requirement to levy a recurring tax on residential property. The measure was highly politicised. It came under considerable pressure both in- and outside Parliament, with several MPs and activist organisations organising non-payment campaigns. The two governing parties had little reputation of supporting the measure, as neither actively promoted the introduction of a levy on residential properties before the Programme and the larger coalition partner, Fine Gael, even denounced the measure during its 2011 election campaign as 'unfair'. In line with the theoretical expectations, the analysis of blame avoidance strategies shows that the Irish government employed blame shifting more frequently than any other blame avoidance strategy in this case.

Second, I examine the reform of Irish water services, which constituted compliance with the EU's requirement to establish a single utility responsible for water supply and introduce water charges covering the supply cost. The measures were highly politicised. They raised significant resistance in- and outside Parliament and, in 2014, led to the biggest anti-austerity protests in Ireland in the context of the financial and the Euro crisis. Unlike the property tax, the governing parties had a reputation for supporting the water services reform, with Fine Gael advocating for reform as early as 2009. In line with the theoretical expectations, the analysis of the government's blame avoidance strategies shows that the Irish government focused on self-defence more than on any other blame avoidance strategy in this case.

Third, I analyse the reform of wage setting mechanisms, which was introduced under the Programme requirement to review the existing wage setting system and introduce necessary reforms to improve competitiveness. Unlike the two previous cases, the reform of the wage setting mechanisms did not meet with significant politicisation. The largest opposition party, Fiánna Fail, remained quiet on the matter, as it had proposed similar measures, and trade unions refrained from industrial action and remained in negotiations with the government throughout the reform process. Similar to the local property tax case, the Irish government did not have a reputation for policy support, as other parties had previously proposed most measures, and neither of the two coalition partners had campaigned to reform the wage setting system before their entering government in March 2011. In line with the theoretical expectations, the government focused on circling the wagons rather than other strategies. Yet, the analysis also shows a significant share of self-defence statements. This is surprising in a case of low politicisation and requires further explanation. A more detailed look into the case shows that a High Court ruling in July 2011 allowed the government to portray the reform as a reinstatement of the wage setting system, a measure for which it would eventually be able to claim credit.

Each of the three case studies probes the theoretical expectations developed in Chap. 2 in a case that exhibits a specific combination of the two independent variables and thus allows for a first evaluation of the theoretical framework within each case. What is more, the cases I present in this chapter form the basis for two pairwise comparisons, which allow me to probe the theoretical expectations of the framework across cases in Chap. 6.

The remainder of the chapter is divided into four parts. The next three sections are dedicated to the three case studies. For each case, I will, first, give a brief description of the cases to provide an overview of the reform process and establish that the introduced reforms were requirements whose fulfilment was necessary to comply with Programme conditionality. Second, I describe the two independent variables, politicisation of the policy and reputation for policy support. Third, I present the analysis of blame avoidance strategies and evaluate the findings against the theoretical framework. The final section summarises the results of the three case studies and concludes.

4.1 Introduction of a Local Property Tax

Before the crisis, Ireland was an outlier among European countries in that it did not have an annually recurring property tax, which it had abolished in 1978 (European Commission, 2015, p. 21). In this subchapter, I depict the introduction of the local property tax and the blame avoidance strategies the government used in its course. The introduction of a levy on residential property, a condition of the Irish Programme, was introduced in two steps between 2012 and 2013. The measure was highly politicised, with a country-wide non-payment campaign in 2012, and neither governing party had a reputation for policy support. The analysis of the blame avoidance strategies employed by the government reveals a predominant reliance on blame shifting.

Description of Reforms

In lieu of an annually recurring tax on residential property, the Irish state derived significant revenue from property sales via stamp duties before 2011. While these transaction-related taxes provided the Irish state with continuous revenue during the years of the real estate boom, they decreased sharply after the onset of the financial crisis (European Commission, 2011a, pp. 15–17). The conditionality attached to the Programme required the Irish government to introduce an annually recurring tax for all residential properties to broaden the tax base and provide an income stream for sub-national administration (European Commission, 2011a, p. 56). The Programme did not specify the form of the property tax.

The 2011 budget published in January included in its revenue calculations a 100 Euro charge for all owners of residential property (Collins & Larragy, 2011; Minihan, 2011). Yet, the government consisting of Fianna Fáil and the Green Party did not introduce the charge before the elections. The task of introducing a levy in compliance with conditionality thus fell to the successor government formed by Fine Gael and the Labour Party. In June 2011, it announced that it would introduce a 100 Euro property charge from 2012, which would be replaced by a site valuation tax on residential properties by 2014 (McGee, 2011b). The charge was introduced into law by the Local Government (Household Charge) Act 2011 in December 2011. Subsequently, the Fine Gael/Labour government introduced the local property tax with the Finance (Local Property Tax) Act 2012. The property tax took effect from the second half of 2013. Property owners were required to assess the value of their residential property and register with the Revenue Commissioners. The estimated value of each property used for tax calculation was fixed until 2016 and subject to re-evaluation by the Revenue Commissioner every 3 years after that. While the property tax was fixed at 0.18% of the site value at first, from 2015 onwards, local authorities received the option to adjust the rate upwards or downwards by up to 15%. The tax is collected centrally by the Revenue Commissioner then distributed back to local authorities, which will retain up to 80% of tax revenue collected in their area from 2014, while the rest will be distributed via an Equalisation Fund. The Local Property Tax Amendment Bill of March 2013 specified exemptions from the tax (Department of Finance, 2019; Thornhill, 2015).

The EU recognised that the government had fulfilled Programme requirements for a levy on residential property and that the measure 'moved property taxation to a more stable value-based annual tax—and hence more permanent sources of income—rather than being reliant on stamp duties which are more immediately tied to the state of the housing market' (European Commission, 2015, p. 71). It remarked that the revenues derived from the property tax were one of the most significant sources of revenue increase in the 2013 budget (European Commission, 2015, p. 70).

Politicisation of the Local Property Tax

While the predecessor government already included a flat-rate property tax in their 2011 budget calculations, it refrained from introducing specific measures before the March 2011 elections. The introduction of a property tax in line with the loan conditionality thus fell to the new government coalition of Fine Gael and the Labour Party. The newly elected government announced in June 2011 that the introduction of a property tax based on site valuation was technically challenging and required long-term planning so that it would levy an interim flat-rate charge of 100€ on residential property in 2012 (Minihan & O'Brien, 2011).

All opposition parties criticised the proposed charge as a regressive tax that disproportionately affected low-income households. Left-wing parties promised the organisation of a mass campaign against the measure, urging people to refuse payment (The Irish Examiner, 2011e; McGee, 2011b). Especially members of the Socialist Party and the People Before Profit Alliance were actively involved in the campaign against household and water charges launched by an alliance of left-wing parties, trade unions and community organisations in September 2011, which organised local meetings all over Ireland (The Irish Examiner, 2011g). The campaign gained prominence because several MPs pledged to refuse payment of the new property charge. Socialist MPs Clare Daly announced that '[a]ll of us as TDs [short for Teachta Dála, Irish equivalent to Member of Parliament; the author] pledge to be at the forefront of a non-payment campaign—a mass campaign of civil disobedience where we intend to make this charge uncollectible' (The Irish Examiner, 2011h). The campaign continued in 2012, when a hotline was launched to support people who were unwilling to pay and protesters gained public attention, for instance by disrupting a meeting of the Galway City Council (The Irish Examiner, 2012a; The Irish Times, 2012). Protests drew out thousands protesters in cities all over Ireland (Burke-Kennedy, 2012; The Irish Examiner, 2012c; O'Halloran, 2012). The biggest protest in Dublin drew a crowd of between 5000 and 10,000 protesters, the largest anti-austerity protest in Ireland during the Programme (Hearne, 2015,

p. 20; The Irish Examiner, 2012d). The campaign efforts can be considered to be successful in so far as the payment of the property charge before the deadline on March 31st was proceeding slowly. By end-February, 93% of property owners had yet to pay the flat-rate charge (The Irish Examiner, 2012b), by the end of March, over 50% of payments were still outstanding. Despite warning letters on payment arrears, by September 2012, around 40% of property owners still refused to pay the household charge (Hearne, 2015, p. 20).

The property tax, which was supposed to follow up on the household charge and transform flat payments to a site value-based payment, did not fare significantly better as it faced opponents both inside and outside Parliament. Already in 2012, the largest opposition party Fianna Fáil announced that in the 'current state of the economy', 'now is not the right time to introduce a property tax. It risks damaging an already weak domestic economy and would fall disproportionately hard on families already struggling to meet mortgage payments'. Therefore, it continued to oppose the tax throughout 2012 and 2013 (The Irish Examiner, 2012i; The Journal, 2012; Minihan, 2013). Sinn Féin announced that it would bring legislation to repeal the property tax to Parliament until summer 2013 (The Irish Examiner, 2013b, 2013e). MPs, who had previously refused to pay the household charge, announced their refusal to pay the new property tax upon its introduction in 2013 (The Irish Examiner, 2012h, 2013d). Protests against the property tax, which was to come into effect in July 2013, continued in the first half of the year (Holland, 2013; The Irish Examiner, 2013a, 2013c; O'Brien, 2013).

Registration for the new property tax commenced slowly but, unlike the household charge, surged right before the deadline at the end of May, so that over 80% of property owners registered for the new tax (The Irish Times, 2013). While the salience of the tax decreased somewhat after the registration deadline in May, the issue re-emerged in November 2013, when it became public that the Revenue Commission, which was responsible for tax collection, required property owners to pay the 2014 property tax in advance in 2013 (The Irish Examiner, 2013f; McGee, 2013a, 2013b). What is more, the mobilisation against the household charge and the property tax found a more institutionalised form when the Anti-Austerity Alliance, which had been formed to protest the measures in 2012, applied for the status of a political party in December 2013 to take part in the 2014 local elections (O'Halloran, 2013).

In sum, the government's plans to introduce a property tax were highly contested from the onset. While the protests in- and outside the Parliament quieted down somewhat after spring 2013, the policy can thus be characterised as highly politicised.

Reputation for Policy Support

Before the property tax found its way into the Irish Programme, the issue had disappeared from the political agenda for a long time. After abolishing a previous property tax had dominated election campaigns in the mid-1970s, the then-Fianna Fáil government eventually made true on an election promise and abolished it in 1978. Since then, there had been no successful attempts to reintroduce a tax on residential property. Instead, during the years of the property boom, governments had profited from high revenue from stamp duties on property sales (Collins & Larragy, 2011). In the 2007 election campaign, neither Fianna Fáil, nor Fine Gael, nor Labour touched upon the issue of a recurring property tax. The measure first appeared in the Revised Programme for Government of the Fianna Fáil/Green Government in 2009 (Collins & Larragy, 2011: 3). It was reiterated as a requirement in the Programme negotiated with the EU and the IMF in late 2010. The Fianna Fáil/Green government announced introducing a property charge of 100 Euros, which was to be introduced after the elections in March 2011 and complemented with a 'value-based addition' in 2013 (Minihan, 2011).

During their 2011 election campaigns, Fine Gael and Labour presented somewhat different positions towards introducing a new tax on property. In its programme, Labour accepted that 'it will be necessary to introduce a site value charge, in order to prevent higher taxes on work' (Labour, 2011a: 16), but criticised existing plans were not well prepared and did not take into account differences in the value of property in different regions. In contrast, Fine Gael rebuffed the government's plan 'to introduce by 2014 an annual, recurring residential property tax on the family home' as 'unfair' (Fine Gael, 2011a, b: 59). The Programme explicitly states that alternatives to a residential property tax would entail 'no extra local taxes' (Fine Gael, 2011a, b: 60). Party representatives reiterated this position throughout the electoral campaign. Spokesperson Michael Noonan ruled out introducing a tax on residential property, arguing that the majority of deficit reductions had to come via spending cuts that did away with 'waste' in the public sector (The Irish Examiner, 2011a). Local authorities, the party proposed, could introduce after 2014 a levy on property sales to gain revenue (Cullen and O'Halloran, 2011; Minihan, 2011). What is more, in a heated electoral campaign that saw Fine Gael and Labour competing for votes, Fine Gael criticised Labour for endorsing the government's plans for a property tax and for becoming a 'seriously high-tax party' (Minihan, 2011).

Consequently, the issue became a bone of contention during coalition talks between Fine Gael and Labour in March, 2011 (Collins et al., 2011). In their Government Programme, the two parties postponed a decision on the topic stating that the new government would 'consider, arising from the previous Government's deal with the IMF, various options for a site valuation tax' (Labour, 2011b: 16). While Fine Gael thus gave up its strong resistance to the measure once in government, neither of the two government parties had a strong reputation of supporting the introduction of a property tax.

Blame Avoidance Strategies

In this section, I analyse how the Irish government employed blame avoidance strategies to confront blame and criticism for the introduction of the local property tax. In the previous subsections, I established that the policy was highly politicised and both coalition partners had little reputation for supporting the policy. In line with the theoretical framework, I thus expect that the Irish government relied more often on blame shifting than all other strategies. The analysis shows that the theoretical expectation indeed bears out in the case of the introduction of the local property tax.

During the introduction of the household charge and its subsequent replacement for a property tax based on site value, the coalition government consisting of Fine Gael and the Labour Party predominantly followed a blame shifting approach. Government representatives often admitted that the levies signified an additional burden to Irish taxpayers and justified the measures by highlighting the Programme requirements its predecessor negotiated with the EU and the IMF. As Fig. 4.1 shows, a majority of 52% of blame avoidance statements follow this pattern and can thus be labelled blame shifting. A disaggregation of the statements by year confirms that blame shifting is consistently the most frequently employed strategy. While its share is initially higher in 2011 (75%), it remains constant at around 50% in 2012 and 2013, when the government introduced the household charge and the site value-based property tax.[1]

Furthermore, the following statements illustrate that government representatives relied on this approach throughout the Programme. During a debate on the introduction of the household charge in December 2011, for instance, Phil Hogan, the Minister for the Environment, Community and Local Government, admitted:

> No Government wants to be in the position of having to introduce new taxes or charges on a public that has been subject to austerity measures over recent budgets. We are in a difficult financial situation and we have to take the necessary action. The household charge is one of the steps along the path to economic recovery. It is also required under the EU-IMF programme of financial support, a programme entered into by the previous Fianna Fáil-Green Party Government. The legislative measures in the Bill give effect to one of the major requirements of the EU-IMF programme. (Dáil Éireann, 2011g, p. 79)

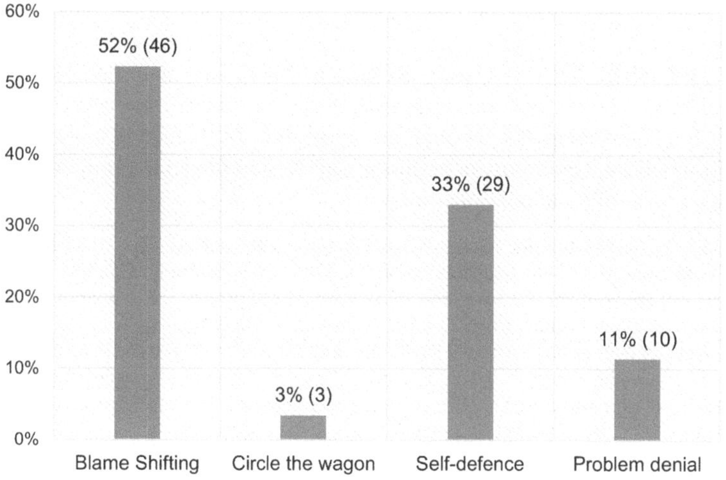

Fig. 4.1 Share of blame avoidance strategies—the local property tax introduction

[1] The disaggregated results can be found in Table A9 in the Appendix.

In December 2012, Minister Hogan reiterated:

> Nobody in any government of which I am aware would desire to introduce a new tax, but it has to be done if we are to comply with the memorandum of understanding which was negotiated by our predecessors. […] The need for it arose due to the economic and fiscal difficulties which we inherited. People were coming in the door from the troika and the Members of the then Government did not even know they were on their way. This is the serious matter we have inherited. (Dáil Éireann, 2012g, p. 89)

Similarly, when opposition politicians criticised the tax, government representatives often did little to negate the criticism but shifted responsibility for the measures to the troika and the predecessor government. Communications Minister Pat Rabbitte stated in March 2013:

> It is difficult to listen to Deputy McGrath bleeding for the citizens when his Government authored the property tax […] and made it a condition that must now be implemented to comply with troika funding. It was a Fianna Fáil proposition. The party was in favour of property tax then and now because it is in the middle of a by-election it pretends to be opposed to it. (Dáil Éireann, 2013c, p. 322)

These examples show that the government employed a similar blame shifting statements throughout the Programme's duration.

Figure 4.2 disaggregates the blame shifting statements by target shows that the troika institutions are the predominant target of the government's blame shifting efforts. Almost 60% of the statements single out the troika institutions as the culprit for the introduction of the tax on residential property. One-third of the statements further shifts blame to both the troika and the predecessor government, which negotiated and signed the Programme. Only a small minority of the government's blame shifting statements singles out the predecessor government as the responsible party (8%).

A considerable share of blame avoidance statements underlines the positive effects of the measure for local administrations, for whom this source of revenue provides financial independence and an opportunity to finance essential local services. For instance, Environment Minister Phil Hogan linked the property tax to an extensive reform of local administration:

> I remind the Deputy that the local government system has not been reformed for a long time. I am doing what I can to devolve more functions from central government and agencies to local government. […] We have introduced a local property tax—with which Sinn Féin has a problem in this jurisdiction but no problem in Northern Ireland—which gives councillors an opportunity to have a say in the priorities for their own local areas and how they can access the funds. […] This will ensure we have a body of powers at the lowest possible level to assist in giving our people a better and more effective service with fewer councillors. (Dáil Éireann, 2013d, pp. 775–776)

Figure 4.1 shows that the share of self-defence statements is considerably lower than the share of blame avoidance statements, yet, at 33%, it is still significant. Self-defence is consistently the second most frequent strategy, and its use increases throughout the Programme duration. While only 17% of statements defend the government's policy in 2011, the share rises to around 35% the following years. Taken together, blame shifting and self-defence statements amount to 85% of the

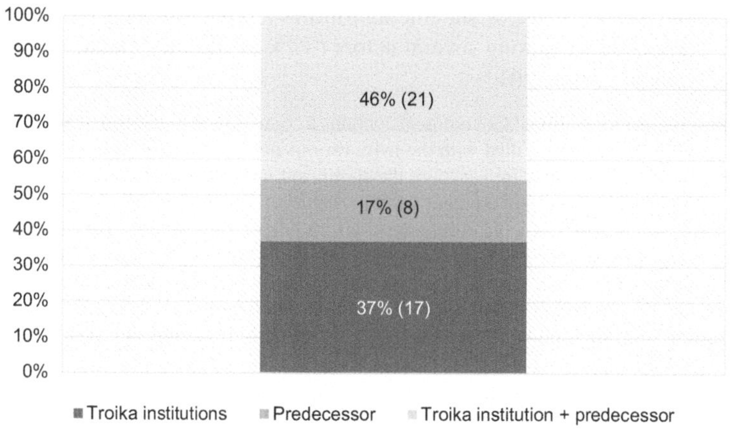

Fig. 4.2 Blame shifting statements by target—the local property tax introduction

government's blame avoidance statements. The government thus focused on strategies that centre responsibility. What is more, a closer look at the statements shows that government representatives sometimes underline the positive effects of government policy while still shifting blame to the troika institutions and the predecessor government. For instance, after underlining the requirement of complying with conditionality, Finance Minister Michael Noonan added:

> The arguments in favour of a property tax go beyond our obligations under the EU-IMF programme. The introduction of a property tax is part of a broader approach to the taxation of property. The aim is to replace some of the revenue from transaction-based taxes, which have proven to be an unstable source of Government revenue, with an annual recurring property tax, which international experience has shown to be a stable source of funding. [...] Ireland was the only country in the OECD that had no recurring property tax and allowed tax relief on rent, on mortgage interest payments, on capital gains by way of principal private residence relief and on capital acquisitions by way of dwelling house relief. This was previously compensated for by way of relatively high rates of stamp duty. Government policy has seen this mix changed through the phased abolition of interest relief, radical reductions on stamp duty rates and the introduction of the local property tax. This is a much more sensible policy mix reflective of what is seen in many other jurisdictions. (Dáil Éireann, 2013d, p. 63)

One explanation for the combination of blame shifting and self-defence strategies could be that the government is balancing short-term and long-term advantages. While shifting blame for the introduction of the local property tax by highlighting the constraints imposed by the Programme can help the government avoid public blame at the moment, framing the measure as a good fit for government efforts to modernise the Irish tax system can open a potential for credit claiming in the long run that comes with a strategy of self-defence. This may help account for the comparatively frequent use of self-defence as a blame avoidance strategy that increases slightly throughout the Programme duration.

While the government thus predominantly employed high-politicisation strategies that centre responsibility, I find evidence for other strategies as well. A considerably smaller share of statements follows a circle the wagons approach of blurring responsibility among several actors (3%), as did the Minister of Finance, Michael Noonan in June 2011:

> The programme for National Government contains a commitment to 'consider, arising from the previous Government's deal with the IMF, various options for a site valuation tax. Any site valuation tax must take into account the significant number of households in mortgage distress and provide local government with a reliable stream of revenue'. Initial consultation on the implications of a recurrent annual tax on property has taken place with relevant stakeholders. [...] At this stage, a decision has yet to be taken on the precise legal mechanism to be used to introduce a site value tax and whether this will be done in tax legislation such as the Finance Bill or through other legislation which may fall within the ambit of the Department of Environment, Community and Local Government. (Dáil Éireann, 2011b, p. 469)

Finally, a small share of statements follows a strategy of problem denial (11%). This example from Minister of State Brian Hayes illustrates that problem denial statements present the introduction of the property levies as a technical matter without palatable alternatives:

> As a society, a Government and a people, we need to chart a way forward. The point has already been made about the need to have a sustainable tax base. In that context, we should not forget one simple statistic. Under Fianna Fáil, in a 12-month period in 2008, tax revenues went from €51 billion to €37 billion. They collapsed because of the collapse of the property market. The task of this Government or indeed any Government, even one involving the Communist Party of Ireland or Sinn Féin, is relatively simple. The task of the Government is to broaden the tax base and take in more taxes. In reducing the deficit we are doing that. Any party, including Sinn Féin, whatever about the nonsense of the debate yesterday and today, which proposes the abolition of a property tax will be laughed out of court. (Dáil Éireann, 2013d, p. 860)

All in all, the observed pattern confirms the theoretical expectation that the high politicisation of the property levies and the lack of reputation for policy support should lead government representatives to focus on blame shifting rather than other strategies of blame avoidance. Regarding the two most frequently used strategies, the observed pattern is stable throughout the Programme duration.

4.2 Reform of the Water Supply System

Until the 2010s, Ireland stood out among the OECD countries as the only country that supplied water free at the point of use (European Commission, 2015, p. 82). Irish water services were traditionally tax-financed and supplied by 34 local authorities. In this subchapter, I give a detailed account of the reform of the Irish water supply system between 2011 and 2014. As a significant reform requirement of the Irish Programme was not introduced until after Ireland exited the Programme at the end of 2013, the period of analysis in this case is extended to 2014, the first year of post-Programme surveillance.

The reform was a requirement of the Irish Programme and highly politicised, as it fundamentally changed the provision of water. The government had a reputation for policy support, as Fine Gael had championed a reform of the water supply system since 2010. My analysis of the blame avoidance strategies employed by the coalition government consisting of Fine Gael and the Labour Party reveals a strong focus on self-defence.

Description of Reforms

When the troika institutions negotiated the loan programme with Irish authorities in 2010, the Irish water provision was fragmented, and the water network suffered from under-investment, which negatively affected water provision (European Commission, 2015, pp. 14–15). The Programme made obligatory a reform of the water supply system. First, it committed Irish authorities to establish a single water utility responsible for water supply in line with expert assessment by the end of 2011. Second, it required introducing water charges within the following 2 years (European Commission, 2011a, p. 70).

The progress with the reform of the water sector was slow. The Fine Gael/Labour Party government commissioned a report from Price Waterhouse Cooper on the alternatives for a water supply utility in early 2011. However, it was not until March 2013 that the Water Services Act established Irish Water as a state-owned, private company, which could take out loans to finance investments in the water infrastructure. Also, the Act provided for the installation of water meters and abrogates a prior ban on water charges for private households (European Commission, 2013b, p. 29). While the installation of water meters commenced in the summer of 2013, the government and the troika institutions agreed to postpone the introduction of charges until 2014. The Water Services (No. 2) Act 2013 was introduced in December 2013 and transferred all water service functions, assets and liabilities from local authorities to Irish Water. It granted the power to regulate water tariffs in line with government provisions to the Commission for Energy Regulation (CER), which regulates gas and electricity services (Dukelow, 2016, p. 153). Finally, the Irish Water Services Act (2014) introduced a water charge system from 2015 on. The Act departed from the envisioned charging structure based on individual use and introduced until 2018 a capped flat charge of 160 € for a single household and 260 € for larger households. Unit charges apply only when metered usage is lower than the flat charge. Furthermore, it provides that a future decision to privatise Irish Water had to be subjected to a referendum (see also Dukelow, 2016, p. 154; Hourigan, 2017, p. 119).

In its post-programme surveillance report, the troika institutions recognised that the government had completed significant adjustments in the Irish water supply system. Nevertheless, they observed that the 'introduction of a national water utility, Irish Water, and household water charges proved practically and politically challenging' (European Commission, 2015, pp. 14–15). They criticised that the reforms' effect was limited due to service-level agreements between Irish Water and the local water authorities and the capped charges (European Commission, 2015, pp. 85–86).

Politicisation of the Reform

Much like the introduction of the local property tax, the reform of the Irish water system met with resistance from the onset. Both water charges and the new water utility foreseen in the Irish Programme faced considerable resistance from Unions and left-wing parties, who saw the charges as an additional burden on Irish taxpayers and suspected that the government would eventually privatise water supply (Holland, 2011; The Irish Examiner, 2010). Protests against the household charge in 2011 and early 2012 were often combined with a rejection of future water charges, especially after the government announced introducing water charges on a flat-rate basis before switching to a usage-based charge after the installation of water meters (The Irish Times, 2011a). This announcement united the opposition in its refusal of the government's plans. Fianna Fáil, which had previously recognised the need to introduce a water charge when in government, now denounced the measure as a 'stealth tax' (McGee, 2011a).

While the government had to retract from the plan of flat-rate water charges due to internal opposition in the Labour Party (Roche, 2011), the opposition continued to accuse the government of disproportionately burdening Irish households (The Irish Examiner, 2011f; Minihan & O'Brien, 2011). Opposition to water charges gained additional impetus in April 2012, when the government made public plans to charge people for water meters and announced that refusal to pay water charges would lead to household's cut-off from the water supply. Opposition MPs cautioned that the additional charges would spark protests similar to those against the household charge (The Irish Examiner, 2012e, 2012f) and activist threatened: 'We successfully made the household tax one of the biggest campaigns in recent decades. Water charges will be even more forcefully opposed' (The Irish Examiner, 2012g).

Protests against water charges did not gain real momentum until 2014, mainly because of a lack of progress on the reform. The introduction of the 2013 Water Services Act was accompanied by criticism from opposition MPs. When the government curtailed the debate on the law, opposition MPs left the Parliament in protest (The Irish Examiner, 2013g). When the government finally presented its first plans for the charging system in April 2014, opposition MPs from all parties criticised that charges were a disproportional burden for low- and middle-income households and that the government continued to threaten cut-offs in cases of non-payment (Hearne, 2015).

Simultaneously, local protests against water charges started to disrupt meter installation (Hilliard, 2014; The Irish Examiner, 2014a, 2014b, 2014c; Roche, 2014). As public discontent with the proposed water charges grew, an alliance of activists, left parties (namely Sinn Féin, People Before Profit and the Anti Austerity Alliance) and trade unions, already acquainted from the protests against the property tax, formed the Right2Water campaign, to organise protests against the government's water charge plans. The first rally in Dublin on October 21 mobilised between 80,000 and 100,000 people to protest against the proposed measures. On November 1, protests all over the country saw up to 150,000 protesters take to the streets on a national action day (Dukelow, 2016; Finn, 2015; Hearne, 2015). In light of the sustained protests against the water charges, the government conceded to shelf its plans for usage-based water charges and proposed smaller, flat-rate payments until 2018 (European Commission, 2015, p. 86). In sum, the government's plans for reforming water services were highly politicised from the onset. The protests against water charges in 2014 were the biggest anti-austerity protests in Ireland in the context of the financial and the Euro crisis.

Reputation for Policy Support

Before the crisis, water services were a minor issue, and in the 2007 elections, the major parties' electoral programmes revolved mostly around necessary water infrastructure investments. Fine Gael campaigned for investments in the water infrastructure, focusing on the provision of clean and safe drinking water and rural development (Fine Gael, 2007). Similarly, the Irish Labour Party advocated for clear drinking water and investments in water treatment facilities and spoke out against the privatisation of water supply (Labour, 2007).

However, in 2009, Fine Gael published plans for 'bringing all of Ireland's water assets under the ownership of one State company, "Irish Water". [...] The fragmented nature of the water industry, in which 34 local authorities are responsible for investment and maintenance, also means that there are currently no real economies of scale' (Fine Gael, 2009, pp. 20–21). The new national water utility company was part of a stimulus package that aimed at job creation through investments in water, energy, and communication infrastructure (Hennessey, 2009). The cost of these investments was supposed to be levied via consumer charges (Fine Gael, 2009, p. 14). This plan preceded the negotiation of the bailout agreement with the European Union and the IMF. The so-called NewEra plan was a central part of Fine Gael's 2011 election campaign (Fine Gael, 2011a, p. 43). Party spokesperson Phil Hogan repeated during the campaign party's position that 'there are 34 entities in the State dealing with water and a new way is required if Ireland is to meet its objectives under the EU water framework directive' and to provide high-quality water supply for Irish households (O'Halloran, 2011).

The Labour Party initially remained silent on a single water utility company in its electoral programme (Labour, 2011a) and refuted the idea of water charges during its electoral campaign (The Irish Examiner, 2011b). Consequently, the topic was controversial during the coalition talks between Labour and Fine Gael (Collins et al., 2011). Nevertheless, Labour seemingly bowed to the Fine Gael plan, as the government programme published in March 2011 included the promises to create a single water utility, 'to install water meters in every household in Ireland and move to a charging system that is based on use above the free allowance' (Labour, 2011b, p. 17). In sum, while Labour may have been cautious about reforming the water system initially, the government, especially Fine Gael, had a reputation of supporting plans to reform the water supply system.

Blame Avoidance Strategies

In this section, I analyse how the Irish government employed blame avoidance strategies to confront blame and criticism for reform of the water supply system. In the previous subsections, I established that the policy was politicised and that the government, and especially Fine Gael, had a reputation for policy support because the latter had championed a reform of the system since 2010. In line with the theoretical framework, I expect that the Irish government employed relied more often on self-defence than all other strategies. The analysis shows that the theoretical expectation indeed bears out in the case of the reform of the water supply system.

The coalition government consisting of Fine Gael and the Labour Party focused predominantly on a self-defence approach and framed its water services reforms as a matter of clean drinking water, environmental protection, and economic growth. It underlined that the new water utility and the charging system would help overcome existing infrastructure deficiencies so that Irish households would have access to clean drinking water in the future. It also emphasised that infrastructure improvements and a metering system would help conserve valuable drinking water. According to the government, these developments would make Ireland an attractive location for water-intensive industries and bring jobs and revenue. Government representatives consistently used these arguments throughout the implementation of the water services reform.

In September 2011, for instance, Minister of State Fergus O'Dowd argued:

> The programme for Government states that 'to achieve a better quality water and environment we will introduce a fair funding model to deliver clean and reliable water'. [...] We want to improve water services and funding is badly needed. There is an inadequate water supply in Dublin, so water will have to be pumped from the Shannon to protect the city's supplies in future. [...] In addition, as a result of climate change, it may not be available to those living in the greater Dublin area. Counties from Donegal to Dublin will not be able to attract industry without an adequate water supply. Some 44% of water produced currently never reaches the taps because it is wasted. (Dáil Éireann, 2011d, p. 629)

This statement pattern is visible throughout the reform's implementation process. In May 2012, Environment Minister Phil Hogan emphasised the deficiencies of the current system and the potential for water conservation:

> The reality is that water leakage on the customer side is not being caught, with substantial losses arising in all local authority areas. That is totally unacceptable. Our objective is to address this issue by eliminating fragmentation and establishing a single public water utility to deal with these matters once. That will ensure we have adequate quantities of quality water for consumers, particularly on the east coast where a water shortage will develop if we do not plan for it now. I am determined, together with Bord Gáis and my Government colleagues, that we will do this in the shortest period of time, notwithstanding the difficulties and hiccups that will inevitably arise along the way. (Dáil Éireann, 2012e, p. 258)

Minister of State Paudie Coffey reiterated these arguments in November 2014, when the protests against the introduction of water charges mobilised large protests:

> The Government has a clear vision for the reform of water services in this country. The central planks of the water reform programme, namely, a new national water utility, a sustainable funding model and independent economic regulation, have been considerably advanced. The objectives of the programme are to protect public health, increase economic competitiveness and conserve our environment. Ireland needs a clean, reliable drinking water supply and coastal waters, rivers and lakes that are free of pollution. (Dáil Éireann, 2014b, p. 94)

As Fig. 4.3 shows, a majority of 66% of blame avoidance statements follow this line of argumentation and, thus, a self-defence strategy. A disaggregation of the statements by year shows that self-defence is consistently the strategy most frequently used by the government, and its share increases over time. While it starts at 58 and 54% in the years 2011 and 2012, it subsequently rises to 62% in 2013 and reaches 72% in 2014, when the government faced large protests against the introduction of water charges.[2]

A considerably smaller share of statements follows a blame avoidance approach. Figure 4.3 shows that 16% of blame avoidance statements engage in blame shifting. Disaggregating the blame shifting statements by target, Fig. 4.4 shows that the government predominantly shifts responsibility for the reforms of water services to the troika institutions. While government representatives often single out the troika institutions (33%), they combine blame to the troika and the predecessor government, which negotiated the loan agreement, even more frequently (59%). For instance, in September 2012, Environment Minister Phil Hogan pointed out in response to criticism of the governments' reform plans:

> As the Deputy knows from the troika agreement, water charges are to be introduced in 2014. This is what the previous Government negotiated. Whether or not there are meters there will be water charges in 2014. (Dáil Éireann, 2012f, p. 11)

Similarly, in October 2014, PM Enda Kenny renounced any responsibility for the water charges, highlighting the role of the troika institutions and the predecessor government instead:

> When the troika came into Ireland, the guys opposite—they are all guys—decided to sign off [...] When the guys signed off on it, they agreed with the troika there would be a comprehensive change in relation to water in Ireland in line with every other European country. They agreed a flat rate charging arrangement, or something like that, which came out at €400 per household. (Dáil Éireann, 2014a, p. 43)

Both entities were not solely blamed for the measures themselves but also for the tight schedule under which the government was operating, as did Minister of State Fergus O'Dowd in March 2013:

> One of the difficulties is that we do not have time because of the time pressures of the troika agreement signed by the previous Fianna Fáil-led Government. [...] Sitting in this seat was the former Taoiseach, Mr. Brian Cowen, who signed a deal with the troika. On behalf of the State he signed up to introducing charges by 1 January 2014. That is what he signed and as the succeeding Government, we have to accept that commitment. That is what the previous Government did—that is the way the country was at the time. (Dáil Éireann, 2013b, p. 26)

A disaggregation of the blame shifting statements by year shows that the share of blame avoidance statements remains relatively stable. Blame shifting statements are the second most frequent type of statement between 2011 and 2013, but their share decreases over time. While they account for 32% of all blame avoidance statements in 2011, their share decreases to 22 and 18% in 2012 and 2013 and reached 11% in

[2]The disaggregated results can be found in Table A11 in the Appendix.

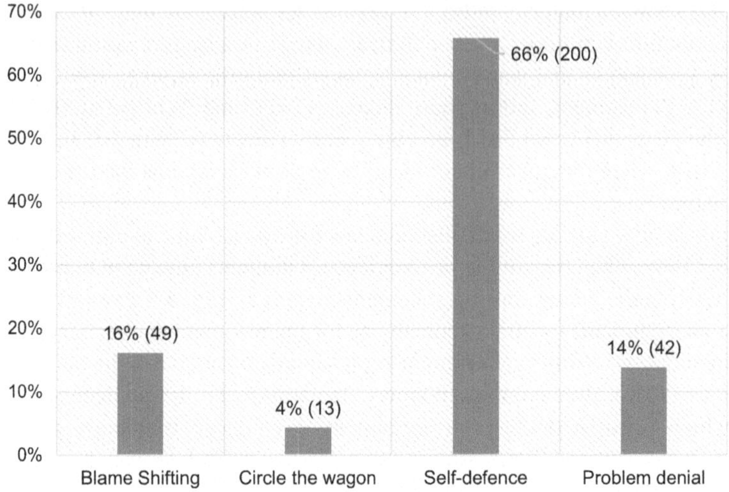

Fig. 4.3 Share of blame avoidance strategies—the water services reform

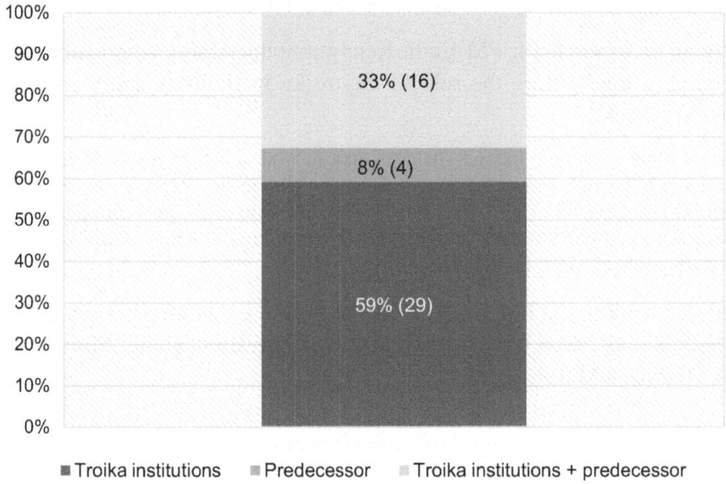

Fig. 4.4 Blame shifting statements by target—the water services reform

2014.[3] Nonetheless, the examples show that the Irish government continued to shift responsibility for water services reforms to the troika institutions even after the end of the Programme. When discussing the water services reform, the Irish government thus consistently focused on high-politicisation strategies that centre responsibility. Together, these strategies account for more than 80% of all blame avoidance statements.

[3] The disaggregated results can be found in Table A11 in the Appendix.

While the government thus predominantly employed high-politicisation strategies, I find evidence for other strategies as well. A considerable share of statements follows a problem denial strategy (14%) that attempted to portray the reforms as an alignment with international standards, as did Minister of State Fergus O'Dowd in September 2011:

> Ireland is unique among OECD countries in not charging households for water. The programme for Government provides for the introduction of water charges based on a new and fair funding model and this is also a requirement of the agreement between Ireland and the European Union and the International Monetary Fund. The programme for Government proposes that water meters will be installed in households connected to public water supplies and that a new charging system will be introduced with water charges based on usage. Experience from the metering of the non-domestic sector and from metering of some group water supplies would suggest that customer side leakage levels are a significant factor in overall unaccounted-for water. Installing water meters encourages households to reduce consumption, use water efficiently and fix leaks where these are identified. Metered charges are also the fairest way to charge for water. (Dáil Éireann, 2011f, p. 766)

The smallest share of statements follows a circle the wagons approach (5%), as did Environment Minister Phil Hogan in May 2011 when he did not negate the cost of the reforms, but blurred the responsibility for the design of a new water utility:

> The Programme for National Recovery 2011–2016 states that the Government will create Irish Water, a new State company that will take over key water/waste water functions from the 34 existing local authorities. The Programme of Financial Support for Ireland agreed between the Government and the EU/IMF refers to the conduct of 'an independent assessment of the transfer of responsibility for water services provision from the local authorities to a water utility'. The independent study required under the EU/IMF agreement is being progressed and will guide the implementation of the strategy set out in the Programme for Government, identifying the optimum role and functions of the proposed company. (Dáil Éireann, 2011b, p. 188)

All in all, the observed pattern confirms the theoretical expectation that the high politicisation of the water services reform and the government's reputation for policy support should lead government representatives to focus on self-defence rather than other strategies of blame avoidance. The disaggregation of statements of the two most frequently used strategies by year shows that the observed pattern is relatively stable throughout the reform implementation process.

4.3 Reform of the Wage Setting System

Before the introduction of the national minimum wage in 2000, Employment Protection Orders (EROs) and Registered Employment Agreements (REAs) had been the only wage setting system that established sectoral minimum wages (O'Sullivan & Wallace, 2011, p. 19). In this subchapter, I provide a detailed account of the reform of this wage setting system, which was part of the Programme conditionality. Unlike the two previous measures, the reform was not highly politicised and the government did not have a reputation for policy support. My analysis of the blame avoidance strategies employed by the Irish government reveals a focus on strategies of low politicisation, with at least some indication for an emphasis on a circle the wagons strategy.

Description of Reforms

While the Irish labour market was already characterised by a high degree of flexibility before the financial crisis,[4] the troika institutions recorded a rise in unemployment to three times the pre-crisis level and noted that unit labour costs had risen sharply since the early 2000s. The Programme pointed out that the comparatively high minimum wage and sectoral wage agreements hampered wage adjustment necessary to improve competitiveness (European Commission, 2011a, pp. 34–37). Therefore, the Programme requested a review of wage setting by EROs and REAs, to establish whether they stood in the way of wage adjustment and required that reforms of the mechanisms should subsequently be negotiated with the Commission.[5] Furthermore, the Programme required introducing 'inability to pay' clauses, which allowed employers to depart from the terms agreed under the EROs and REAs for consecutive periods in case of economic difficulties (European Commission, 2011a, p. 63).

Both EROs and REAs are wage setting mechanisms that cover low-paid employment sectors. Before the Programme, EROs regulated sectoral wages and employment conditions in several specified sectors, including catering, the hotel industry and hairdressers. The agreements were negotiated by Joint Labour Committees (JLC), consisting of trade union and employer representatives. REAs extended collective agreements across a specific sector, such as the construction and electrical industry. This meant that agreements on sectoral minimum wages and terms of employment became legally enforceable even for employers that have not been party to the agreement (Regan, 2013, p. 13). In 2011, 68 REAs were registered with the Labour Court (The Irish Examiner, 2011a).

In February 2011, Labour Court Chairman Kevin Duffy and Economist Frank Walsh were commissioned to conduct the review required by the Programme (The Irish Examiner, 2011a). The government formed by Fine Gael and the Labour Party in March 2011 received the expert review in late May. The report found that while the ERO and REA system should be maintained, it required radical reforms to 'make it fairer and more responsive to changing economic circumstances' (Wall, 2011c). A High Court decision declaring the Joint Labour Committee system unconstitutional on 7 July 2011 subsequently stalled the government's reform

[4] According to the OECD's strictness of employment protection index, Ireland ranked third after the UK and Denmark in the EU in 2009 and 2010.

[5] The reform requirement was subsequently specified after the publication of the review and required legislative reforms of both EROs and REAs, see for example European Commission (2011b, p. 51).

proposal (Wall, 2011g). Consequently, the 2012 Industrial Relations (Amendment) Act, which restored the system, was not introduced until July 2012.

The reform reduced the scope of EROs from 12 sectors to 6, decreased the number of minimum wages that could be set by each order and excluded the regulation of special rates, such as Sunday pay rate (European Commission, 2012, p. 60). What is more, the new Act introduced inability to pay clauses for both EROs and REAs, made mandatory the examination of several factors, such as the impact on employments and relative wage levels in other EU countries, before registration of an agreement and made both types of agreement subject to Ministerial approval (European Commission, 2013a, p. 38). A subsequent High Court ruling declared the REA system unconstitutional on 9 May 2013, prompting the Commission to observe that while it was satisfied that the reforms would improve labour market flexibility, the government's legislative efforts were 'partly overtaken by judicial developments' (European Commission, 2015, p. 83). The REA system was not reformed until July 2015, when the 2015 Industrial Relations (Amendment) Act was introduced.

Politicisation of the Reform of the Wage Setting System

The February 2011 announcement of a review of wage setting mechanisms yielded mixed reactions from the social partners. While employer associations argued that the system was outdated and mandated wages that were damaging Irish businesses and thus welcomed a change of the system, the Irish Congress of Trade Unions called the review an 'attack on incomes' (Slattery, 2011). However, the topic did not stay in the public spotlight as the then-government refrained from further actions before the March 2011 elections, and an alliance of firms from the fast-food sector brought a constitutional challenge on the wage setting mechanism in the catering sector to the High Court (Wall, 2011a).

In April, the issue briefly re-emerged when the incoming government coalition of Fine Gael and the Labour Party reinstated the minimum wage, which had been cut by its predecessor and announced it would wait for the Duffy-Walsh report's review of the wage setting mechanisms before engaging in reform negotiations with the social partners and the troika. Opposition politicians from Sinn Féin and the Socialist party cautioned that in return for the reversal of the minimum wage cut, the government would dismantle wage setting mechanisms, which guaranteed higher wages for low paid workers (O'Regan, 2011a).

The government received the Duffy-Walsh report in May 2011 and announced that while the report supported that the wage setting system should be maintained, it required a 'radical overhaul' (Wall, 2011b). The Minister for Enterprise and Jobs, Richard Bruton, announced that a system reform would exclude the regulation of Sunday and overtime pay rates from future agreements (Wall, 2011d). The reaction to the government's reform plans was almost exclusively adverse. While employer associations had expected reforms to go further and even abolish the ERO and REA systems, unions and some Labour backbenchers opposed the plans because they would effectively cut the wages of low paid workers. Union representatives warned that implementing the government's plans could lead to industrial action (Wall,

2011e). Despite the discontent, contestation remained limited and orbited the issue of special premium payments. Labour Party leader Eamon Gilmore confirmed that the government was united in its plans to reform the wage setting mechanisms (The Irish Examiner, 2011c). After negotiation with the social partners, representatives of the Irish Congress of Trade Unions (ICTU) confirmed that a 'broad agreement' (Wall, 2011f) had been reached between the government and the trade unions on the reform plans. The largest opposition party, Fianna Fáil, remained silent on the issue, as it had presented similar reform plans when still in office (Government of Ireland, 2010; Wall, 2011i). Negotiations over Sunday and overtime premium payments continued throughout June 2011 but were side-lined by the High Court ruling on 7 July 2011, which declared the Irish JLC system, under which EROs were negotiated, unconstitutional (Wall, 2011g).

The High Court ruling effectively ended discussions about the government's reform of wage setting mechanisms, as it called in to question the validity of existing EROs (Wall, 2011g). While this technically would not change the wage and employment conditions of workers with existing contracts, politicians and unions cautioned against employers replacing workers to decrease costs. Consequently, up to 200,000 low paid workers were directly affected by the court ruling and calls for action to reinstate the wage setting mechanisms arose (The Irish Examiner, 2011d). The discussions after the court ruling were thus concerned predominantly with the timing of legislation on the wage setting mechanisms. While unions and opposition parties asked for immediate action to secure workers affected by the ruling, the government underlined that the reform required extensive preparation to rule out further constitutional challenges to the wage setting mechanisms (Bréadun, 2011; O'Regan, 2011b). In late July 2011, the government reached an agreement on the reform plans and announced that a bill would enter Parliament in the fall (Wall, 2011h). The social partner's reactions to the proposed reforms were mixed. While employer associations criticised that the wage setting system would be reinstated, trade unions welcomed the return of the JLC system but criticised the reform provisions relating to the inability to pay clauses and Sunday and overtime payments. There were, however, no threats of further actions against the bill (Duncan, 2011; Hunt, 2011). The issue subsequently disappeared from the public debate. The government published the Industrial Relations Bill in December 2011 (The Irish Times, 2011b), and there were no further discussions on the topic until a further High Court ruling declared unconstitutional the REA system in May 2013 (Burke-Kennedy, 2013).

While the content of the reform of wage setting mechanisms was controversially discussed by Irish politicians and the social partners, it becomes evident from this description that the reform process was a lot less politicised than in the other two reform cases. On the one hand, the largest opposition party, Fianna Fáil, mostly remained quiet on the reforms plans, having developed similar plans before the March 2011 elections. What is more, there was no significant opposition to the reforms outside the Parliament. This observation is backed by the literature, which confirms that trade unions offered only weak opposition to labour market reforms throughout the Programme. For instance, ICTU did not organise any protest against measures introduced by the government between 2011 and 2013 and 'did not even participate in the European Confederation of Trade Unions' coordinated day of "Action and Solidarity" against austerity in October 2012' (Hearne, 2015, p. 311). Instead, trade unions remained committed to dialogue and coordination with both the government and employers, at least in part because of union leaders' belief that in the crisis, industrial action was not sustainable and would not lead to results (Geary, 2016, p. 12).

Another reason for unions' restraint was the Labour Party's participation in government, as unions 'supported the Labour Party in government and thus any hint of potential opposition was considered disloyal and counterproductive' (Hearne, 2015, p. 311).[6] In December 2012, the leader of the largest trade union, the Services, Industrial, Professional and Technical Union (SIPTU), argued that the Labour Party had secured the restoration of the wage setting mechanisms and ensured that a 'threshold of decency' (Wall, 2012) remained in the government. A notable deviation from this pattern is the active participation of smaller unions, such as the union Unite, in the campaigns against the property tax and water charges (O'Connor, 2017, p. 79).

In sum, we do not observe principled groups opposing and contesting the reform of wage setting mechanisms. While some opposition politicians criticised the government's reform plans and the slow reaction to the High Court ruling in 2011, many, and especially the largest opposition party, Fianna Fáil, agreed on the necessity of reforms (an issue that Fianna Fáil previously backed when in office). Similarly, while critical of the reforms, the trade unions refrained from outright opposition and engaged in negotiations with the government and employer representatives throughout the reform process. Finally, there was no public protest against the measures. While the introduction of the local property tax led to a countrywide refusal of payment campaign in 2012 and the water charges brought many Irish citizens to the streets, we do not observe similar protest behaviour in the case of the wage setting reforms. Instead, the reinstatement of the wage setting system after the High Court ruling in 2011 was perceived as a success despite the introduction of more flexibility and inability-to-pay clauses. Therefore, the reform of the wage setting system faced low levels of politicisation.

Reputation for Policy Support

Reforms of the wage setting system were not a new topic of the Fine Gael/Labour Party government. The issue first emerged in 2009, after a challenge to the system's constitutionality by employer representatives from the hotel sector (O'Sullivan & Wallace, 2011, p. 32). The predecessor government introduced reform plans to prevent further legal challenges to the system, including the introduction of an inability to pay clause for wage setting mechanisms and ministerial oversight over wage agreements (Dáil Éireann, 2010, p. 31; The Irish Examiner, 2009). The plans did not

[6] The only exception was the ICTU protest against Anglo debt in February 2011.

proceed beyond the stage of Parliamentary debates in early 2010.[7] However, the then-governing parties Fianna Fáil and the Green Party included a commitment to review and amend the sectoral wage agreements in their recovery plan in November 2010, which served as a base for subsequent negotiations with the troika institutions (Government of Ireland, 2010, p. 37; MacCarthaigh & Hardiman, 2020, p. 184). In February 2011, the predecessor government raised the possibility that special premium payments, such as Sunday or overtime pay, should no longer be regulated by wage setting mechanisms (Wall, 2011i). In sum, the most significant—and controversial—aspects of the reform were already on the agenda before Fine Gael and the Labour Party came into office in March 2011.

Before coming into office, neither Fine Gael nor the Labour Party promoted plans to reform the wage setting system. Fine Gael committed itself to review existing EROs in its 2011 election manifesto and promoted firm-level agreements (Fine Gael, 2011a, pp. 56–57) but did not argue in favour of a reform of the overall system. Furthermore, Fine Gael highlights in a strategy paper in February 2011 that the reform is a project of the predecessor government, stating: 'We note that the Government had agreed to review the JLC and JIC wage setting mechanism' (Fine Gael, 2011b, p. 52). The Labour Party is traditionally in favour of social partnership and collective wage agreements. I had called for an extension of the REA system in its 2007 manifesto (Labour, 2007) and in 2011 underlined the importance of collective bargaining after the 2010 breakdown of social partnership and coordinated wage bargaining, while admitting the necessity of wage restraint in wage agreements (Labour, 2011a, p. 17).

The topic of reforms of the wage setting mechanisms first appears in the government agreement between the two parties negotiated in March 2011. It states that, to support small and medium enterprises, the government will 'reform the Joint Labour Committee structure, beginning with the appointment of independent chairpersons to JLCs' and opens the possibility to review 'premium pay for atypical hours, such as Sunday pay' (Labour, 2011b, p. 11). While the government agreement commits to reform the wage setting system, neither of the two parties had a reputation for supporting the measure beforehand. The reform was a project of the predecessor government, with substantial aspects of the reform discussed as early as 2009.

Blame Avoidance Strategies

In this section, I analyse how the Irish government employed blame avoidance strategies to confront blame and criticism for reforming the wage setting mechanisms. In the previous subsections, I established that politicisation of the measures was low and that the governing parties did not have a long-standing reputation for policy support. In line with the theoretical framework, I expect that the Irish government employed circling the wagons more than other blame avoidance strategies. The analysis shows that the theoretical expectation partly bears out.

[7] The government bill did not progress beyond a first debate in the Irish Parliament in February 2010 and ultimately lapsed with the elections in March 2011, see https://www.oireachtas.ie/en/bills/bill/2009/56/ (accessed on 18 March 2021).

During the reform of the wage setting mechanisms, the Irish government employed various blame avoidance strategies. The largest share of statements follows a circle the wagons approach. In these statements, the government refrained from justifying the reforms by underlining positive aspects or highlighting policy failures that make the reforms necessary or desirable. Instead, they stress that several actors are involved in the reform process, such as the previous government, the social partners and the troika institutions. Figure 4.5 shows that the largest share of statements followed this circle the wagons approach (34%), thus blurring the responsibility for reforming the wage setting mechanisms. The following statements illustrate that the described pattern was visible throughout the Programme. For instance, in May 2011, the Minister for Enterprise, Trade and Innovation, Richard Bruton, replied to a question inquiring about the consequences of the abolition of special rates for atypical hours by highlighting that the Government was building on the work of its predecessor and was getting input from experts and social partners on the issue:

> The inconsistent approach to atypical hours has been raised as an issue. The terms of reference were set by the previous Government and explicitly referred to anomalies, obsolete provisions and inflexibilities. (Dáil Éireann, 2011a, p. 637)

Similarly, after the High Court ruling, PM Enda Kenny underlined the necessity to reform the wage setting system along the lines of the Duffy/Walsh report and the High Court ruling:

> [I]n the case of reform of the joint labour committees, JLCs, and registered employment agreements, REAs, the process of making employment regulation orders, EROs, was found by the High Court to be unconstitutional [...] That supports the case for the main features of the recommendations for reform put forward in the Duffy Walsh report. Following the High Court ruling of July 2011, the Government's priority has been to prepare and deliver a comprehensive reform package because the implications of the judgment are not confined to the joint labour committee system. A programme of reform of the JLC and REA systems is required to address all the recommendations for reform put forward in the report, as well as the broad implications of the High Court ruling [...] (Dáil Éireann, 2012c, p. 30)

A disaggregation of the results by year shows that the government's reliance on a circle the wagons approach was consistent throughout the Programme, with the share of statements ranging between 31 and 36%. Yet, the strategy is not consistently the most frequently used blame avoidance approach.

It is notable that the government used the strategy of problem denial in a similarly large share of statements (33%). The share of problem denial statements is variable and decreases over time. While problem denial is the most frequently used strategy in 2011 (37%), it decreases to 31% in 2012, thus drawing level with the share of circle the wagons statements.[8] No problem denial statements were found in 2013. Yet, due to the overall small number of statements in this year ($n = 6$), the results for this year are hard to interpret. In these statements, the governments portray the reforms as necessary in the light of the Duffy/Walsh report and blur

[8] The disaggregated results can be found in Table A7 in the Appendix.

responsibility by emphasising the involvement of the social partners and EU experts. For instance, Minister Bruton argues that the reforms are a matter of technical expertise rather than a political choice, stating that:

> Equally, the reform of the system of sectoral wage agreements offers scope to further generate jobs across the wider economy. I recently received the Report of the Independent Review of Employment Regulation Orders and Registered Employment Agreements, which indicates that the system requires radical overhaul to make it fairer and more responsive to changing economic circumstances and labour market conditions. (Dáil Éireann, 2011e, p. 517)

Furthermore, the government used the High Court ruling in July 2011 to underline the importance of reforming the system and emphasised that the reform protects workers in the aftermath of the court ruling. Take the following example by Minister Bruton:

> The main purpose of the [Industrial Relations, the author] Bill is to implement the commitment in the Programme for Government to reform the Joint Labour Committee system. The reform of the legal framework for our statutory wage setting mechanisms is aimed at increasing employers' ability to retain and employ workers, particularly in sectors hard hit by the prevailing economic circumstances [...] The fact that the process of making EROs has been found by the High Court to be unconstitutional, together with the identified lack of adequate Oireachtas scrutiny of this process, only underscores some of the main features of the recommendations for reform that were put forward by the Independent Review Report on these statutory wage setting mechanisms—the Duffy/Walsh report. (Dáil Éireann, 2012a, pp. 168–169)

Overall, low-politicisation strategies that blur responsibility thus amount to 67% of the blame avoidance statements the Irish government used when discussing the reforms of the wage setting system. Yet, Fig. 4.5 also shows a considerable share of statements follows a self-defence approach, which account for 29% of all government statements. The share of self-defence statements increases over time. Starting

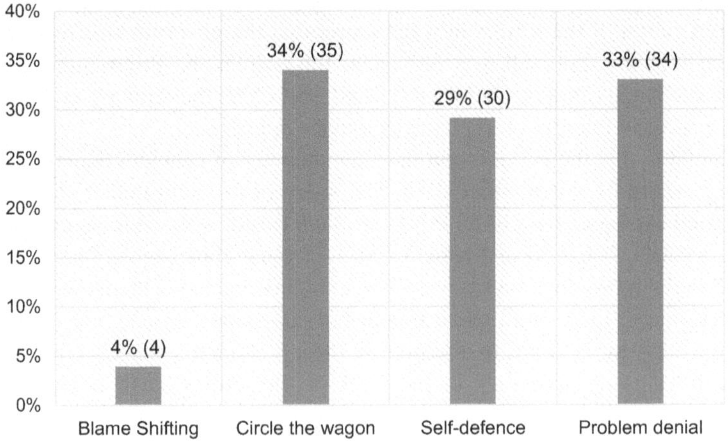

Fig. 4.5 Share of blame avoidance strategies—the reform of wage setting mechanisms

at 24% of all blame avoidance statements in 2011, the government used this strategy significantly less frequently than the other two. The share of self-defence statements then rises to 34% in 2012 and 67% in 2013, making it the most frequently used blame avoidance strategy in these years.[9]

Only a small fraction of 4% of the statements shifts blame. In these statements, the government points to the responsibility of the troika institutions, which require the reform as part of the Programme conditionality, and—especially after the 2011 court ruling—the predecessor government, which did not follow through with necessary reforms to ensure the constitutionality of the wage setting system. A disaggregation of the blame shifting statements yields little insight due to the overall low number of statements.[10]

While the overall picture thus confirms the theoretical expectation, this impression is weakened when disaggregating the data over time. The high shares of problem denial and especially of self-defence statements, which take turns in surmounting the share of circle the wagons statements in all years, contradict the theoretical framework. As the use of a strategy of self-defence should be most likely in cases with high politicisation and high reform ownership, the frequent use of this strategy is especially puzzling in light of the theoretical expectations.

However, one event that took place during the Irish Programme can help explain the divergent findings. The High Court ruling in July 2011 declared existing ERO wage agreements void. Consequently, workers in the affected industries retained the wages obtained in the wage agreements because they were stipulated in their individual contracts but were in danger of being replaced by 'cheaper' workers, as employers were no longer bound by existing EROs. The discussion, thus, shifted from reforming the wage setting mechanisms to reinstating the system. The government was thus in a position to frame the Industrial Relations Bill as a reinstatement of the system by amending those parts that had been declared unconstitutional. It could thus portray itself as rescuing rather than reforming the wage setting system, which opened up the potential to go beyond blame avoidance and claim credit in the long run.

Figure 4.6 presents the shares of blame avoidance strategies before and after the High Court ruling and supports this explanation. While 41% of statements were using a circle the wagons strategy before the ruling, the use of this strategy declines to 29% after the ruling. Conversely, the share of self-defence statements is, at 20%, considerably lower than the share of circle the wagons statements before the ruling but subsequently surpasses it. After the ruling, the predominant share of statements employs a self-defence strategy (36%). The share of problem denial statements remains relatively constant over both periods and is consistently the second most frequently used blame avoidance strategy.

[9] The disaggregated results can be found in Table A7 in the Appendix.

[10] The government is apparently not fixed on one specific target—two statements target the troika institutions, two target the predecessor government.

Indeed, looking at specific statements, this explanation of the high share of self-defence statements after the ruling bears out. For instance, Minister Bruton argued:

> On 8 May last, the Government approved a number of amendments to the Industrial Relations (Amendment) (No. 3) Bill 2011. It should be remembered that the main purpose of the Bill is to implement reform proposals in line with the commitment in the Government's Programme for National Recovery to reform the JLC system to make them more flexible and responsive to the needs of the economy [...] These reforms, and this Bill, is all the more important in the light of deficiencies in the original legislation identified in the judgment of the High Court [...] which struck down the whole ERO/REA system of wage settlements. So, this Bill is not just reforming the ERO/REA system it is actually rebuilding them and replacing a system that wasn't legally robust with a system that is better designed to meet the challenges of the Irish economy in the twenty-first century. (Dáil Éireann, 2012b, p. 686)

Similarly, Deputy PM Eamon Gilmore stated:

> As the Deputy is aware, a number of important pieces of legislation from the Department of Jobs, Enterprise and Innovation relating to the rights of workers are being progressed. [...] there is also legislation on the joint labour committees and the EROs. That legislation arose because the High Court struck down the joint labour committee system and the employment regulation order. The Government decided that the system would be reinstated on a reformed basis and that legislation is progressing. (Dáil Éireann, 2012d, pp. 10–11)

The temporal disaggregation shows that, in this case, the government's choice of blame avoidance strategies is not stable over time. It is also notable that the absolute number of statements decreases steeply over time. While 68 blame avoidance statements by the government are coded in 2011, the number decreases to 29 in the following year, and only six statements are found for the year 2013. Two factors can help explain the steep decrease in statements. First, the reform of the wage setting mechanisms was introduced relatively early on. The government presented its Bill in December 2011, and the Industrial Relations (Amendment) Act was signed into action by the President in July of the following year. This does, however, not explain the almost complete silence after the 2013 court ruling. Second, the early decrease in attention for the reform may be related to the low politicisation of the issue. While other reforms gathered significant attention both in- and outside Parliament, thus making necessary a more constant use of blame avoidance strategies, the reform of the wage setting mechanism was comparatively uncontested. Especially after the ruling in July 2011, most political actors agreed on the necessity to reform the wage setting system. The lacking reaction to the 2013 court ruling can also be explained along these lines, especially as the REA system was not reformed until 2015.

All in all, the observed pattern of blame avoidance strategies provides some evidence that confirms the theoretical expectation that the low politicisation of the reform of the wage setting system and the lack of reputation for policy support leads government representatives to focus on the strategy of circle the wagons rather than other strategies of blame avoidance. Yet, the high shares of problem denial and especially self-defence statements are puzzling from the point of view of the theoretical framework. A disaggregation of the statements showed that the high share of self-defence statements could be explained by an event external to the theoretical framework. A High Court ruling in July 2011 declared the existing wage setting system unconstitutional and changed the discourse from reform to reinstatement of the system. This allowed the government to employ a strategy of self-defence, which then allowed it to claim credit for the reinstatement of the wage setting system in the long run.

4.4 Conclusion

In this chapter, I presented three case studies of reforms introduced in Ireland under Programme conditionality. The cases varied with regard to both politicisation and reform ownership. Therefore, each case came with specific expectations about the Irish government's pattern of blame avoidance strategies. The empirical analysis showed that the theoretical framework developed in Chap. 3 had explanatory leverage in each of the three cases.

First, the introduction of a local property tax in Ireland was highly politicised. Several members of Parliament and activist organisations mobilised an extensive campaign against the payment of the household charge and the local property tax in 2012 and 2013. The two governing parties did not have a reputation for supporting this measure, as neither actively promoted the introduction of a levy on residential properties before the Programme and the larger coalition partner, Fine Gael, denounced the measure during its 2011 election campaign as 'unfair'. For these reasons, I expected that the Irish government relied upon blame shifting more frequently than on any other blame avoidance strategy. The government of PM Enda Kenny strongly relied on the high-politicisation strategies of blame avoidance and self-defence and predominantly shifted responsibility for introducing the property tax to the troika institutions and the predecessor government. The consistent results

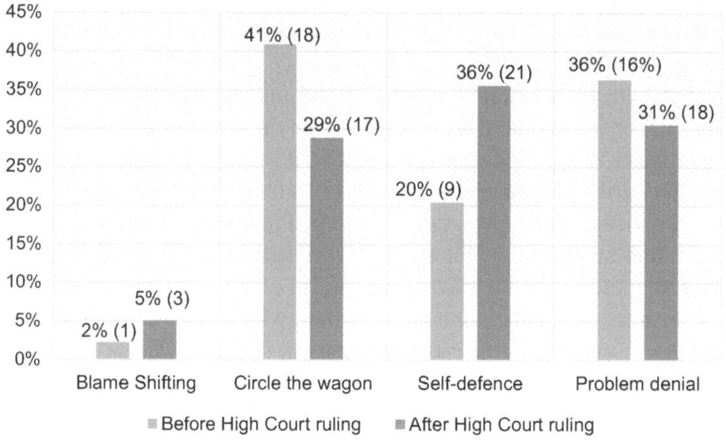

Fig. 4.6 The reform of wage setting mechanisms (before and after the High Court ruling)

throughout the Programme's duration increase the confidence in the observed pattern of blame avoidance.

Second, the reform of Irish water services was also highly politicised. Building on structures developed during the campaign against the local property tax, activists mobilised against the installation of water meters and a charging system. In 2014, these mobilisation efforts led to the biggest anti-austerity protests in Ireland in the context of the financial and the Euro crisis. This led me to expect that the Irish government also focused on the high-politicisation strategies of blame avoidance and self-defence in this case. Unlike the property tax, however, the governing parties had a reputation for supporting the reform of water services, with Fine Gael advocating for the reform as early as 2009. Therefore, I expected that the Irish government relied more on self-defence than any other blame avoidance strategy during the water services reform. The analysis showed a strong reliance on the high-politicisation strategies of blame avoidance and self-defence. In line with the theoretical expectations, I observed a predominant focus on a strategy of self-defence, which was stable throughout the reform implementation process.

Third, when reforming the wage setting system of Employment Regulation Orders and Registered Employment Agreements, the government faced little politicisation. The largest opposition party, Fianna Fáil, agreed on the necessity of reforms (an issue that Fianna Fáil previously backed when in office). Similarly, while critical of the reforms, the trade unions refrained from outright opposition and industrial action and engaged in negotiations with the government and employer representatives throughout the reform process. Finally, there was no public protest against the measures. Similar to the local property tax case, the two governing parties, Fine Gael and the Labour Party, did not have a reputation for policy support, as the reform was a project of the predecessor government, with substantial aspects of the reform discussed as early as 2009. Therefore, I expected that the government to predominantly employ a circle the wagons approach. The results were less clear in the third case. While the government relied heavily on low-politicisation strategies and especially focused on a circle the wagon approach, it employed the strategies of problem denial and circle the wagons in almost equal shares. What is more, a significant share of statements follows a self-defence approach. A closer look at the case revealed a change of strategy after a High Court ruling declared the wage setting system unconstitutional in July 2011. While the government previously relied predominantly on low-politicisation strategies, it increasingly used a self-defence approach afterwards, that opened up possibilities for credit claiming.

In sum, the theoretical expectations developed in Chap. 2 mostly bore out in the three case studies analysing the blame avoidance behaviour of the Irish government. The change in strategies in the case of the reform of the wage setting system seems to have been triggered by the High Court ruling, which allowed the government to shift strategies to make possible credit claiming in the long run.

The subsequent Chap. 5 continues to analyse blame avoidance strategies in two cases of reforms introduced under conditionality in Portugal. In Chap. 6, I evaluate the explanatory power of the theoretical framework in four pairwise comparisons of the studied cases.

References

Burke-Kennedy, E. (2012). Countryside rallies against charges. *The Irish Times,* 1 March 2012.

Burke-Kennedy, E. (2013). Court ruling casts doubt on wage deals: Supreme Court strikes down wage agreements as 'unconstitutional'. *The Irish Times,* 10 May 2013.

Collins, M. L., & Larragy, A. (2011). *A site value tax for Ireland: Approach, design and Implementation* (Trinity Economic Papers No.1911). Dublin: Trinity College Dublin.

Collins, S., McGee, H., & Cullen, P. (2011). Kenny and Gilmore to renew talks on forming coalition. *The Irish Times,* 1 March 2011.

Dáil Éireann. (2010). *26 January 2010: Official Report - unrevised* (Parliamentary Debates), *700 (1).*

Dáil Éireann. (2011a). *17 May 2011: Official Report - unrevised* (Parliamentary Debates 732(3)).

Dáil Éireann. (2011b). *25 May 2011: Official Report - unrevised* (Parliamentary Debates). *733 (1).*

Dáil Éireann. (2011c). *5 May 2011: Official Report - unrevised* (Parliamentary Debates), *731 (3).*

Dáil Éireann. (2011d). *7 June 2011: Official Report - unrevised* (Parliamentary Debates), *734 (3).*

Dáil Éireann. (2011e). *15 September 2011: Official Report - unrevised* (Parliamentary Debates), *740 (2).*

Dáil Éireann. (2011f). *20 September 2011: Official Report - unrevised* (Parliamentary Debates), *740 (3).*

Dáil Éireann. (2011g). *13 December 2011: Official Report - unrevised* (Parliamentary Debates), *749 (4).*

Dáil Éireann. (2012a). *06 March 2012: Official Report - unrevised* (Parliamentary Debates 758 (1)).

Dáil Éireann. (2012b). *07 June 2012: Official Report - unrevised* (Parliamentary Debates 767 (2)).

Dáil Éireann. (2012c). *10 July 2012: Official Report - unrevised* (Parliamentary Debates 772(1)).

Dáil Éireann. (2012d). *10 May 2012: Official Report - unrevised* (Parliamentary Debates 765 (1)).

Dáil Éireann. (2012e). *3 May 2012: Official Report - unrevised* (Parliamentary Debates), *764 (2).*

Dáil Éireann. (2012f). *18 September 2012: Official Report - unrevised* (Parliamentary Debates), *774 (1).*

Dáil Éireann. (2012g). *14 December 2012: Official Report - unrevised* (Parliamentary Debates), *787 (1).*

Dáil Éireann. (2013a). *7 March 2013: Official Report - unrevised* (Parliamentary Debates), *795 (3).*

Dáil Éireann. (2013b). *21 March 2013: Official Report - unrevised* (Parliamentary Debates), *797 (2).*

Dáil Éireann. (2013c). *11 June 2013: Official Report - unrevised* (Parliamentary Debates), *806 (1).*

Dáil Éireann. (2013d). *12 June 2013: Official Report - unrevised* (Parliamentary Debates), *806 (2).*

Dáil Éireann. (2014a). *23 October 2014: Official Report - unrevised* (Parliamentary Debates), *855 (3).*

Dáil Éireann. (2014b). *18 November 2014: Official Report - unrevised* (Parliamentary Debates), *858 (1).*

de Bréadun, D. (2011). Bruton rejects emergency legislation on pay deals. *The Irish Times,* 13 July 2011.

Department of Finance. (2019). *Review of local property tax: The report of the interdepartmental group.*

Dukelow, F. (2015). Pushing against an open door': Reinforcing the neo-liberal policy paradigm in Ireland and the impact of EU intrusion. *Comparative European Politics, 13*(1), 93–111.

Dukelow, F. (2016). Irish water services reform: Past, present and future. In M. Murphy & F. Dukelow (Eds.), *Irish welfare state in the twenty-first century: Challenges and change* (pp. 141–165). Palgrave Macmillan.

Duncan, P. (2011). Mixed response from unions, business. *The Irish Times,* 29 July 2011.

European Commission. (2011a). *The Economic Adjustment programme for Ireland* (Occasional Papers No. 76). Brussels: European Commission.

European Commission. (2011b). *Economic adjustment programme for Ireland: Autumn 2011 review* (Occasional Papers No. 88). Brussels: European Commission.

European Commission. (2012). *Economic adjustment programme for Ireland: Winter 2011 Review* (Occasional Papers No. 93). Brussels: European Commission.
European Commission. (2013a). *Economic adjustment programme for Ireland: Autumn 2012 Review* (Occasional Papers No. 127). Brussels: European Commission.
European Commission. (2013b). *Economic Adjustment programme for Ireland: Winter 2012 Review* (Occasional Papers No. 131). Brussels: Directorate General for Economic and Financial Affairs (DG ECFIN).
European Commission. (2015). *Ex-post evaluation of the economic adjustment programme: Ireland, 2010–2013* (European Economy Institutional Papers No. 4). Bussels: Directorate General for Economic and Financial Affairs (DG ECFIN). https://doi.org/10.2765/755597
Fine Gael. (2007). *General election manifesto 2007*. https://manifesto-project.wzb.eu/
Fine Gael. (2009). *New ERA*. http://www.paschaldonohoe.ie/wp-content/uploads/2010/01/NewERA1.pdf
Fine Gael. (2011a). *Manifesto 2011: Let's get Ireland working*. https://manifesto-project.wzb.eu/
Fine Gael. (2011b). *Working for our Future: A Jobs and Economic Development Strategy for Ireland 2011–2016*. https://source.southdublinlibraries.ie/bitstream/10599/10236/3/GE%202011%20DSW%20-%20Fine%20Gael%2001%20OCR.pdf
Finn, D. (2015). Ireland's water wars. *New Left Review*, 95. https://newleftreview.org/issues/ii95/articles/daniel-finn-ireland-s-water-wars
Geary, J. (2016). Economic crisis, austerity and trade union responses: The Irish Cse in Cmparative perspective. *European Journal of Industrial Relations, 22*(2), 131–147. https://doi.org/10.1177/0959680115616526
Government of Ireland. (2010). *National Recovery Plan 2011–2014*. Government Publications. http://www.budget.gov.ie/RecoveryPlan.aspx
Hearne, R. (2015). *The Irish water war, austerity and the 'risen people': An analysis of participant opinions, social and political impacts and transformative potential of the Irish anti water-charges movement*. Department of Geography, Maynooth University. Maynooth.
Hennessey, M. (2009). Fine Gael publishes plan to create 100,000 Jobs. *The Irish Times*, 27 March 2009.
Henning, C. R. (2017). *Tangled governance: International regime complexity, the troika, and the euro crisis*. Oxford: Oxford University Press.
Hick, R. (2018). Enter the troika: The politics of social security during Ireland's bailout. *Journal of Social Policy, 47*(1), 1–20. https://doi.org/10.1017/S0047279417000095
Hilliard, M. (2014). Water charges Taoiseach meets tide of protest. *The Irish Times*, 13 June 2014.
Holland, K. (2011). Candidates protest over water services. *The Irish Times*, 4 February 2011.
Holland, K. (2013). Protest rally considers boycott of property tax. *The Irish Times*, 14 January 2013.
Hourigan, N. (2017). Austerity, resistance and social protest in Ireland: Movement outcomes. In E. Heffernan, J. McHale, & N. Moore-Cherry (Eds.), *Debating austerity in Ireland: Crisis, experience and recovery* (pp. 115–128). Royal Irish Academy.
Hunt, J. (2011). Mixed response from unions and employers. *The Irish Times*, 23 December 2011.
Labour. (2007). *The fair society: Labour manifesto 2007*. https://manifesto-project.wzb.eu/
Labour. (2011a). *One Ireland. Jobs, reform, fairness: Manifesto 2011*. https://manifesto-project.wzb.eu/
Labour. (2011b). *Towards Recovery: Programme for a National Government. 2011–2016*. https://www.socialjustice.ie/content/policy-issues/programme-government-2011-2016-full-text
MacCarthaigh, M., & Hardiman, N. (2020). Exploiting conditionality: EU and international actors and post-NPM reform in Ireland. *Public Policy and Administration, 35*(2), 179–200. https://doi.org/10.1177/0952076718796548
McGee, H. (2011a). Property and water taxes at flat rate next year. *The Irish Times*, 7 May 2011.
McGee, H. (2011b). Minister defends new 100€ charge ahead of full property tax. *The Irish Times*, 27 July 2011.

McGee, H. (2013a). Property tax now on Shakier ground over what householders see as early payment: Minister says row comes from revenue offering too many payment options. *The Irish Times*, 3 November 2013.

McGee, H. (2013b). Revenue faces questions on property tax. *The Irish Examiner*, 4 November 2013.

Minihan, M. (2011). Site valuation tax to be contained in finance bill. *The Irish Times*, 10 January 2011.

Minihan, M. (2013). Martin criticises FG over 'unfair budgets'. *The Irish Times*, 7 January 2013.

Minihan, M., & O'Brien, T. (2011). Households face two new annual bills for property and water. *The Irish Times*, 1 June 2011.

O'Brien, T. (2013). Thousands attend anti-austerity protest in Dublin. *The Irish Times*, 15 April 2013.

O'Connor, F. (2017). The presence and absence of protest in austerity Ireland. In A. Della Porta, M. Andretta, T. Fernandes, F. O'Connor, E. Romanos, & M. Vogiatzoglou (Eds.), *Late neoliberalism and its discontents in the economic crisis: Comparing social movements in the European periphery* (pp. 65–98). Palgrave Macmillan. https://doi.org/10.1007/978-3-319-35080-6_3

O'Halloran, M. (2011). FG Calls for Single National Water Company. *The Irish Times*, 13 January 2011.

O'Halloran, M. (2012). Protest Rally Planned Against €100 Fee. *The Irish Times*, 27 February 2012.

O'Halloran, M. (2013). New Anti-Austerity Party to be Formed for Local Elections; Alliance will have 200 Candidates If All Left-Wing and Anti-Austerity Groups Join. *The Irish Times*, 16 December 2013.

O'Regan, M. (2011a). SF Warns Wages of 240,000 May Be Hit. *The Irish Times*, 15 April 2011.

O'Regan, M. (2011b). Legislation on low earners due 'as early as possible' after break. *The Irish Times*, 20 July 2011.

O'Sullivan, M., & Wallace, J. (2011). Minimum labour standards in a social partnership system: The persistence of the Irish variant of wages councils. *Industrial Relations Journal*, *42*(1), 18–35.

Pisani-Ferry, J., Sapir, A., & Wolff, G. B. (2013). *EU-IMF assistance to Euro-area countries: An early assessment* (Bruegel Blueprint).

Regan, A. (2013). *The impact of the Eurozone crisis on Irish social partnership: A political economy analysis* (DIALOGUE Working Paper No. 3). Governance and Tripartism Department.

Roche, B. (2011). No water levy until meters installed, says Hogan. *The Irish Times*, 10 May 2011.

Roche, B. (2014). Protesters vow to continue blocking water meters. *The Irish Times*, 24 April 2014.

Slattery, L. (2011). Review of wage deals in certain sectors 'A Fresh Attack on Incomes'. *The Irish Times*, 10 February 2011.

The Irish Examiner. (2009). Bill to strengthen worker agreements. *The Irish Examiner*, 8 August 2009.

The Irish Examiner. (2010). Unite Up Pressure with Call for Industrial Action. *The Irish Examiner*, 3 December 2010.

The Irish Examiner. (2011a). Wage agreements to be reviewed. *The Irish Examiner*, 9 February 2011.

The Irish Examiner. (2011b). Still undecided? Here's a last-minute summary. *The Irish Examiner*, 24 February 2011.

The Irish Examiner. (2011c). Government 'Committed' to reforming wage deals. *The Irish Examiner*, 30 May 2011.

The Irish Examiner. (2011d). U-turn on legislation to protect low-paid. *The Irish Examiner*, 13 July 2011.

The Irish Examiner. (2011e). Govt to fine householders who do not pay new household charge. *The Irish Examiner*, 26 July 2011.

The Irish Examiner. (2011f). €100 Charge to Hit 1.8m Households. *The Irish Examiner*, 27 July 2011.

The Irish Examiner. (2011g). Householders urged not to pay charges by left-wing groups. *The Irish Examiner*, 8 September 2011.

The Irish Examiner. (2011h). Unions and opposition groups say 'Enough' to Government Cuts. *The Irish Examiner,* 14 September 2011.
The Irish Examiner. (2012a). Protesters launch anti-household charge hotline number. *The Irish Examiner,* 11 January 2012.
The Irish Examiner. (2012b). Public urged to join anti-taxprotests. *The Irish Examiner,* 25 February 2012.
The Irish Examiner. (2012c). 'It's not our debt': Thousands of protesters attend anti-household charge Rally. *The Irish Examiner,* 24 March 2012.
The Irish Examiner. (2012d). Protest Group Claim 10,000 Attend Household Charge March. *The Irish Examiner,* 31 March 2012.
The Irish Examiner. (2012e). Threats of mass revolt over meter costs. *The Irish Examiner,* 17 April 2012.
The Irish Examiner. (2012f). Backlash deepens over water crisis. *The Irish Examiner,* 18 April 2012.
The Irish Examiner. (2012g). Group to fight water charges. *The Irish Examiner,* 19 April 2012.
The Irish Examiner. (2012h). Higgins Vows not to Pay Property Tax. *The Irish Examiner,* 21 September 2012.
The Irish Examiner. (2012i). Fianna Fáil launches campaign against property tax. *The Irish Examiner,* 10 October 2012.
The Irish Examiner. (2013a). Six hundred turn out for anti-austerity meeting. *The Irish Examiner,* 12 January 2013.
The Irish Examiner. (2013b). FG faces revolt over property tax plan. *The Irish Examiner,* 16 January 2013.
The Irish Examiner. (2013c). Gardaí called as protesters stop Cork City Council Meeting. *The Irish Examiner,* 28 January 2013.
The Irish Examiner. (2013d). Collins: Property tax the rock Govt Will Perish on. *The Irish Examiner,* 10 March 2013.
The Irish Examiner. (2013e). SF to launch bill to remove property tax. *The Irish Examiner,* 25 March 2013.
The Irish Examiner. (2013f). Revenue to appear before Dáil Committee on Property Tax. *The Irish Examiner,* 3 November 2013.
The Irish Examiner. (2013g). Opposition TDs stage walkout of 'Sham Debate' on water bill. *The Irish Examiner,* 19 December 2013.
The Irish Examiner. (2014a). Cork residents stop Irish water work. *The Irish Examiner,* 22 April 2014.
The Irish Examiner. (2014b). Call for wave of water meter protests. *The Irish Examiner,* 24 April 2014.
The Irish Examiner. (2014c). Tensions mount at water meter blockade as two injured. *The Irish Examiner,* 1 May 2014.
The Irish Times. (2011a). Enda Kenny's Immediate Goals. *The Irish Times,* 5 May 2011.
The Irish Times. (2011b). Bill on Joint Labour Committees Approved by Government. *The Irish Times,* 21 December 2011.
The Irish Times. (2012). House tax protest disrupts meeting. *The Irish Times,* 10 January 2012.
The Irish Times. (2013). Property tax returns filed by 1.5m Homes: Compliance rate of more than 80 per cent secured after extension deadline. *The Irish Times,* 30 May 2013.
The Journal. (2012). Property tax: Where do the political parties stand? *Thejournal.Ie,* 7 October 2012. https://www.thejournal.ie/party-positions-property-tax-621790-Oct2012/
Thornhill, D. (2015). *Review of the Local Porptery Tax (LPT).* http://www.budget.gov.ie/Budgets/2016/Documents/Review_of_Local_Property_Tax_pub.pdf
Wall, M. (2011a). Fast food group brings constitutional challenge. *The Irish Times,* 14 March 2011.
Wall, M. (2011b). Reform of overtime pay needed, says Bruton. *The Irish Times,* 7 May 2011.
Wall, M. (2011c). Wage-setting deals backed but call for radical Overhaul. *The Irish Times,* 21 May 2011.

Wall, M. (2011d). Thousands Face Pay Cuts in Proposed Reform of Wage Deals. *The Irish Times,* 26 May 2011.

Wall, M. (2011e). For Unions, Bruton's reforms will slash wages and may be straw that breaks camel's back. *The Irish Times,* 27 May 2011.

Wall, M. (2011f). Bruton to keep to schedule for reform of wage mechanisms. *The Irish Times,* 3 June 2011.

Wall, M. (2011g). JLCs ruling devastating for workers, says Union. *The Irish Times,* 8 July 2011.

Wall, M. (2011h). Bruton says reforms will protect workers. *The Irish Times,* 29 July 2011.

Wall, M. (2011i). Sunday Pay change raised in February. *The Irish Times,* 2 August 2011.

Wall, M. (2012). Labour maintaining threshold of decency, says Siptu Leader. *The Irish Times,* 3 December 2012.

Chapter 5
Blame Avoidance Strategies in Portugal: Two Cases of Reforms

In the early 2000s, Portugal experienced sluggish economic growth and low productivity, which, together with increasing employment in the public sector, led to a continuous increase in public debt. In the first decade of the 2000s, the Commission set into motion the process of an Excessive Deficit Procedure (EDP) three times (Henning, 2017; Viegas & Ribeiro, 2014). After the financial crisis, the Portuguese government followed the strategy of many EU member states to counter the consequences of the global crisis and introduced stimulus packages in 2008 and 2009. The consequent increases of sovereign debt, together with the onset of the Euro crisis, led to a steep increase in risk premiums on government debt, which increased the costs of servicing public debt (Pereira & Wemans, 2015). To counter these processes, the Socialist minority government under Prime Minister José Sócrates introduced three rounds of austerity measures from 2010 onwards. Yet, the economic outlook worsened throughout 2010 and 2011, and opposition to the government's austerity measures grew. When the Sócrates government's fourth austerity package failed to win Parliamentary support in March 2011, this not only caused the government to resign and open the way for elections but also forced it to request financial assistance from the EU and the IMF (Zartaloudis, 2014).

The negotiations of the Portuguese Programme included not just the governing Socialist Party (Partido Socialista, PS) but also the PSD and the CDS, as negotiations took place before the Parliamentary elections on 5 June 2011. The Programme was signed in May 2011 and envisaged to run until 2014 (European Commission, 2011b, p. 4). The Programme parties agreed that the Programme's implementation would start after the Parliamentary elections and fall to the new Portuguese government. On 5 June 2011, the elections delivered a heavy blow to the governing PS and the PSD, which emerged as the strongest party, and the CDS formed a coalition government under PM Pedro Passos Coelho (Lütz et al., 2019). The Portuguese Programme consisted of three pillars. First, it aimed at reducing the public deficit by introducing a fiscal consolidation strategy that would also streamline the public

L. Kriegmair, *Responsiveness and Responsibility in the Euro Crisis*, Contributions to Political Science, https://doi.org/10.1007/978-3-031-84473-7_5

sector. Second, it introduced financial sector safeguards. Third, it foresaw significant structural reforms to improve the competitiveness of the Portuguese economy and encourage growth (European Commission, 2011b, p. 6).

This chapter analyses the Portuguese government's use of blame avoidance strategies in two cases of reform required by Programme conditionality. While the Portuguese government had a reputation for policy support in both cases, the cases vary with regard to politicisation. Following the theoretical framework, I thus expect to find a different pattern of blame avoidance strategies in the analysis of each case. While I do not argue that governments will commit consistently to one strategy of blame avoidance, I expect a clear pattern that shows their preference for the predominant strategy.

First, I study the labour market reforms the Portuguese government introduced to comply with Programme conditionality. The government of PM Passos Coelho faced considerable headwinds when introducing labour market reforms, and the social partners increasingly politicised the measures. The government had a reputation for policy support, with both governing parties having long-standing commitments to reforming the labour market since their last term in office when they introduced far-reaching labour market reforms, which the successor government partially reversed. In line with the theoretical framework, the analysis of blame avoidance strategies shows that the Portuguese government primarily employed a self-defence approach.

Second, I examine the measures introduced to liberalise regulated professions in compliance with the conditionality included in the Portuguese Programme. The liberalisation of regulated professions faced low politicisation, with professional associations and opposition parties mounting little resistance to the reforms. Similar to the case of labour market reforms, the Portuguese government, or at least the larger coalition partner PSD, had a long-standing commitment to easing regulations of the goods and services markets and had voted in favour of liberalising regulated professions in the past. Confirming the theoretical expectations, the analysis of blame avoidance strategies shows that the PSD-CDS coalition government mainly focused on problem denial.

Each of the two case studies probes the theoretical expectations developed in Chap. 2 in a case that exhibits a specific combination of the two independent variables and thus allows for a first evaluation of the theoretical framework within each case. What is more, the cases I present in this chapter form the basis of a pairwise comparison, which allow me to probe the theoretical expectations of the framework across cases in Chap. 6.

The remainder of the chapter is divided into three sections. The following two sections are dedicated to the case studies. For each case, I will, first, give a brief description of the cases to provide an overview of the reform process and establish that the introduced reforms were indeed requirements that needed to be fulfilled to comply with Programme conditionality. Then, I describe the two independent variables, politicisation and the governing parties' reputation for policy support. Finally, I present the analysis of blame avoidance strategies and evaluate the findings against the theoretical framework. The third section summarises the results of the two case studies and concludes.

5.1 Introduction of Labour Market Reforms

During the early 2000s, Portugal experienced an increase in structural unemployment, and, in reaction, two rounds of labour market reforms were introduced in 2003 and 2009. However, these reforms had limited success in ameliorating what were considered the problems of the Portuguese labour market. For one, the reforms sustained a high level of protection for labour market insiders, thus perpetuating labour market dualisation (Cardoso & Branco, 2018, pp. 35–36). Furthermore, the reforms did not change the fundamental principles of favourability and continuity of collective agreements, which are perceived as problematic rigidities of the Portuguese labour market.[1] In this section, I analyse the labour market reforms introduced during the Programme and the blame avoidance strategies the government used in its course. The PSD-CDS coalition government introduced a wide range of reforms related to the labour market. Both opposition parties and the social partners contested these reforms and politicisation of the measures grew over the Programme's duration. The governing parties had a long-standing commitment to reforming the Portuguese labour market and thus had reform ownership. In line with the theoretical expectations, the analysis of the blame avoidance strategies employed by the government shows a solid commitment to the strategy of self-defence.

Description of Reforms

The troika institutions found nominal labour costs had been consistently above productivity growth in Portugal since the late 1990s and identified the 'downward rigidity of nominal wages' as a 'major reason for the increase in unemployment since 2011' (European Commission, 2011b, p. 12). Furthermore, they pointed out that the solid employment protection and the ridged collective bargaining system led to a dualisation of the Portuguese labour market, with solid protection for workers with permanent contracts and lower wages and little protection for atypical workers. The Programme thus required four sets of measures to reform the Portuguese labour market. First, it demanded the introduction of flexible working time arrangements, such as a 'bank of hours', the reduction of compensation for overtime, and the easing of requirements for short time working schemes. Second, it further demanded a freeze of the national minimum wage for the Programme duration,[2] the limitation of the extension and survival of collective agreements, and the decentralisation of collective bargaining. Third, it comprised requirements to

[1] The favourability principle commits collective agreements to lay down conditions that are more favourable than minimum legal provisions. The principle of continuity holds that agreements could only expire when the social partners agreed on their expiration unanimously or when they are replaced Campos Lima (2019, p. 491). Together with the quasi-automatic extension of collective agreements, these measures guaranteed Portuguese trade unions a critical role in labour relations despite comparatively low membership Campos Lima and Abrantes (2016, p. 11).

[2] The Programme required a commitment that increases of the national minimum wage would take place only with troika agreement and 'if justified by economic and labour market developments', see European Commission (2011b, p. 78).

reduce employment protection, including significant decreases in severance payments and a reform of the rules for individual dismissals. Finally, the Programme required the Portuguese government to strengthen Active Labour Market Policies but remained vague on specific measures (see also Campos Lima & Abrantes, 2016; European Commission, 2011b, pp. 78–81; Theodoropoulou, 2015).

After coming into office in June 2011, the centre-right PSD-CDS coalition immediately set to work on the Programme implementation. Law 53/2011 of 14 October 2011 lowered the costs of dismissals to employers by reducing severance pay for new contracts.[3] In 2012, the duration of fix term contracts was extended (Law 3/2012 of 10 January),[4] and a new Labour Code (Law 23/2012) significantly changed provisions for employment protection and collective bargaining. Most notably, the new law extended the rules on severance pay to all existing work contracts and eased conditions for individual dismissals. What is more, the law increased working time in the private sector by reducing vacation time and the number of public holidays, and cut overtime payments. The law also decentralised collective bargaining by allowing for company level agreements and the derogation from higher level agreements. Furthermore, wage setting in collective agreements was restricted in that the new Labour Code suspended provisions for annual holidays, overtime payment and compensatory rest higher than the legal provisions (Campos Lima & Abrantes, 2016, pp. 9–11; Cardoso & Branco, 2018, 39–43).

The centre-right government further weakened the Portuguese collective bargaining system by imposing stricter conditions on the extension of collective agreements (Resolution 90/2012). In August 2013, it further decreased severance payments to align with European averages (Law 69/2013) and created an employer fund for severance payments that ensured payments in cases where companies faced economic difficulties or insolvency (Law 70/2013) (Távora & González, 2016, pp. 341–342).

A Constitutional Court ruling reversed parts of the new labour legislation on 20 September 2013. The Court declared unconstitutional the suspension of collective agreements setting more favourable conditions for compensatory rest and holiday entitlements and partially revoked restrictions to agreements on overtime pay. Moreover, the ruling repealed provisions for individual dismissals, most prominently the definition of criteria for dismissals by employers. The latter part of the ruling made necessary further legal action to regulate individual dismissals. In May 2014, the government's new criteria were approved in Parliament (Law 27/2014) (Cardoso & Branco, 2018, p. 39; Távora & González, 2016, pp. 342–345).

In addition to the reforms, the government introduced several active labour market policies from 2012, which included employment subsidies (for example, the Estímulo Emprego 2012 programme), as well as internships and financial incentives for employers to tackle youth unemployment (for example, the Impulso Jovem

[3] Severance pay was cut from 30 to 20 days per year of work, with a cap of 12 months, or 240 minimum wages, see Campos Lima and Abrantes (2016, p. 13).

[4] The extension was prolonged by Law 76/2013.

programme and the Youth Guarantee Scheme). However, the financing of activation measures remained well below pre-Programme standards throughout the 2011–2014 period (Cardoso & Branco, 2018, p. 45).

The troika recognised the reforms the PSD-CDS coalition government had introduced to reform the Portuguese labour market during the Programme's duration: 'Severance payments have been reduced and individual dismissals eased; [...] working time flexibility has been increased; steps were taken to reform the wage-setting mechanism, particularly through the introduction of a quantitative threshold for the extension of collective agreements' (European Commission, 2014, p. 61). Yet, the Commission cautioned that further reforms were necessary to reduce unemployment and labour market segmentation after the Programme.

Politicisation of Labour Market Reforms

In the past, agreements with the social partners had helped Portuguese governments gain support for reforms of the Portuguese economy and labour market. While two social pacts, reached in 2011 and 2012 respectively, contained parts of the Programme's labour market conditionality, the reforms became increasingly politicised during the Programme's duration.

Upon coming into office, the government could build on preparations by the predecessor government. Parts of the measures required in the Programme were part of the Social Pact the preceding PS government and the social partners had approved in March 2011.[5] However, of the two big trade union associations UGT (União Geral de Trabalhadores) and CGTP (Confederação Geral dos Trabalhadores Portugueses-Intersindical Nacional), only the UGT approved the agreement. The CGTP organised a large protest against the social pact and the PS government's austerity measures in March 2011 (Távora & González, 2016, p. 311). The 2011 social pact thus secured the new PSD-CDS government the support of parts social partners and the PS, which was now the largest opposition party, for the introduction of the reductions of severance pay for new contracts in late August 2011, as well as the extension of fixed-term contracts in January 2012. The smaller left-wing opposition parties, like the Portuguese Communist Party (Partido Comunista Português, PCP) and the Left Block (Bloco de Esquerda, BE), and the CGTP opposed the measures.

Subsequent reforms required additional coordination between the government and the social partners, either because measures foreseen in the Programme were not part of the previous social pact or because the specific content of reforms remained unclear in the agreement. In November 2011, the trade union associations jointly organised a general strike to protest the government's austerity policies (Campos Lima & Abrantes, 2016, p. 17). While a decline in the social partnership

[5] The *Acordo Tripartido para a Competitividade e Emprego* provided for an extension of the duration of fixed-term contracts, changes of collective bargaining rules such as the introduction of firm-level agreements, a revision of the causes for individual dismissals and a reduction of severance payment to 20 days per year and capping payments at 12 months for new contracts, see Conselho Económico e Social (2011, 19, 24–26).

was, in part, a result of tax increases and pension cuts introduced without prior consultations and that adversely affected workers both in the public and private sector (Campos Lima, 2012a), labour market reforms increasingly became a bone of contention among social partners as well.

The government postponed some measures, such as the creation of a fund for severance payments, which were controversial among the social partners (Campos Lima, 2011; Tiago, 2011) and initiated negotiations on changes of the Labour Code which included measures not previously foreseen in the 2011 Social Agreement (Távora & González, 2016, p. 334). The government's plans for working time increases in the private sector ignited conflict among the social partners (Jornal de Notícias, 2011; Rodrigues, 2012). While the centre-right government reached a compromise with the UGT and the employer associations and signed a tripartite agreement in January 2012 (Comissão Permanente De Concertação Social, 2012, pp. 40–46; Jornal de Notícias, 2012a), the CGTP refrained from signing the agreement and went to strike against the agreement in March 2012 (Wise, 2012a). The UGT justified the agreement by highlighting that the government had agreed not to pursue additional labour market reforms that were not part of the Programme and the social pact (Campos Lima, 2012a), but peace was brittle. In April 2012, the UGT threatened to shred the agreement, accusing the government of concentrating solely on liberalising the labour market while neglecting other aspects of the 2012 social agreement (Martins, 2012a).

Opposition parties were also divided on the agreement. While the Socialist Party, the largest opposition party, accepted the necessity of reforming the labour market, other parties, like the PCP and the Left Block, condemned the agreement's 'attacks on workers' (Correia & Roque, 2012) and questioned the constitutionality of the reforms (Campos Lima, 2012b). Based on the compromise with the social partners, the new Labour Code found Parliamentary approval on 11 May 2012, with the abstention of the Socialist Party (Jornal de Notícias, 2012b; Martins, 2012b). The government had thus managed to only partially contain the conflicts over the changes to the Labour Code, and the contestation of labour market reforms was increasing.

The conflict over labour market reforms further grew after the introduction of the new Labour Code for two reasons. First, the government decided unilaterally to limit the extension of collective agreements and, in addition, proposed a cut in employers' social security contributions while simultaneously raising workers' contributions. Both measures were presented as strategies to decrease labour costs and were met with significant protest by opposition parties and social partners. The plan to increase workers' social contributions led to protests in September 2012 and forced Prime Minister Passos Coelho to renounce the plans (Távora & González, 2016, p. 338; Wise, 2012b). Similarly, the changes in the extension of collective agreement raised loud criticism from the social partners, with both unions and employer associations condemning the government's unilateral action as endangering the collective bargaining system (Bulfone & Afonso, 2020, pp. 833–834; Campos Lima, 2013; Távora & González, 2016, pp. 335–336). These developments lead to an erosion of trust between the social partners in the second half of 2012 and, in part, the general strike held by the CGTP and parts of the UGT's unions in November 2012 (Campos Lima & Abrantes, 2016, p. 17).

Second, the 2012 Social Pact provided for a general agreement between the government and the social partners regarding the reforms to be implemented as part of the Programme but refrained from specifying the form of some measures, such as the final level of severance pay, the fund for severance pay and changes in collective bargaining. Conflicts on the specificities of reforms thus increased throughout 2012 and 2013. In December 2012, the government announced that an alignment with the European average would decrease Portuguese severance payment to 12 days per year of tenure and that an alignment would be introduced in concert with the severance pay fund. The proposed cut in severance pay was rejected by the unions and led the UGT to threaten to leave the negotiation table and 'tear up the tripartite agreement' (Rodrigues, 2013, translation by the author). UGT leader João Proença conditioned union support on a differentiation between severance pay for existing and new contracts, as well as the simultaneous introduction of an alignment with EU averages and the severance pay funds (Correia & Tiago, 2013; Ribeiro, 2013). Employer associations insisted on the 12-day provision and urged for a postponement of the fund as it posed an additional burden to employers (Público, 2013; Rodrigues, 2013). To propitiate both sides, the government offered concessions, proposing the creation of two funds covering both collective dismissals and dismissals in cases of insolvency and promising to cover employers' contributions to the funds for the first 18 months (Correia, 2013; Martins, 2013b). Nevertheless, trade unions still opposed a renewed adjustment of severance pay, and the UGT reiterated its threat to consider the tripartite agreement void if the government did not change the level of severance pay (Martins, 2013a). In reaction to the union's opposition, the government was forced to renegotiate the requirement for an alignment for severance pay with the troika institutions (Martins & Rodrigues, 2013). The government's compromise[6] was adopted in Parliament with the votes from the governing parties and the PS in June 2013 (Jornal de Notícias, 2013).

The reform of severance pay did not provide for a long breathing pause for the government, however. Upon request by the opposition parties (Martins, 2013c), the Constitutional Court ruled unconstitutional parts of the 2012 Labour Code in October 2013. The Court's decision revoked the suspension of provisions for compensatory rest and holidays, and found inadmissible parts of the Labour Code's provisions easing employment protection. This decision forced the government to define criteria for individual dismissals in cases of job extinction (Távora & González, 2016, pp. 342–345). In December 2013, the PSD-CDS coalition government presented a proposal consisting of six criteria to determine a rank order for dismissals in cases of extinction of working position.[7] The definition of these

[6] The government's final proposal included a transitory regime that retained acquired rights and henceforth offered workers 18 days of severance pay for the first 3 years of contract and 12 days thereafter.

[7] The government proposed six criteria, including the performance of workers, their education and professional qualifications, the costs of employee maintenance, the seniority of workers in job and

criteria proved highly contentious, with the unions criticising that they gave employers too much leeway, promoted wage dumping, and constituted an invasion of workers' privacy (Martins, 2013d, 2014a, b). To reach a compromise with the unions, the government offered a ranking of the criteria in January 2014 (Pinheiro, 2014). However, the UGT threatened that the proposal would not receive union support unless the government removed certain elements from the list. What is more, the ranking of criteria and the possible elimination of elements from the list raised the criticism of employer associations, especially the Confederation of the Portuguese Industry (CIP) (Martins, 2014b; Tiago, 2014).

The conflict with the social partners did not abate before the government met with the troika institutions on 20 February 2014. Instead, calls by the CIP to reinstate, in some form, the suspensions of collective agreements the Constitutional Court had revoked in its September 2013 ruling aggravated the conflict (Martins, 2014c). To reach an agreement, the government offered further concessions. Nevertheless, a compromise failed with both the unions and the CIP opposing the new criteria for individual dismissals, and the government had to introduce the criteria without the support of the social partners (Martins, 2014d; Público, 2014). In consequence, the opposition parties heavily criticised the government's proposal. The Left Block called the criteria for dismissal 'one of the most violent projects of the PSD/CDS Government' (Correia, 2014; translated by the author), and opposition parties were united in their disapproval of the government's proposal (Jornal de Notícias, 2014a, b).

In sum, the government's plans to reform the Portuguese labour market grew increasingly contested over time. While the government could initially build on the support of the largest opposition party, the PS, and at least parts of the social partners, relations with the latter deteriorated over time. The social partners grew more and more critical of the government's reform plans, making compromise agreements more and more difficult. While some of the government's plans led to public protests, like the plans to increase worker's social security contributions, others lead to public conflicts between the government and the social partners, like the alignment of severance payments and the criteria for dismissals. All in all, the Portuguese labour market reforms were highly politicised.

Reputation for Policy Support

The two parties governing throughout the Programme, the PSD and CDS, have engaged in significant labour market reforms before coming into office in 2011. During the last PSD-CDS coalition government under PM Barroso, a new Labour Code entered into force in 2003. The reform of Portuguese labour market legislation foresaw significant steps towards a liberalisation of the Portuguese labour market. It extended the maximum duration of fixed term contracts and reformed collective bargaining by allowing for unilateral requests for expiry of collective agreements and doing away with the favourability principle, which required collective

firm, and the financial and family situation of employees.

agreements to improve upon legal provisions on wage setting and employment conditions. It thus 'represented a major shift' (Campos Lima, 2019, 485) in Portuguese labour law (see also Cardoso & Branco, 2018, p. 35). The PDS's 2005 electoral programme highlighted the reform as an essential step towards removing labour market rigidities in Portugal (PSD, 2005, 19).

While neither party campaigned in favour of changes in labour market legislation in the 2009 elections, the topic emerged in the context of the 2011 austerity measures. Both parties supported efforts to reform labour legislation under the predecessor government. The predecessor PS government proposed reforms of the severance pay system in early 2011, which included reductions of severance pay and the introduction of a fund for severance payments (Figueira, 2011; Penedos, 2011). The PSD and the CDS did not oppose their plans to reform the labour market. Instead, the PSD repeatedly stressed the importance of structural reforms in general and, specifically, labour market reforms (Aníbal et al., 2011). Especially the PSD's proposals to liberalise the rules for individual dismissals[8] and extend the duration of fixed term contracts were very controversial and received significant public attention (Martins, 2011; Rodrigues, 2011).

The PSD reiterated its calls for a reform of the labour market during the 2011 election campaign. It campaigned for reform of the labour market as specified in the Programme to promote economic growth. The election manifesto called for the removal of rigidities. It contained specific proposals for the decentralisation of collective bargaining, the flexibilisation of working time, and the extension of temporary contracts (PSD, 2011, pp. 39–40; Ramos, 2011). Similarly, the CDS' programme contained a commitment to labour market reform, explicitly calling for the extension of fixed term contracts, less restrictive labour legislation for small and medium enterprises, the decentralisation of collective bargaining, wage moderation, and a reduction of public holidays (CDS-PP, 2011, pp. 39–40). The programme for government reiterated the commitment to reforming the labour market, albeit without reference to specific reforms (Público, 2011b; Simas & Rodrigues, 2011).

In sum, the two parties responsible for implementing the Portuguese Programme from June 2011 had a long-standing reputation for supporting reforms of the Portuguese labour market. Both parties had been responsible for a previous change to the Labour Code in 2003, which significantly changed the collective bargaining system. When involved in the Programme negotiations, especially the PSD publicly advocated for labour market reforms, such as the liberalisation of individual dismissals. The reform commitment was reiterated during the election campaign and in the Programme for government.

---

[8] The calls for liberalisation of dismissals were dropped during the election campaign, see Público (2011a). Yet, the PS continued to attack the PSD for the proposal throughout the election campaign, see G. Pereira and Pinto (2011). Therefore, the liberalisation of dismissals continued to be closely linked with the PDS's political agenda even after the elections, see Lourenço (2011).

Blame Avoidance Strategies

In this section, I analyse how the Portuguese government employed blame avoidance strategies to confront blame and criticism for labour market reforms. In the previous sections, I established that the reforms were politicised and both coalition partners had a reputation of supporting the measures introduced as part of the Programme conditionality. In line with the theoretical framework, I thus expect that the Portuguese government relied on self-defence more than on all other strategies. The analysis shows that this expectation bears out in the case of the reforms of the Portuguese labour market.

The PSD-CDS coalition government focused predominantly on self-defence to avoid blame for the labour market reforms introduced between 2011 and 2014. Representatives of the Portuguese government consistently justified the government's reform efforts by underlining the current shortcomings of the Portuguese labour legislation and the potential of the reforms to foster economic growth and employment. Figure 5.1 shows that half of all blame avoidance statements follow this self-defence approach. A disaggregation of the results by year shows that the government's predominant reliance on a self-defence approach was consistent throughout the Programme, with the share of self-defence statements ranging between 39 and 56%.[9]

Furthermore, the following statements illustrate that the described self-defence pattern was visible throughout the Programme. In a Parliamentary discussion of the first reduction of severance pay in July 2011, the Secretary of State for Employment, Pedro Silva Martins, underlined the deficiencies of the current Portuguese labour legislation and advocated for the Government's reform plans:

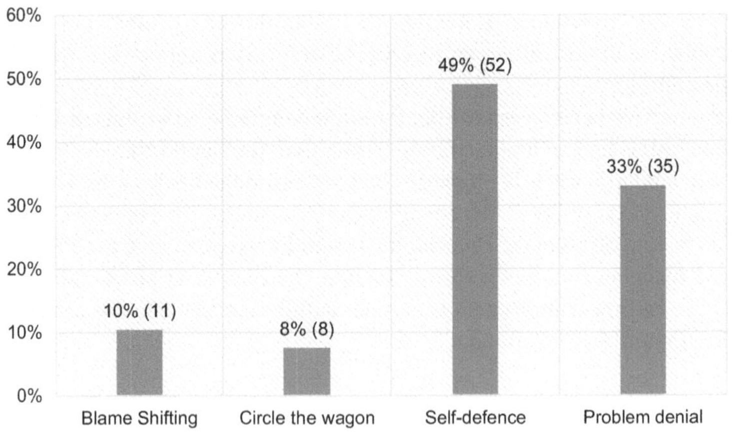

Fig. 5.1 Share of blame avoidance strategies—the labour market reforms

[9]The disaggregated results can be found in Table A15 in the Appendix.

> The purpose of these amendments is quite clear and it is to foster job creation. As soon as employers are faced with lower compensation payments, job creation will become more interesting, more profitable, from the employers' point of view. [...] The current situation in Portugal [...] discourages job creation. That's why, as I said earlier, our young people go and look for jobs in other countries, where compensation is lower. Employers in other countries find it easier to create jobs, labour markets are more flexible, less ossified, more mobile, with large productivity gains, which in turn allow for higher salaries. [...] Everyone wins since it is possible to create jobs more easily. This is the main goal of the Government's proposal: to facilitate job creation and thereby combat unemployment and segmentation. (Diário da Assembleia da República, 2011b, pp. 36–37)

Similarly, PM Paolo Passos Coelho stated in a speech in Parliament in March 2012:

> There is therefore another alternative, the one we took on from the first day we took office, the alternative we embodied when we were elected to govern in such difficult circumstances: that of attacking the causes of the crisis, of the difficulties faced by companies, of unemployment, of the lack of competitiveness, of the closure of the Portuguese economy and society, of poverty, of the lack of mobility and of inequality. [...] But to achieve all these objectives requires change and reform and this is the opposite of complacent and incomprehensible satisfaction with the status quo. For this Government, the Portuguese deserve more, much more than what is as it is! Thus, it was necessary to reform the labour market in order to increase employment and give more opportunities to young people and the unemployed, and that is what we did! [...] We had to respond to the worsening youth unemployment, and that is what we did! (Diário da Assembleia da República, 2012b, pp. 8–9)

The Minister of Economy and Employment, Álvaro Santos Pereira, underlined the benefits of the government's labour market reforms in a discussion on ways to foster investment in Portugal in March 2013:

> Deputy Oliveira asked me what we can do to attract new investment to Portugal. [...] Investors may be interested if there are important economic reforms that can attract more investment. Therefore, we [...] have to act, as we did, at the level of labour legislation, making hiring more flexible and making our labour legislation more attractive. (Diário da Assembleia da República, 2013a, p. 26)

Finally, PM Passos Coelho stated in a discussion on the criteria for fair dismissals in February 2014:

> [F]irst of all, I want to say that, in fact, unemployment is not a disaster generated by this Government, it is a disaster generated by policies that were followed for many years and that led the country to bankruptcy. [...] The policies we have been promoting are aimed at reviving the country. Do not confuse the medicine with the disease! Second: regarding performance evaluation, I cannot agree with the Honourable Member. It is essential that there is the greatest possible objectivity whenever a company has to make choices regarding the identification, when terminating a job, of the worker that may have to be dismissed. The performance evaluation is perhaps, with the prior knowledge and involvement of the worker, the most objective thing that can be done. [...] I think it is very important that Portuguese companies, [...] that want to be more productive, more competitive and generate more sustained employment, may also themselves develop performance assessment processes that are not only good for companies but also fair for workers. (Diário da Assembleia da República, 2014a, pp. 24–25)

Problem denial was the second most frequent strategy the government employed to avoid blame for the labour market reforms. The Portuguese government thus heavily relied on strategies that framed the labour market reforms in a positive light. Figure 5.1 shows that in one-third of statements, government representatives did not stop at underlining the benefits of labour market reforms and also diffused responsibility by underlining the role of the social partners, the Portuguese voters and international commitments. A disaggregation by year shows that problem denial was consistently the second most frequently used strategy, ranging between 19 and 41%.[10] A closer look at the content of the statements confirms that the government consistently relied on a pattern of argumentation that underlined the necessity to reform the labour market to create employment and presented the reforms as an endeavour supported by domestic as well as international actors. For instance, the Minister of Economy and Employment, Álvaro Santos Pereira, argued in a Parliamentary debate on unemployment and changes to the labour legislation in October 2011:

> [...] labour law reform is essential for job creation and for fostering the competitiveness of our economy. It is not by chance that these are the points that we find foreseen in the Memorandum of Understanding as integral elements of the structural reforms for the Portuguese labour market. The inflexibility of the labour laws has evident consequences internally, namely in the segmentation of the labour market, which is especially visible in the most vulnerable groups of workers. [...] It is also important to realise that the Portuguese labour market is not attractive to many potential investors and it is necessary to realise, once and for all, that there can be no employment without companies. [...] the government wants to encourage mobility and the adaptation of workers to the new demands of the labour markets. It is not intended, nor would it be possible under our Constitution, to eliminate the concept of just cause for dismissal. This is a value that the Government recognises and values as an integral principle of the democratic rule of law. Thus, it is not true that there is an attempt to allow dismissals at the employer's discretion. In fact, all the measures that the Government proposes to implement are measures that result from the Memorandum of Understanding and were voted for by the Portuguese people in the last elections. (Diário da Assembleia da República, 2011c, pp. 11–12)

Similarly, in June 2014, the Minister of Solidarity, Employment and Social Security, Pedro Mota Soares, diffused responsibility for the labour market reforms between the government and the social partners:

> I want to reaffirm the importance of the concertation agreement we were able to conclude with the social partners. The Commitment to Growth, Competitiveness and Employment represented a milestone of enormous added value for Portugal. Never before had an agreement with the social partners been so structural, so extensive and so profound as this one, and it was thanks to it that Portugal advanced in a profound set of reforms to achieve a labour market that is more prodigal in job creation, more capable of adjusting to the pace of change in the global economy, and more friendly to innovation, investment and entrepreneurship. But the social dialogue did not end on January 18, 2012, with the signing of this agreement, but intensified in its implementation. It is in close dialogue that we have been honouring the Commitment to Growth, Competitiveness and Employment and, in this sense, it is a social agreement that is fulfilled when the Government, employers and workers' representatives implement it on a daily basis and if we all implement the reforms that will allow us to achieve a labour market that is more prodigal in job creation, more friendly to innovation, investment and entrepreneurship, but, above all, more capable of adjusting to

[10] The disaggregated results can be found in Table A15 in the Appendix.

> the pace of change in the global economy. (Diário da Assembleia da República 2014c, pp. 16–17).

Overall, harm-denying strategies account for more than 80% of the statement. Yet, I find evidence for other strategies as well. A considerably smaller share of statements follows a blame shifting approach. Figure 5.1 shows that 10% of the government's blame avoidance statements focused on shifting responsibility for the labour market reforms to other actors, such as the troika or the predecessor government. A disaggregation of statements by year shows that the share of blame avoidance statements is consistently low, ranging between zero and 19%. Government representatives repeatedly linked measures, like easing employment protection or the freeze of the national minimum wage, to commitments vis-à-vis the troika institutions, which the predecessor government negotiated. For instance, PM Passos Coelho argued in a Parliamentary debate in June 2011:

> Finally, the Honourable Member says that we want cheaper and faster dismissals. What is in the Memorandum of Understanding's commitment will be fulfilled by us and, in this particular regard, is the result of a social concertation agreement that was reached by the previous government. (Diário da Assembleia da República, 2011a, p. 44)

Similarly, the Minister of Economy and Employment deflected calls for an increase of the national minimum wage in February 2013 by denying responsibility in this realm:

> We also know that at the moment there is no room to increase the minimum wage because in the original Memorandum of Understanding, as the Deputy rightly said, it is written very clearly that during the assistance programme this cannot happen. [...] In this case, we know who negotiated the Memorandum of Understanding and we know why there is no margin. There is no margin because you [the PS, comment by the author] did not allow for that margin in the Memorandum of Understanding. (Diário da Assembleia da República, 2013a, p. 21)

Figure 5.2 shows that the government's blame shifting statements predominantly target the EU, either alone or in concert with the preceding PS government, while a few statements target the predecessor alone.

Finally, a small share of statements follows a circle the wagons approach. Figure 5.1 shows that 8% of the statements do not attempt to reframe labour market reforms in a positive light but blur responsibility among several actors by highlighting the role of the social partners and international commitments.

Overall, the observed pattern mostly confirms the theoretical expectation that the high level of politicisation of labour market reforms and the reform ownership of the governing parties should lead the PSD-CDS government to predominantly rely on a self-defence approach. The Portuguese government consistently preferred self-defence statements, which amounted to around half of all blame avoidance statements. The significant share of problem denial statements shows that, overall, the government put significant effort into a positive portrayal of the labour market reforms. The observed pattern is stable across years. The consistent results throughout the Programme's duration increase the confidence in the observed pattern of blame avoidance. The consistently high share of self-defence and problem denial

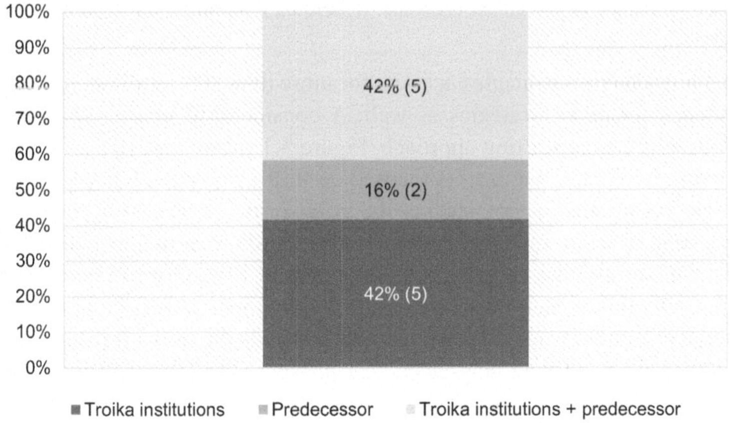

Fig. 5.2 Blame shifting statements by target—the labour market reforms

statements may suggest that high ownership for the reforms and the Programme as a whole drove the government's choice of blame avoidance strategies in this case.

5.2 Liberalisation of Regulated Professions

The regulation of professions has the function to provide certain standards for specific services. Regulated professions are often found in the legal sector, the technical field, the financial accountancy sector, and the healthcare sector. Regulation typically covers both entry criteria and the conduct of professional activities. While the regulation can be beneficial in overcoming information asymmetries and thus increase trust in a specific profession, overly restrictive criteria on entry and exercise of a profession can inflate prices of service provision and thus hamper economic growth (OECD, 2018, p. 24). Therefore, the regulation of professions has caught the eye of EU regulators, who identify excessive regulation as a hindrance to economic competitiveness and mobility within the single market (Canton et al., 2014, pp. 7–8).

In this section, I analyse the liberalisation of restricted professions during the Programme in Portugal and the blame avoidance strategies the government used in its course. Reforms of regulated professions, which were part of the conditionality, were implemented throughout the Programme. I find little evidence of politicisation of the measures and at least the larger governing party, the PSD, had a reputation for policy support. In line with theoretical expectations, the analysis of the blame avoidance strategies employed by the government reveals a predominant reliance on problem denial.

Description of Reforms

Regulated professions play an important role in the Portuguese economy (OECD, 2018, p. 43). Next to many legally regulated professions, Portugal has witnessed a steady growth of the number of professions governed by professional bodies since the revolution in 1974, and especially since the 1990s (Rego, 2013, p. 62). A reform of the regulated professions system initiated by the governing PS in 2008 took the first steps to liberalise professions regulated by independent bodies but did not cover already existing professional bodies (Rego, 2013). The troika institutions found that a high degree of regulation in many Portuguese service sectors hampered competition and led to excessive rents. To lift the regulatory burden, the Programme required a complete transposition of the Services and the Professional Qualification Directives and the reform of the regulation of professions (European Commission, 2011b, 12, 27). Specifically, it required the abolition of restrictions to advertising for restricted professions, the liberalisation of access and exercise restrictions for professionals from the EU, the reduction of professions regulated by law, and the review and reform of professions regulated by independent professional bodies (European Commission, 2011b, pp. 86–87; Martins, 2014, p. 29).

In July 2011, the PSD-CDS coalition government published Decree Law 92/2011, which established a new and simplified system regulating access to professions (Sistema de Regulação de Acesso a Profissões, SRAP). Furthermore, it abolished the legal restrictions to 170 professions, including carpenters, hairdressers, and firefighters (Araújo, 2011), and introduced a commission (Comissão de Regulação do Acesso a Profissões, CRAP) that would revise all remaining regulations of legally restricted professions (European Commission, 2011b, p. 27; Ministério do Trabalho e da Solidariedade Social, 2011). The CRAP issued a report analysing 122 regulated professions and proposed deregulation steps in March 2012. As the Portuguese Constitution required that Parliament approve changes to the regulation of access and exercise of professions, the government, in agreement with the troika institutions, focused its liberalisation efforts on seven professions with a significant economic impact in a first step (European Commission, 2012a, p. 38, 2012b, 40, 2013, p. 37).[11] A second part of the CRAP's report was issued in 2013 and prompted further steps to ease access and exercise provisions for legally regulated professions. All in all, the two-step process of deregulation eased access and exercise requirements for 183 professions (European Commission, 2014, p. 67).

The deregulation of professions regulated by professional associations was delayed throughout 2012. In November 2012, the framework law for regulated professions with professional bodies, such as lawyers, notaries, architects, and pharmacists, was approved by Parliament and subsequently published as Law 2/2013 (European Commission, 2013c, p. 52). The framework law abolished regulations that could harm competition when they were not necessary to protect public interests. The law required revising professional associations' bylaws, prohibited the

---

[11] In this way, in January 2013, three legally regulated professions were deregulated by Laws 5/2013 and 6/2013 (owner/manager of freight companies, companies involved in the transport of children, and of taxi companies); see European Commission (2013, p. 52).

fixing of professional quotas, and abolished some reserved activities (OECD, 2018, p. 26). Yet, the revision processes were delayed, and reforms of the associations' bylaws did not occur until after the Programme's end (European Commission, 2014, pp. 67–68). Finally, Law 41/2012 transposed in August 2012 the EU's professional qualifications directive (Assembleia da República, 2012),[12] and the government implemented 67 sector-specific regulations to fulfil the Services directive (European Commission, 2014, p. 67).

The troika institution's evaluation of the liberalisation of regulated professions in Portugal was mixed. While the government of PM Passos Coelho had considerably eased legal restrictions, there was less progress in the realm of the highly regulated professions governed by professional associations. By the end of the Programme, the amended bylaws, which professional associations were required to present to the authorities and which were to abolish restrictions to advertising as foreseen in the Services Directive, had not yet passed Parliament (European Commission, 2014, pp. 67–68).[13]

Politicisation of the Regulated Professions Reforms

Occupational groups in Portugal represent the interests of their profession and function similar to trade unions in this way. The National Council of Professional Orders (Conselho Nacional das Ordens Profissionais, CNOP) represents a majority of Portugal's professional orders and advocates their interests vis-à-vis the Portuguese government (Rego, 2013, pp. 69–71). Previous efforts to liberalise professions regulated by independent bodies have raised criticism of professional bodies and prior reforms thus presented compromises that mostly retained the privileges of existing professional orders and chambers (da Mota, 2008). The general framework law of 2008 did not extend to already existing professional bodies and left the decision to join the new framework free to them. Furthermore, it did little to change the process of establishing professional orders, as the respective rules remained vague (Rego, 2013, pp. 63–66). While interest groups thus opposed previous reform efforts, the reforms taking place throughout the Portuguese Programme did not face high levels of politicisation.

Introducing a new regime to regulate the access and exercise restrictions for professions without a professional body was part of the 2011 tripartite agreement between the predecessor government and the social partners (Araújo, 2011; Conselho Económico e Social, 2011, p. 19). Furthermore, its status as a decree-law meant that the government did not require Parliamentary approval. As such, it faced little public opposition. Similarly, the full implementation of the Services and Professional Qualifications Directives did not spark public opposition from opposition parties or in the media.

Professional orders and the CNOP criticised the horizontal framework law on the governance of regulated professions. Points of criticism concerned ministerial

[12] The government additionally adopted Executive orders 328/2012, 325/2012, 367/2012 to complement law 41/2012 between August and November 2012.

[13] Bylaws for 13 regulated professions were passed in 2015; see OECD (2018, p. 62).

oversight of professional orders, the possibility for the public prosecution to launch disciplinary proceedings against members of professional orders, and the liberalisation of some professional tasks, especially in the healthcare sector (Jornal de Notícias, 2012c; Monteiro, 2012; Rego, 2013, p. 70). The final version of the framework law represented a compromise in so far as it removed initial government proposals for the involvement of public prosecutors and the abolition of the right of professional orders to create entry hurdles in the form of mandatory fees of professional associations (Simões, 2012). Yet, more substantial opposition to the new framework law by some professional associations, such as the Portuguese bar association and the medical association, did not lead to further actions against it. There was no consensus among the professional associations on a common position against the new law (Jornal de Notícias, 2012d; Pinto, 2013). What is more, there are no reports on protest events around the adoption of the laws on professional restrictions. The horizontal framework law passed unanimously in Parliament, with the biggest opposition party, PS, voting in favour of the law, and other opposition parties abstaining from the vote (Pinto, 2013).

In sum, the liberalisation of regulated professions thus differs significantly from the labour market reform, which became increasingly contested over time. There was little protest against the government's liberalisation efforts within and outside Parliament. This process also stands in stark contrast to the liberalisation efforts in Greece, for instance, where the abolition of restrictions in the freight sector led to weeklong protests in the summer of 2010 (Skrekas, 2010; Smith, 2010). All in all, the level of politicisation was thus low.

Reputation for Policy Support

While the CDS remained quiet on the topic of regulation, the PSD has a longstanding commitment to liberalising the economy to reap benefits from increased competitiveness. In its 2005 election manifesto, the PSD called for barriers to economic growth to be eliminated by '[the] correct economic policies that create more competition in domestic sectors' (PPD/PSD, 2005, p. 19). The election manifesto highlights that barriers arise 'from the inadequacy of regulation to promote the smooth operation of the market, resulting in restrictions on market access for new entrants, the artificial setting of price levels or the introduction of requirements that impede the operational and commercial optimisation of companies' activities' (PPD/PSD, 2005, p. 19). Similarly, the PSD's election manifesto for the 2009 Parliamentary elections included a commitment to 'reduce excessive market and product regulation, which makes it difficult for consumers to access goods and services under better conditions' (PSD, 2009, p. 7). Though these programmes do not specifically target regulated professions and especially the system of professional orders and chambers, the PSD thus has a history of campaigning in favour of less regulation of product and service markets. This commitment also became evident in 2008, when the PSD voted in favour of the new law restricting the powers of new professional orders (da Mota, 2008).

While professional bodies were critical of the measures required by the Programme (Lusa, 2011), the issue of regulated professions did not gain much attention in the 2011 electoral campaign (see, for instance, Ramos, 2011). The PSD's 2011 election manifesto reiterated the commitment to improve the competitiveness of the Portuguese economy. The PSD recognised a general need to overcome weaknesses in the regulatory system, ensuring competition and safeguarding the interests of the public and citizens (PSD, 2011, p. 20). As part of its Program for Growth, Competitiveness and Employment (Programa para o Crescimento, a Competitividade e o Emprego), the PDS promised to implement 'structural policies of quality on the supply side of goods and services [...] to improve productivity, competitiveness and employment' (PSD, 2011, p. 36). The election manifesto included specific commitments to increase the flexibility of service market regulation and eliminate legal entry barriers to goods and services markets (PSD, 2011, pp. 37–38), yet remain silent on reforming professional bodies.

The PDS and CDS' agreement for government highlighted the necessity to comply with the requirements of the EU's Economic Adjustment Programme. While not containing specific measures, it reiterated a general commitment to further economic growth by reforming regulatory bodies and eliminating competition impediments (Público, 2011b; Simas & Rodrigues, 2011).

In sum, regulated professions did not receive ample attention in the decade before the Portuguese Programme or during the 2011 electoral campaign. The CDS has long remained silent on the topic of liberalisation in general and regulated professions in specific. The larger coalition partner, the PSD, has long spoken out in favour of increasing competitiveness and decreasing regulation in Portugal. This commitment becomes evident in two instances. First, the PSD—then in opposition—voted in favour of the PS's proposal to reform professions regulated by professional bodies in 2008. Second, during the 2011 election campaign, professional associations voiced some concerns about the troika's requirements regarding regulated professions. In this context, while remaining silent on reforming professional associations, the PSD explicitly calls for the deregulation of services markets. All in all, the government thus had a reputation of supporting the reforms of regulated professions implemented during the Portuguese Programme.

Blame Avoidance Strategies

In this section, I analyse how the Portuguese government employed blame avoidance strategies to confront blame and criticism for the reforms they implemented in the realm of regulated professions. In the previous sections, I showed that the policy was not strongly politicised and that at least the larger coalition partner, the PSD, had a reputation for supporting the measures. In line with the theoretical framework, I thus expect that the PSD-CDS coalition government employed problem denial more than other blame avoidance strategies. The analysis shows that this expectation bears out in the case of the reform of regulated professions.

Throughout the Programme duration, the PSD and CDS coalition government relied predominantly on a problem denial approach when discussing reforms of regulated professions. Government officials consistently painted a positive image of these reforms by linking them to general government commitments to reduce context costs in goods and services markets and create a more flexible labour market open to all Portuguese and European citizens. At the same time, they underlined the additional benefit of meeting international commitments, either in the form of Programme conditionality or European law. In many statements, government representatives also highlighted the support the reforms received from social partners and professional bodies, thus effectively diffusing responsibility for the measures among a broad coalition of actors.

As Fig. 5.3 shows, a majority of 57% of statements follow this pattern of problem denial. Checking the consistency of the results by disaggregating statements by year is difficult because the overall low number of statements makes the interpretation of the results difficult.[14] However, looking at the content of the statements, the described problem denial pattern is visible through the Programme's duration. For instance, in July 2012, Secretary of State for Employment, Pedro Silva Martins, maintained:

> I would like to say that I think we all agree that the country needs qualified professionals and a more flexible labour market to modernise and grow. In this sense, the draft laws that we had the opportunity to present and that are currently being considered by this Assembly aim to eliminate unjustified obstacles to the access and exercise of professional activity, to increase the possibilities of entering and remaining in the labour market and, consequently, to increase competition in the provision of services, within the framework of compliance with the international commitments that Portugal has undertaken. These objectives are achieved without jeopardising the rights of workers, consumers or other service recipients. Regarding professional qualifications, it is important to deepen knowledge in search of best practices, which allow an effective exchange of experiences and ensure real freedom of movement and provision of services in the European area. (Diário da Assembleia da República, 2012c, p. 28)

The Secretary of State of Public Works, Transport and Communications, Sérgio Monteiro, gave a similar statement when discussing reforms of professions in the realm of driving education in June 2013:

> As we know, this alignment of the regime is urgent, indispensable and necessary, taking into account the commitments assumed by the Portuguese State under the Memorandum of Understanding with the Troika. In general terms, the reformulation of this regime is intended to simplify and to make less bureaucratic the activity of companies that operate driving schools, of the certification of associated professions and also of the respective training entities, making it less costly and more in line with the European directives regarding the freedom of access and exercise of professions. It is also important to mention that a driving education model is proposed, aimed at enhancing skills with a view to safe and responsible driving, thus contributing to the reduction road accidents. The increase of road safety is a strategic goal of this Government—and I know that it is also a goal of the associations of the sector—that we wish to pursue in its various aspects, in particular, and at this

[14] Totalling 44 blame avoidance statements throughout the Programme duration, no government statements regarding the reforms of regulated professions were found in 2011. This may be the result of the overall low level of politicisation of the reforms. The predominant share of statements fits a problem denial approach in 2012 and 2014, with respectively 62% and 82% of statements from this category. In 2013, the share of problem denial statements was considerably lower. Of a total of 12 blame avoidance statements, only three follow a problem denial approach so that the share is considerably lower at 25%. The disaggregated results can be found in Table A13 in the Appendix.

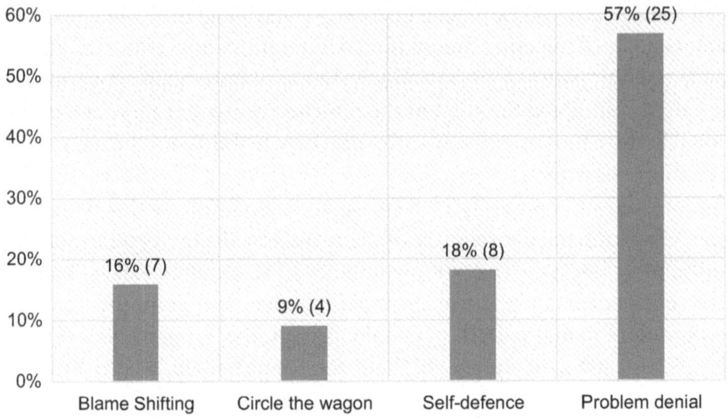

Fig. 5.3 Share of blame avoidance strategies—the reforms of regulated professions

> moment with the approval of the present draft law. (Diário da Assembleia da República, 2013b, p. 25)

The pattern is also visible in the statement made by Monteiro when discussing a reform of professional activities in the construction sector in May 2014:

> One of this government's priorities is to reduce the context costs that companies face when carrying out economic activity in our country. For this reason, and as this Chamber is aware, the largest legislative reform carried out in the services sector in Portugal is already in its final stages, driven by the need to implement the Services Directive across the sector, which has already resulted in the amendment of over 100 pieces of legislation.[…] Preceded by a broad and active process of hearing representatives of the sector and social partners […] we, therefore, hope that the draft laws now under discussion will be welcomed by this Assembly, as we consider that they are, in both cases, projects that, by removing context costs, as well as other barriers currently existing to the exercise of construction activity, will contribute to the promotion of a favourable business environment and, consequently, to the growth of the economy and job creation. (Diário da Assembleia da República, 2014b, p. 40)

A considerably smaller amount of statements follows a self-defence approach. At 18% of statements, this is the second most frequently used strategy. When using a self-defence strategy, the PSD-CDS coalition government accepts responsibility for the reforms in the realm of regulated professions and links them to a broader government commitment to remove obstacles to economic growth and improve labour market access. For instance, in April 2012, the Minister of Economy and Employment, Álvaro Santos Pereira, stated regarding the reform of professions regulated by a professional association:

> The idea of this diploma, which will now be in public consultation, mirrors and reflects well the government's vision for the economy, that is, less state and more regulation. The state's role is exactly to remove obstacles to economic growth and the normal functioning of the economy. And we are committed, from the very first moment, to promoting free access to the labour market. We know that there is a lot to do at the level of regulated professions, namely at the level of professional associations and chambers […]. (Diário da Assembleia da República, 2012a, p. 38)

A disaggregation by year shows that throughout the years 2012 to 2014, self-defence is consistently the second most frequent type of blame avoidance statement employed by the government when discussing reforms of regulated professions.[15]

A similarly large share of statements (16%), engages in blame shifting. In these statements, government representatives linked the necessary reforms to commitments arising from EU law, such as the Services and Qualification Directives, and highlighted the binding nature of Programme conditionality. For instance, during a debate on the reform of the profession of driving instructor, the Secretary of State of Public works, transport and communication, Sérgio Monteiro, highlighted the constraints the government faced:

> I would like to say that some of the issues raised by the Deputies Bruno Dias and Ana Drago were the subject of an attempt to reach a consensus with the European Commission, within the scope of the regular evaluations, and we arrived at the formulation that was possible in that context. The territorial issue was proposed, but it was impossible to reach a consensus with the European Commission. (Diário da Assembleia da República, 2013b, p. 31)

Figure 5.4 shows that all statements target EU institutions, either as part of the troika or as a policymaker responsible for EU law that necessitated domestic transposition. However, it becomes clear that the government predominantly stresses general EU commitments when talking about reforms of regulated professions rather than the specific requirements arising from the Programme.

Finally, a considerably smaller amount of statements follows a circle the wagons approach. Figure 5.3 shows that 9% of statements blur responsibility across several actors but do nothing to portray the introduced measures in a positive light. For instance, in July 2012, Secretary of State for Employment, Pedro Silva Martins, highlighted the involvement of several actors in the transposition of the professional qualification directive:

> I would like to say that the Government has every interest in ensuring that this proposal receives the broadest possible consensus. It is an initiative that stems from international commitments entered into by the Portuguese State, it is obviously subject to the restrictions that result from those commitments, but in any case, we certainly have every interest in trying to ensure that this proposal has the broadest and widest possible consensus. Regarding the more specific questions you addressed to me, I would like to mention that this proposal was discussed within the scope of the Commission for the Regulation of Access to Professions, which, as you know, includes in its composition representatives of all social partners. (Diário da Assembleia da República, 2012c, pp. 20–21)

Overall, the observed pattern confirms the theoretical expectation that the low policy politicisation and the reputation for policy support should lead government representatives to focus on problem denial, to avoid blame for the introduced measures. Self-defence is the second most frequently used government strategy. The Portuguese government once more focused on a positive portrayal of the measures introduced to liberalise regulated professions. While the overall low number of blame avoidance statements makes the results of disaggregating the data by year hard to

[15] The disaggregated results can be found in Table A13 in the Appendix.

interpret, I find that the results are relatively stable with the years 2012 and 2014 following the overall pattern.

5.3 Conclusion

In this chapter, I presented two case studies of reforms introduced in Portugal under conditionality. The cases varied in the level of politicisation of the respective policies and each case thus came with specific expectations about the pattern of blame avoidance strategies employed by the Portuguese government. The empirical analysis showed that the theoretical framework developed in Chap. 2 had explanatory leverage in both cases.

First, the labour market reforms in Portugal were contested from the outset and the politicisation of the measures increased throughout the Programme. While the trade union federation CGTP rallied its members in opposition to the measures required by the Programme from the start, the rest of the social partners grew increasingly averse to the reforms introduced by the government throughout the Programme, making compromise agreements more and more difficult. Similarly, opposition parties became more united in their disapproval of the measures throughout the Programme. The government had a reputation for policy support, with both governing parties having long-standing commitments to reform the labour market, which date back to previous reform efforts in 2003. For these reasons, I expected the PSD-CDS coalition government to rely primarily on self-defence. Indeed, the government of PM Passos Coelho predominantly employed self-defence as a blame

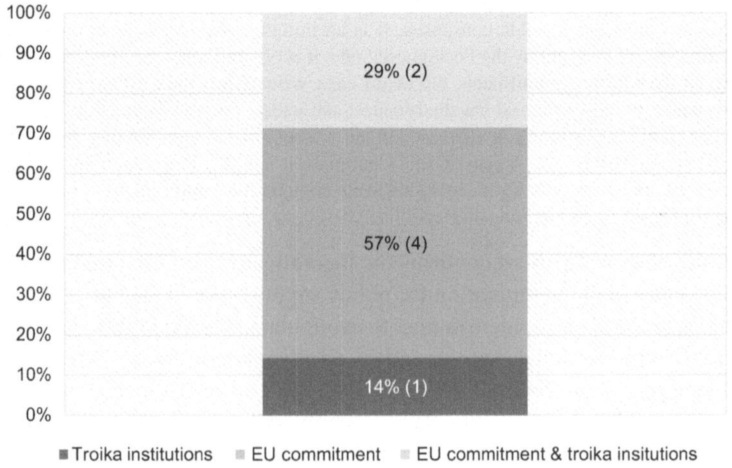

Fig. 5.4 Blame shifting statements by target—the reforms of regulated professions

avoidance strategy. The consistent results throughout the Programme's duration increase the confidence in the observed pattern of blame avoidance. Problem denial was the second most frequently employed strategy of the Portuguese government. The observed pattern suggests that the government put significant effort into a positive portrayal of the labour market reforms.

Second, the liberalisation of regulated professions in Portugal did not receive ample public attention and faced low levels of politicisation. Most opposition parties did not actively oppose the measures. Even professional associations, which are responsible for representing the interests of their professions vis-à-vis the government, offered little opposition to the reform plans because they failed to find a common position. While the CDS remained silent on the issue, the PSD had a long-standing commitment to liberalising goods and services markets and thus had a reputation for supporting the measures introduced to liberalise regulated professions. Therefore, I expected the Portuguese government to focus mainly on problem denial. Indeed, the analysis showed that government representatives employed relied heavily on the strategy of problem denial. Self-defence was the second most frequently used government strategy. Thus, the Portuguese government focused once more on a positive portrayal of the measures introduced to liberalise regulated professions. While the overall low number of blame avoidance statements makes the results of the disaggregated data hard to interpret, I find that the results are relatively stable with the years 2012 and 2014 following the overall pattern.

Overall, both case studies thus follow the expected pattern of blame avoidance strategies. However, the small number of blame avoidance statements made it difficult to establish whether the observed pattern was consistent in the case of regulated professions. The low number of statements may be a result of the low level of politicisation of the reforms. As the government faced little opposition both in- and outside Parliament, the issue simply appeared in Parliamentary debates less frequently than other topics. Moreover, the theoretical framework cannot explain the high share of statements that positively portray the reforms in both cases. The consistently high share of self-defence and problem denial statements in both cases may suggest that the high ownership for the reforms and the Programme as a whole drove the government's choice of blame avoidance strategies in both cases.

The last two chapters provide in-depth accounts of reforms introduced in Ireland and Portugal under Programme conditionality, and I showed that the theoretical expectations developed in Chap. 2 mostly bore out in each of the case studies. The subsequent chapter will analyse whether the theoretical framework has explanatory leverage across the cases and can account for variation in the two explanatory factors, politicisation and reputation for policy support.

References

Aníbal, S., Botelho, L., & Faria, A. R. (2011). *Troika moderada no corte do défice e radical nas reformas estruturais* [Troika Moderate on Deficit Cutting and Radical on Structural Reforms]. Público, 5 May 2011.

Araújo, P. (2011). Cabeleireiro será uma das profissões visadas pelo decreto-lei ontem aprovado [Hairdresser Will Be One of the Professions Covered by the Decree-Law Approved Yesterday]. *Jornal De Notícias*, 20 May 2011.

Assembleia da República. (2012). *Lei n.° 41/2012 de 28 de agosto* (n.° 166/2012).

Bulfone, F., & Afonso, A. (2020). Business Against Markets: Employer Resistance to Collective Bargaining Liberalization During the Eurozone Crisis. *Comparative Political Studies, 53*(5), 809–846. https://doi.org/10.1177/0010414019879963

Campos Lima, M. da Paz (2011). *Deadlock over proposal on severance pay*. https://www.eurofound.europa.eu/de/publications/article/2011/deadlock-over-proposal-on-severance-pay

Campos Lima, M. da Paz (2012a). *Unions split over tough labour agreement*. https://www.eurofound.europa.eu/publications/article/2012/unions-split-over-tough-labour-agreement

Campos Lima, M. da Paz (2012b). *Controversial new Labour Code comes into force*. https://www.eurofound.europa.eu/publications/article/2012/controversial-new-labour-code-comes-into-force

Campos Lima, M. da Paz (2013). *Dramatic decline in collective agreements and worker coverage*. https://www.eurofound.europa.eu/publications/article/2013/dramatic-decline-in-collective-agreements-and-worker-coverage

Campos Lima, M. da Paz (2019). Portugal: Reforms and the turn to neoliberal austerity. In T. Müller, K. Vandaele, & J. Waddington (Eds.), *Collective bargaining in Europe: Towards an endgame* (Vol. III, pp. 483–504). European Trade Union Institute (ETUI).

Campos Lima, M. da Paz & Abrantes, M. (2016). *DIASDSE - Dialogue for advancing Social Europe: Country Report: Portugal*. CESIS - Centro de Estudos para a Intervenção Social.

Canton, E., Ciriaci, D., & Solera, I. (2014). *The economic impact of porfessional service liberalisation* (European Economy Economic Papers No. 533). Brussels: Directorate General for Economic and Financial Affairs (DG ECFIN).

Cardoso, D., & Branco, R. (2018). Liberalised dualisation: Labour market reforms and the crisis in Portugal. *European Journal of Social Security, 20*(1), 31–48. https://doi.org/10.1177/1388262718763668

CDS-PP. (2011). *Este é o momento: Manifesto eleitoral 2011 - Por ti.* Por todos. Portugal. https://manifesto-project.wzb.eu/.

Comissão Permanente De Concertação Social. (2012). *Compromisso para o Crescimento, Competitividade e Emprego*: [Commitment to Growth, Competitiveness and Employment]. https://www.ces.uc.pt/observatorios/crisalt/documentos/cronologia/2012118_Acordo_Concertacao.pdf

Conselho Económico e Social. (2011). *Acordo Tripardido para Competitividade e Emprego* [Tripartite Agreement on Competitiveness and Employment]. http://www.smav.pt/documentos/legislacao/acordotripartidocompemp2011.pdf

Correia, R. A. (2013). *Empresas terão de descontar para dois fundos deindemnizações* [Companies Will Have to Pay into Two Compensation Funds]. Público, 10 January 2013.

Correia, A. P. (2014). Catarina estende a mão ao PS, Semedo critica Seguro [Catarina Reaches Out to PS, Semedo Criticises Seguro]. *Jornal De Notícias*, 17 February 2014.

Correia, A. P., & Roque, T. (2012). Passos amarrou Seguro ao acordo de concertação [Passos Ties Seguro to the Concertation Agreement]. *Jornal De Notícias*, 21 January 2012.

Correia, A. P., & Tiago, L. (2013). Não Vale A Pena Negociar Com Quem Não Tem Mandato: [No Sense In Negotiating With Those Who Have No Mandate]. *Jornal De Notícias*, 5 January 2013.

da Mota, I. T. (2008). Estado limita poderes das novas ordens [State Limits Powers of New Orders]. *Jornal De Notícias*, 15 January 2008.

Pinto, M. de (2013). A governamentalização das associações profissionais [The Governmentalisation of Professional Associations]. *Jornal De Notícias*, 4 February 2013.

Diário da Assembleia da República. (2011a). *Reunião Plenária de 30 de Junho de 2011* (I Série - Número 3).

Diário da Assembleia da República. (2011b). *Reunião Plenária de 28 de Julho de 2011* (I Série - Número 9).

Diário da Assembleia da República. (2011c). *Reunião Plenária de 26 de Outubro de 2011* (I Série - Número 35).

Diário da Assembleia da República. (2012a). *Reunião Plenária de 19 de Abril de 2012* (I Série - Número 98).

Diário da Assembleia da República. (2012b). *Reunião Plenária de 25 de Junho de 2012* (I Série - Número 125).

Diário da Assembleia da República. (2012c). *Reunião Plenária de 4 de Julho de 2012* (I Série - Número 129).

Diário da Assembleia da República. (2013a). *Reunião Plenária de 21 de Março de 2013* (I Série - Número 69).

Diário da Assembleia da República. (2013b). *Reunião Plenária de 12 de Junho de 2013* (I Série - Número 101).

Diário da Assembleia da República. (2014a). *Reunião Plenária de 14 de Fevereiro de 2014* (I Série - Número 50).

Diário da Assembleia da República. (2014b). *Reunião Plenária de 28 de Maio de 2014* (I Série - Número 87).

Diário da Assembleia da República. (2014c). *Reunião Plenária de 27 de Junho de 2014* (I Série - Número 101).

European Commission. June (2011a). *The Economic Adjustment Programme for Portugal* (Occasional Papers No. 79). Bussels: European Commission.

European Commission. (September 2011b). *The Economic Adjustment Programme for Portugal: First review- Summer 2011* (Occasional Papers No. 83). Brussels: European Commission.

European Commission. (2012a). *The Economic Adjustment Programme for Portugal: Third Review - Winter 2011/2012*. Brussels: European Commission.

European Commission. (July 2012b). *The Economic Adjustment Programme for Portugal: Fourth Review - Spring 2012* (Occasional Papers No. 111). Brussels: European Commission.

European Commission. (June 2013). *The Economic Adjustment Programme for Portugal: Seventh review - Winter 2012/2013* (Occasional Papers No. 153). Brussels: European Commission.

European Commission. (October 2014). *The Economic Adjustment Programme for Portugal: 2011–2014* (Occasional Papers No. 202). Brussels: European Commission.

Figueira, A. (2011). Governo entregou PEC IV no Parlamento, depois de Sócrates reunir com os líderes partidários [Government Delivered SGP IV in Parliament after Sócrates' Meeting with Party Leaders]. *Jornal De Notícias*, 22 March 2011.

Henning, C. R. (2017). *Tangled Governance: International regime complexity, the Troika, and the Euro Crisis*. Oxford: Oxford University Press.

Jornal de Notícias. (2011). Primeiro Plano - Trabalho [Close-Up - Work]. *Jornal De Notícias*, 14 October 2011.

Jornal de Notícias. (2012a). Fundo de compensação operacional até Maio [Compensation Fund Operational Until May]. *Jornal De Notícias*, 22 January 2012.

Jornal de Notícias. (2012b). Cavaco promulga Código do Trabaho [Cavaco Promulgates Labor Code]. *Jornal De Notícias*, 19 June 2012.

Jornal de Notícias (2012c). ADELINO MEIRELES/GLOBAL IMAGENMS [ADELINO MEIRELES / GLOBAL IMAGES]. *Jornal De Notícias*, 1 August 2012.

Jornal de Notícias. (2012d). Breves [In brief]. *Jornal De Notícias*, 26 September 2012.

Jornal de Notícias. (2013). Prestação sobe para créditos a três meses [Instalments Rise for Three-Month Loans]. *Jornal De Notícias*, 29 June 2013.

Jornal de Notícias. (2014a). Todos contra critérios para despedimentos [All Against the Dismissal Criteria]. *Jornal De Notícias*, 14 March 2014.

Jornal de Notícias. (2014b). Assembleia aprova novos critérios para despedimentos [Assembly Approves New Criteria for Dismissals]. *Jornal De Notícias*, 15 March 2014.

Lourenço, N. S. (2011). *Esquerda avaliza rapidez na indigitação de Passos Coelho* [Left Backs Speedy Appointment of Passos Coelho]. Público, 15 June 2011.

Lusa. (2011). *Ajuda externa: Ordens profissionais querem preservar modelo de autorregulação* [External Assistance: Professional Associations Want to Preserve Model of Self-Regulation]. Lusa Press Agency, 20 June 2011. https://www.cnop.pt/2011/06/presidente-republica-cnop/#more-48

Lütz, S., Hilgers, S., & Schneider, S. (2019). Games borrower governments play: The implementation of economic adjustment programmes in Cyprus and Portugal. *West European Politics, 42*(7), 1443–1463.

Martins, P. (2011). *Se tenho dívidas e não consigo pagá-las, estou nas mãos do credor. O que me causa impressão não é a questão da soberania, é a da dignidade nacional* [If I Have Debts and I Cannot Pay Them, I Am in the Hands of the Creditor. What Strikes Me Is Not the Question of Sovereignty, It Is that of National Dignity]. *Jornal De Notícias*, 15 April 2011.

Martins, R. (2012a). *UGT ameaça rasgar acordo de concertação* [UGT Threatens to Tear Up Concertation Agreement]. Público, 17 April 2012.

Martins, R. (2012b). *Críticos do código laboral à espera de Cavaco Silva* [Critics of the Labour Code Waiting for Cavaco Silva]. Público, 12 May 2012.

Martins, R. (2013a). *UGT volta a acenar com fim do acordo de concertaçãosocial* [UGT Waves Again at the End of the Social Conciliation Agreement]. Público, 18 January 2013.

Martins, R. (2013b). *Estado financia fundo para os despedimentos duranteano e meio* [State Funds Redundancy Fund for a Year and a Half]. Público, 23 January 2013.

Martins, R. (2013c). *TC obriga a rever despedimentos* [TC Forced to Review Dismissals]. Público, 27 September 2013.

Martins, R. (2013d). *Governo propõe critérios para justificar despedimento por extinção de postos de trabalho* [Government Proposes Criteria to Justify Dismissal for Job Losses]. Público, 7 December 2013.

Martins, D. C. (2014). Labour law in Portugal between 2011 and 2014. *Paper presented at the young Scholars Meeting of the XI European Regional Congress 2014*, Dublin.

Martins, R. (2014a). *Nova proposta do Governo não convence e gera dúvidas de aplicação* [The Government's New Proposal Is Not Convincing and Creates Doubts About Its Application]. Público, 30 January 2014.

Martins, R. (2014b). *Exigências da UGT condicionam acordo para despedimentos* [UGT's Demands Condition Agreement on Redundancies]. Público, 31 January 2014.

Martins, R. (2014c). *Governo não desiste do acordo com CIP e UGT nos despedimentos* [Government Does Not Give up on Agreement with CIP and UGT on Dismissals]. Público, 7 February 2014.

Martins, R. (2014d). *Governo volta a analisar despedimentos sem garantia de acordo com UGT e CIP* [Government Revisits Redundancies Without Guarantee of Agreement with UGT and CIP]. Público, 13 February 2014.

Martins, R., & Rodrigues, S. (2013). *Maioria propõe período transitório nas indemnizações* [Majority Proposes Transitional Period on Compensation]. Público, 23 May 2013.

Ministério do Trabalho e da Solidariedade Social. (2011). *Decreto-Lei n.° 92/2011 de 27 de Julho* (n.° 143/2011).

Monteiro, O. d. S. (2012). *Proposta de lei das ordens profissionais: uma oportunidade ou um espartilho?* [Proposed Law on Professional Associations: An Opportunity or a Corset?]. Diário De Notícias, 10 August 2012.

OECD. (2018). *OECD competition assessment reviews: Portugal: Volume II - Self-regulated professions. Paris: OECD.*

Penedos, A. (2011). *Quem tem medo do "fundo de garantia"*? [Who is Afraid of the "Guarantee Fund"?]. Público, 20 May 2011.

Pereira, G., & Pinto, J. (2011). Passos ficou refém das suas próprias propostas [Passos Held Hostage by His Own Proposals]. *Jornal De Notícias*, 21 May 2011.

Pereira, P. T., & Wemans, L. (2015). Portugal and the global financial crisis: Short-sighted politics, deteriorating public finances and the bailout imperative. In J. Wanna, E. A. Lindquist, & J. de Vries (Eds.), *The global financial crisis and its budget impacts in OECD Nations: Fiscal Responses and Future Challenges* (pp. 231–254). Cheltenham, UK: Edward Elgar Publishing. https://www.elgaronline.com/view/edcoll/9781784718954/9781784718954.00015.xml

Pinheiro, A. M. (2014). *Nova proposta do Governo vem estabelecer uma hierarquia de critérios a considerar nas dispensas* [The Government's New Proposal Establishes a Hierarchy of Criteria to be Considered in the Exemptions]. Público, 30 January 2014.

PPD/PSD. (2005). *Um Contrato com os Portugueses: Legislativas 2005. Manifesto Eleitoral* [A Contract with the Portuguese. Parliamentary Elections 2005. Electoral Program]. https://manifesto-project.wzb.eu/

PSD. (2009). *Compromisso de Verdade: Programa eleitoral do Partido Social Democrata 2009/2013* [A Commitment to Truth. Electoral Program of the Social Democratic Party 2009/2013]. https://manifesto-project.wzb.eu/

PSD. (2011). *Recuperar a Credibilidade e Desenvolver Portugal: Programa Eleitoral do Partido Social Democrata. Eleições legislativas 2011* [Recovering Credibility and Developing Portugal. Electoral Program of the Social Democratic Party. Parliamentary Elections 2011]. https://manifesto-project.wzb.eu/

Público (2011a). *Sociais-democratas avançam com proposta que França e Itália não conseguiram aplicar* [Social Democrats Put Forward Proposal that France and Italy Failed to Implement]. Público, 12 May 2011.

Público. (2011b). *Text do acordo político PSD/CDS na íntegra* [Text of the PSD/CDS Political Agreement in full]. Público, 16 June 2011.

Público. (2013). *Empresas terão de descontar para dois fundos deindemnizações* [Companies will have to Pay into Two Compensation Funds]. Público, 11 January 2013.

Público. (2014). *Despedimentos o consenso falhado* [Dismissals, the failed consensus]. Público, 14 February 2014.

Ramos, J. d. A. (2011). *Um programa eleitoral virado para as empresas promotoras do crescimento económico* [An Electoral Programme Aimed at Businesses that Promote Economic Growth]. Público, 9 May 2011.

Rego, R. (2013). Portuguese occupational group trends running counter to EU policies. In R. Rego (Ed.), *Palgrave pivot. The trend towards the European deregulation of professions and its impact on Portugal under the crisis* (pp. 55–77). Palgrave Macmillan.

Ribeiro, L. R. (2013). Fundo das indemnizações avança em breve [Compensation Fund to Go Ahead Soon]. *Jornal De Notícias*, 4 January 2013.

Rodrigues, S. (2011). *PSD quer facilitar contratação a termo de desempregados*: [PSD Wants to Make it Easier for the Unemployed to be Hired on a Fixed-Term Basis]. Público, 29 January 2011.

Rodrigues, R. (2012). João Proença "A UGT não troca a meia hora por nada, não aceita a desregulação laboral" [João Proença "The UGT does not Exchange the Half Hour for Anything, It does not Accept Labour Deregulation"]. *Jornal De Notícias*, 13 January 2012.

Rodrigues, S. (2013). *Maioria PSD/CDS e UGT baixam tensão em torno do corte nas indemnizações* [PSD/CDS Majority and UGT Lowering Tension over Severance Pay Cut]. Público, 9 January 2013.

Simas, N., & Rodrigues, S. (2011). *Nova AD quer ir além da Troika com a revisão da Constituição* (New AD Wants to Go Beyond the Troika with the Revision of the Constitution). Público, 17 June 2011.

Simões, L. (2012). *Governo recua no controlo das Ordens Profissionais* (Government Backs Away from Control of Professional Associations). Diário Económico, 26 November 2012.

Skrekas, N. (2010). Greece's truckers protest austerity. *The Wall Street Journal*, 14 September 2010.

Smith, H. (2010). Greek Truckers Call off Strike After Tourist Industry is Crippled. *The Guardian*, 2 August 2010.

Távora, I., & González, P. (2016). The reform of joint regulation and labour market policy during the current crisis: National report on Portugal. In A. Koukiadaki, I. Távora, & M. Martínez Lucio (Eds.), *Joint regulation and labour market policy in Europe during the crisis* (pp. 321–394). Brussels: European Trade Union Institute (ETUI).

Theodoropoulou, S. (2015). National social and labour market policy reforms in the shadow of EU bail-out conditionality: The cases of Greece and Portugal. *Comparative European Politics, 13*(1), 29–55.

Tiago, L. (2011). Menos subsídio de desemprego [Less Unemployment Benefit]. *Jornal De Notícias*, 20 July 2011.

Tiago, L. (2014). Governo quer aprovar alteração na próxima quinta-feira, mas faltam consensos (Government wants to approve change next Thursday, but lacks consensus). *Jornal De Notícias*, 3 February 2014.

Viegas, M., & Ribeiro, A. P. (2014). The Economic Adjustment Program for Prtugal: Assessing welfare impact in a heterogeneous-agent framework. *Portuguese Economic Journal, 13*(1), 53–70. https://doi.org/10.1007/s10258-014-0098-2

Wise, P. (2012a). Portugal Strike Hit by Trade Union Split. *Financial Times*, 22 March 2012.

Wise, P. (2012b). Portugal swaps pay cuts for tax rises. *Financial Times*, 24 September 2012.

Zartaloudis, S. (2014). The impact of the fiscal crisis on Greek and Portuguese welfare states: Retrenchment before the catch-up? *Social Policy and Administration, 48*(4), 430–449.

Chapter 6
Comparing Blame Avoidance Strategies and Alternative Explanations

Chapters 4 and 5 were dedicated to the analysis of the five case studies and established that the expected pattern of blame avoidance strategies was present in each case. The disaggregation of blame avoidance strategies by year and a closer look at the content of blame avoidance statements showed that governments' choice of strategy was predominantly consistent over time in the analysed cases, thus further strengthening the theoretical conjectures. Solely the Irish government's choice of blame avoidance strategies when talking about the reforms of the collective bargaining system changed over time due to an external event.

In this chapter, I compare governments' blame avoidance strategies across the examined cases. This comparative approach allows me to evaluate whether the two independent variables, politicisation and reputation for policy support, indeed have the expected effect on governments' choice of strategy. As most similar comparisons aim at evaluating the individual explanatory power of independent variables, I hold constant in each comparison one of the independent variables while choosing cases that exhibit variation on the other. To test my argument that both variables work in concert, I evaluate the empirical fit of the theoretical expectations for all combinations of the independent variables. Consequently, I compare the cases in four pairwise comparisons:

- First, I assess the impact of variation in politicisation in cases of governing parties' low reputation for policy support by comparing the reform of the wage setting system and the introduction of a property tax in Ireland.
- Second, I analyse the impact of variation in politicisation in cases of governing parties' high reputation for policy support in a comparison of reforms of regulated professions and the labour market in Portugal.
- Third, I evaluate the impact of variation in governing parties' reputation for policy support in cases of low politicisation in a comparison of reforms of regulated professions in Portugal and the reform of the wage setting system in Ireland.

L. Kriegmair, *Responsiveness and Responsibility in the Euro Crisis*, Contributions to Political Science, https://doi.org/10.1007/978-3-031-84473-7_6

- Fourth, I assess the impact of variation in governing parties' reputation for policy support in cases of high politicisation by comparing the introduction of a property tax with the reform of the water supply system in Ireland.

Furthermore, I contrast the results of these comparisons with the explanatory power of alternative explanations in accounting for the observed variance between the analysed cases. This further strengthens my confidence that the two independent variables, politicisation and reputation for policy support, drive governments' choice of blame avoidance strategy.

In the first section, I evaluate the effect of variance in politicisation in two pairwise comparisons that each hold constant the governments' reputation for policy support. Following the theoretical expectations developed in Chap. 2, the cases in each comparison should exhibit differences in the use of high- and low-politicisation strategies while sharing the governments' evaluation of the policy introduced under EU conditionality. The blame avoidance pattern observed in both comparisons matches these expectations. Within each comparison, the Irish and Portuguese governments consistently chose to focus more on high-politicisation strategies rather than low-politicisation strategies when the policies they had to implement to comply with EU conditionality faced considerable politicisation. Furthermore, both governments consistently chose their predominant strategy among harm-denying and -accepting strategies in line with their reputation for policy support across the two comparisons.

In the second section, I evaluate the effect of variance in governments' reputation for policy support in two pairwise comparisons that each hold constant the level of politicisation. In line with the theoretical framework I developed in Chap. 2, I expect that the cases in each pairwise comparison differ in their evaluation of the policy implemented under EU conditionality while sharing a focus on either high- or low-politicisation strategies. The blame avoidance pattern observed in both comparisons matches these expectations. Within each comparison, the governments' choice of blame avoidance strategies was similar regarding the use of high- and low-politicisation strategies but varied in the evaluation of the policy.

In the third section, I evaluate the empirical fit of three alternative explanations of patterns of blame avoidance in and across the cases. First, I examine the claim in the literature that governments follow a sequential approach that weighs the effectiveness of blame avoidance strategies and the potential for credit claiming. I show that while three cases match the expected initial focus on harm-denying strategies, the cases of the local property tax in Ireland and reforms of the regulated professions in Portugal do not fit the expectations of a sequential approach. Second, I analyse the impact of government ideology and the style of policymaking. I show that only the observed pattern of blame avoidance strategies in the case of the Portuguese reforms of regulated professions matches the expectation that governments focus predominantly on a problem denial approach. Third, I examine whether governments' compliance record shapes their choice of strategy. I show that only the observed pattern of blame avoidance strategies in the cases of the reform of collective bargaining in Ireland and the Portuguese labour market reform matched the expectation that governments focus on harm-denying strategies in cases of good compliance records. Beyond the empirical fit of the alternative accounts, the sequential and compliance conjectures had difficulties in accounting for variation between statements centring and blurring of responsibility and harm-accepting and -denying statements simultaneously.

The final section concludes by giving a critical appraisal of the empirical fit of the proposed theoretical framework compared to alternative explanations. I show that the observed pattern of blame avoidance strategies in and across the cases matches the theoretical expectations and that the empirical fit exceeds that of alternative accounts. This further strengthens my confidence that the two independent variables, politicisation and reputation for policy support, drive governments' choice of blame avoidance strategy.

6.1 Variation in Politicisation

In Chap. 2, I argued that governments' ability to diffuse responsibility is constrained by the degree of politicisation. Governments should be better positioned and thus more likely to blur responsibility when the policies they have to introduce to comply with EU conditionality face low levels of politicisation than in situations of high politicisation. In this section, I evaluate whether this conjecture holds in two pairwise comparisons. As most similar comparisons aim at evaluating the individual explanatory power of independent variables, I hold constant in each comparison the governing parties' reputation for policy support. Consequently, within each case pair, the dominant strategies chosen by the government should share the same evaluation of the policy introduced under EU conditionality.

While I do not argue that governments will commit consistently to one strategy of blame avoidance, I expect a clear pattern that shows their preference for the dominant strategy. To confirm the theoretical framework, clear variation in most frequently used strategy should be visible between the two cases in each comparison. Furthermore, I expect to find clear variation in the overall use of high- and low-politicisation strategies between the cases in each pairwise comparison.

Collective Bargaining and the Property Tax in Ireland

In the first pairwise comparison, I look at two cases where the government did not have a reputation for policy support. First, the Irish government did not have a record of supporting reforms that liberalised the Irish collective bargaining system. The Labour party traditionally supported the ERO and REA systems and favoured their extension, and Fine Gael portrayed any reform of the wage-setting mechanisms as a project of the preceding government formed by Fianna Fáil and the Green Party. Second, the Irish government did not support the introduction of a local property tax. Before coming into office, the larger coalition partner, Fine Gael, denounced the measure as unfair and campaigned against introducing a levy on residential property in its 2011 election campaign. Therefore, in both cases, the Irish government did not have a reputation for supporting the policy it was required to introduce under EU conditionality.

While both cases thus share this property, they differ with regard to the second independent variable, politicisation. First, the reform of the collective bargaining system was not strongly politicised. Parts of the opposition agreed on the necessity to reform the system, and the trade unions engaged in negotiations with the government and employer associations throughout the reform process. In consequence, there were no public protests against the government's reform plans. Second, this stands in stark contrast to the introduction of the local property tax. This endeavour came under considerable pressure both in- and outside Parliament, with several MPs and activist organisations organising non-payment campaigns. The mobilisation against the household charge and the property tax found a more institutionalised form when the Anti-Austerity Alliance applied for political party status in December 2013. This shows that both cases differ significantly in the politicisation dimension.

According to the theoretical framework, the lack of a reputation for policy support should lead the Irish government to draw on strategies that accept the perceived harm that arises from the policies it introduced under EU conditionality rather than harm-denying strategies in both cases. However, the observed differences in politicisation should have led the Irish government to focus on different blame avoidance strategies in the two cases. This allows for specific expectations on the choice of strategy in the two cases. I expect to observe a much larger share of circle the wagons statements in the case of the reform of the collective bargaining system than in the case of the local property tax. Conversely, the share of blame shifting should be larger in the latter case.

This expectation bears out. While the Irish government chose as its dominant strategy a harm-accepting approach in both instances, the cases vary with regard to the specific strategy. In Chap. 4, I showed that the Irish government predominantly used a circle the wagons approach in the wage setting case. Figure 6.1 shows that the share of circle the wagons statements (34%) in this case is ten times larger than in the local property case, where the Irish government employed a circle the wagons approach in only 3% of the statements. Conversely, Chap. 4 showed that the Irish government predominantly used a blame shifting approach in the latter case. The share of blame shifting statements (52%) is ten times higher than in the collective bargaining case, where the government employed blame shifting only 4% of the time.

Furthermore, the Irish government should overall focus on low-politicisation strategies in the case of the reform of the wage setting system, while it should overall favour high-politicisation strategies when talking about the local property tax instead. Figure 6.2 shows that this expectation bears out as well. While low-politicisation strategies amount to 67% in the collective bargaining case, the Irish government used these strategies in only 14% of statements in the local property tax case. Conversely, compared to the wage setting case, the share of high politicisation strategies is more than twice as high in the local property case. In sum, the comparison of the two cases supports the theoretical conjectures.

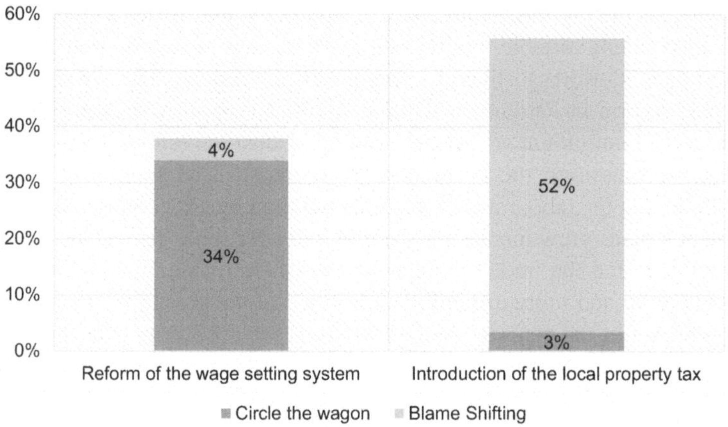

Fig. 6.1 Circle the wagons and blame shifting statements in cases of varying politicisation

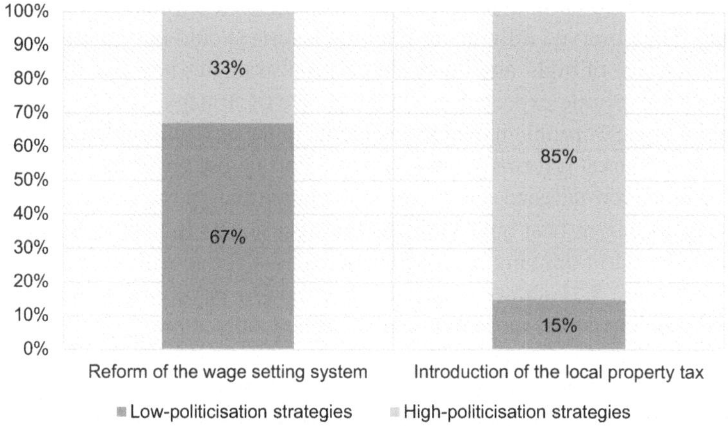

Fig. 6.2 High- and low-politicisation strategies in cases of varying policy politicisation

Regulated Professions and Labour Market in Portugal

In the second pairwise comparison, I look at two cases where the government had a reputation for policy support. First, the Portuguese government, or at least the larger coalition partner PSD, had a long-standing commitment to easing regulations of the goods and services markets and had voted in favour of the preceding government's plans for liberalising regulated professions in 2008. Second, both governing parties had long-standing commitments to reforming the labour market since their last term in office when they introduced far reaching labour market reforms. Furthermore, the PSD spoke out in favour of specific labour market reforms before the 2011 elections. Therefore, the Portuguese government had a reputation for supporting these two reforms it had to introduce to comply with EU conditionality.

Yet, whereas the two cases thus share this property, they differ with regard to the second independent variable, politicisation. First, there was little politicisation of the government's efforts to liberalise regulated professions. The government was able to pass reform in Parliament without significant opposition, and professional associations did not mount significant protests against the reforms. Second, unlike in regulated professions, the Portuguese government faced significant headwinds when introducing the labour market reforms required by EU conditionality, and the government's plans grew increasingly politicised over time. The relations between the government and the trade unions deteriorated over time, making compromise agreements more and more difficult. While some of the government's plans led to public protests, like the plans to increase worker's social security contributions, others lead to public conflicts between the government and the social partners, like the alignment of severance payments and the criteria for dismissals. The two policies thus vary significantly on the politicisation dimension.

According to the theoretical framework, its reputation for policy support should lead the Portuguese government to chose its dominant approach a strategy that denies the perceived harm that arises from the policies it introduced under EU conditionality. The observed differences in politicisation should have motivated a variance in the choice of high- and low-politicisation strategies between the two cases. This allows for specific expectations on the choice of strategy. I expect to observe a much larger share of problem denial statements in the case of regulated professions than in labour market reforms. Conversely, the Portuguese government should have employed more self-defence statements in the latter than in the former.

These expectations bear out. While the Portuguese government chose as its dominant strategy a harm-denying approach in both cases, the specific choice of strategy varied. In Chap. 5, I showed that the Portuguese government predominantly employed problem denial more frequently than any other strategy in the case of the reforms of regulated professions. Figure 6.3 shows that, at 57%, the share of statements is considerably larger than in the case of labour market reforms (33%). Conversely, the share of self-defence statements, the most frequently used strategy in the case of labour market reforms (49%), is more than two times as large as in the case of regulated professions (18%).

Furthermore, I expect the Portuguese government to employ more low-politicisation strategies in the case of the little politicised reforms of regulated professions than in the case of the highly politicised labour market reforms. Conversely, I expect to observe more high-politicisation strategies in the latter. Again, Fig. 6.4 supports this conjecture. Whereas the Portuguese government employed low-politicisation strategies in two-thirds of its blame avoidance statements when talking about the reforms of regulated professions, these strategies amount to just 41% of the government's blame avoidance efforts in the labour market case. In the latter case, the government thus predominantly employed high-politicisation strategies in 59% of its statements, whereas it employed these strategies only 24% of the time in the case of regulated professions reforms.

In sum, the first two case comparisons confirm the theoretical framework's expectations for governments' blame avoidance behaviour in cases of varying

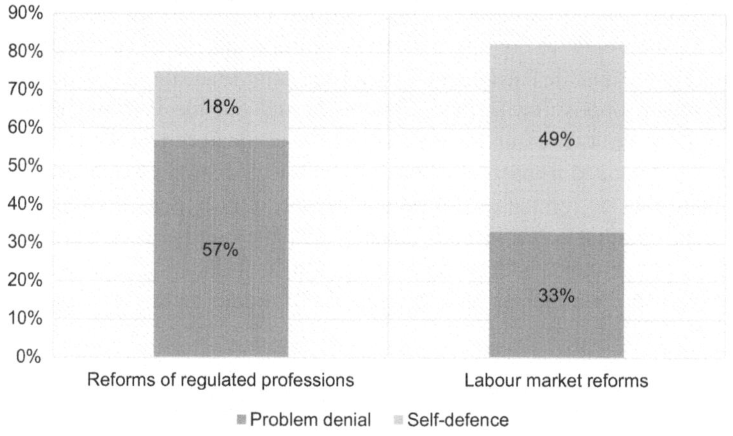

Fig. 6.3 Problem denial and self-defence statements in cases of varying policy politicisation

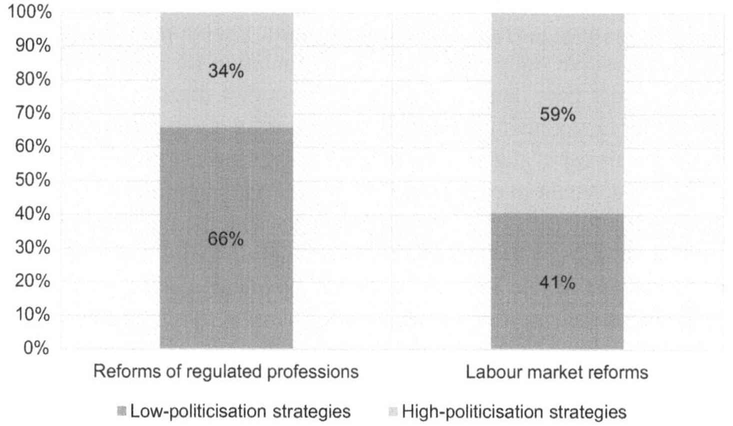

Fig. 6.4 High- and low-politicisation strategies in cases of varying politicisation

politicisation. The Irish government did not have a record for supporting either the introduction of a local property tax or the reform of wage setting systems. In line with the theoretical framework, its use of circle the wagons statements was thus considerably more frequent in the low-politicisation reform of collective bargaining systems than in the highly politicised case of the introduction of the local property tax. Conversely, its share of blame shifting statements was ten times higher in the latter case. The Portuguese government had a reputation for supporting both the reforms of regulated professions and the labour market. In line with the theoretical framework, it employed problem denial more frequently in the low-politicisation reforms of regulated professions than in the case of labour market reforms, which were highly politicised. Conversely, the share of self-defence statements in the latter case is twice as high as in the former. Furthermore, both the Irish and the Portuguese governments chose to focus more on high-politicisation strategies when the policies they had to implement to comply with EU conditionality faced considerable headwinds both in and outside Parliament. Instead, they employed more low-politicisation strategies when opposition to the measures in and outside Parliament was more docile. Finally, the two comparisons support the conjecture that the reputation for policy support indeed impacts governments' choice of strategy. The Irish government, which had no reputation for policy support, chose as its dominant strategy harm-accepting approaches in both cases of the first comparison. Conversely, the Portuguese government, which had a reputation for policy support in both cases, chose to focus predominantly on harm-denying strategies in the second case pair.

6.2 Variation in Reputation for Policy Support

The theoretical framework developed in Chap. 2 posits that governments' reputation constrains the viability of strategies that aim at manipulating the perception of harm: While governing parties' reputation for policy support facilitates reframing the policy in a positive light, those without a reputation for policy support should have a much harder time denying the harmfulness of a measure. In this section, I evaluate whether this conjecture holds in two pairwise comparisons. As most similar comparisons aim at evaluating the individual explanatory power of independent variables, I hold constant in each comparison the level of politicisation of the analysed measures. Consequently, within each comparison, the two cases should share a focus on either high- or low-politicisation strategies. Again, I do not expect governments to commit to one strategy of blame avoidance consistently. Yet, a clear pattern that shows their preference for either a harm-denying or a harm-accepting strategy should emerge. To confirm the theoretical framework, clear variation in the dominant choice of strategy should be visible between the two cases in each comparison.

Collective Bargaining in Ireland and Regulated Professions in Portugal

In the third pairwise comparison, I look at two cases where the policy introduced in compliance with EU conditionality did not face significant levels of politicisation. First, the reform of the wage setting system in Ireland was, as laid out in subsection one, not strongly politicised. Second, as I pointed out in subsection two, there was little protest against the Portuguese government's efforts to liberalise regulated professions in- and outside Parliament. Therefore, both cases share a similarly low level of politicisation.

Yet, these two cases differ with regard to the second independent variable, reputation for policy support. First, neither coalition partner in the Irish government had spoken out in favour of reforming the wage setting system, which was portrayed as the preceding government's plans. Second, and in contrast, the larger coalition partner in the Portuguese government had a long-standing commitment to easing regulations of the goods and services markets. This shows significant differences between the Irish and the Portuguese government regarding their reputation for supporting the two measures required by EU conditionality.

According to the theoretical framework, the low levels of politicisation of the two measures should lead the Irish and Portuguese governments to draw on low-politicisation strategies of circle the wagons and problem denial rather than other strategies. However, the observed differences in the governments' reputation for policy support should have led them to focus on blame avoidance strategies that differ in their policy evaluation. This allows for specific expectations on the dominant choice of strategy in the two cases. I expect to observe a much larger share of circle the wagons statements in the case of the reforms of the collective bargaining system in Ireland than in the case of the reforms of regulated professions in Portugal. Conversely, the Portuguese government should have employed more problem denial statements.

These expectations bear out. In Chap. 4, I showed that the Irish government predominantly followed a circle the wagons approach when talking about the reforms of the wage setting system. Figure 6.5 shows that, at 34%, the share of statements by the Irish government, which follows a circle the wagons approach, is more than three times as high as the share of circle the wagons statements by the Portuguese government when talking about the reforms of regulated professions (9%). Conversely, the share of problem denial statements, the most frequently used strategy employed by the Portuguese government in the reforms of regulated professions (57%), is more almost twice as large as in the case of the reform of the Irish wage setting system, where problem denial is used in 33% of the statements.

Furthermore, I expect both cases to share a focus on low-politicisation strategies of circle the wagons and problem denial rather than other strategies. Again, Fig. 6.6 lends support to this conjecture. Both the Irish and the Portuguese governments employed low-politicisation strategies in more than two-thirds of all blame avoidance statements in the two cases.

The Local Property Tax and Water Services in Ireland

In the fourth and final pairwise comparison, I look at two cases where the policy introduced in compliance with EU conditionality was highly politicised. First, as pointed out in section one of this chapter, the introduction of the local property tax in Ireland was considerably politicised, with several Members of Parliament (MPs) and activist organisations organising non-payment campaigns. Second, the reform of Irish water services was similarly highly politicised and, in 2014, led to the biggest anti-austerity protests in Ireland in the context of the financial and the Euro crisis. Both cases thus share a similarly high degree of politicisation.

However, the measures differ regarding the Irish government's reputation for policy support. First, neither of the governing parties had supported introducing a property tax before the Irish Programme and the larger coalition partner, Fine Gael, denounced the measure as unfair. Second, and in contrast to the local property tax, Fine Gael, had spoken out in favour of reforming the Irish water services system since 2009. Therefore the cases differ significantly regarding the Irish governments' reputation for supporting the measures.

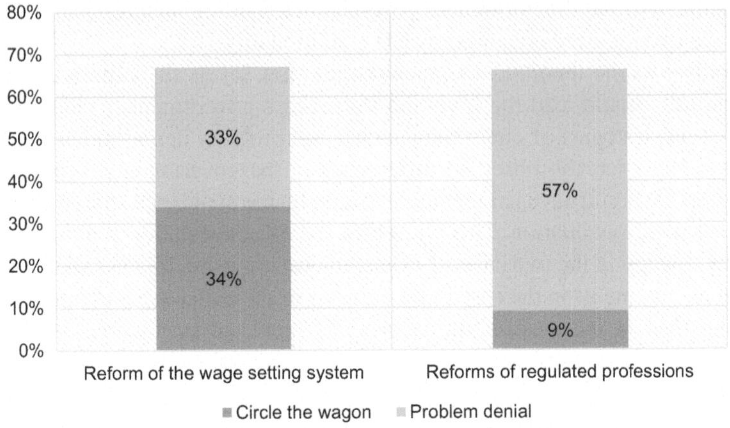

Fig. 6.5 Circle the wagons and problem denial statements in cases of varying reputation for policy support

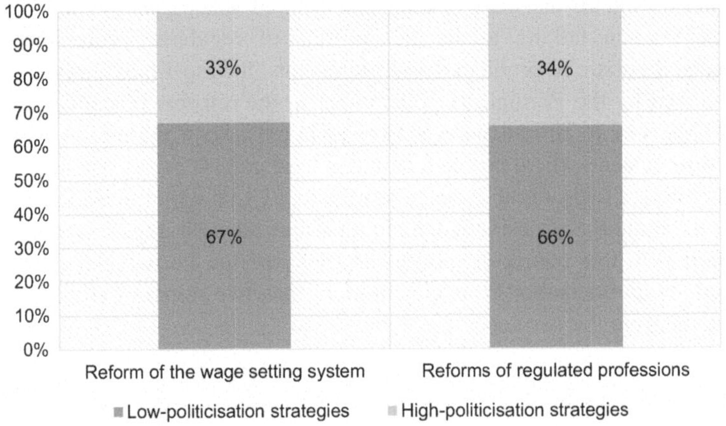

Fig. 6.6 High- and low-politicisation strategies in cases of varying reputation for policy support

According to the theoretical framework, the high level of politicisation should lead the Irish government to draw on strategies of blame shifting and self-defence rather than other strategies. However, the observed differences in the Irish government's reputation for policy support should have motivated a choice in the dominant strategy that differs in the evaluation of the policy. This allows for specific expectations on the dominant choice of strategy in the two cases. I expect a larger share of blame shifting statements in the case of the introduction of the local property tax than in the water services reform case. Conversely, the Irish government should have employed a self-defence approach in a larger share of its statements in the latter case.

These expectations bear out. In Chap. 4, I showed that the Irish government predominantly employed blame shifting statements when talking about introducing the local property tax. Figure 6.7 shows that the shares of blame-shifting differ starkly in the two cases. While the share of blame shifting statements is very high at 52% in the property tax case, it is less than half that size in the water services case (16%). Conversely, the share of self-defence statements, the predominantly employed strategy in the case of the water services reform is twice as high in the latter case (66%) as in the case of the introduction of the local property tax (33%).

These observations strengthen the conjecture that a reputation for policy support makes it more difficult for governments to shift responsibility for the measure onto other actors. Indeed, the following statement by Environment Minister Phil Hogan demonstrates that the Irish government more readily drew the connection between the Programme conditionality and the introduction of the local property tax than the reform of water services:

> The EU/IMF Programme of Financial Support for Ireland under its fiscal consolidation measures commits to the introduction of a property tax for 2012 and to an increase in the property tax for 2013. [...] In light of the complex issues involved, a property tax, requiring a comprehensive property valuation system, would take time to introduce and accordingly, to meet the revenue measure in the EU/IMF Programme, I have already indicated my intention to introduce a household charge in 2012. This will be introduced on a flat-rate basis. I will be bringing proposals to Government in the near future on the legislative and administrative requirements necessary to implement the household charge. [...] The Programme for Government also proposes the installation of water meters in individual households and the introduction of water charges based on usage above a free allowance. My Department is developing proposals to implement the metering programme. (Dáil Éireann, 2011, p. 174)

Furthermore, I expect that the Irish government focuses on high-politicisation strategies of blame shifting and self-defence rather than low-politicisation strategies in both cases. Figure 6.8 supports this expectation. The Irish government relied on

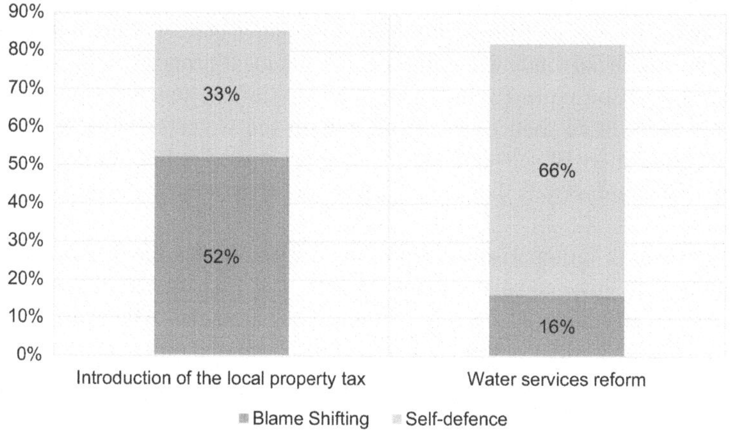

Fig. 6.7 Blame avoidance and self-defence statements in cases of varying reputation for policy support

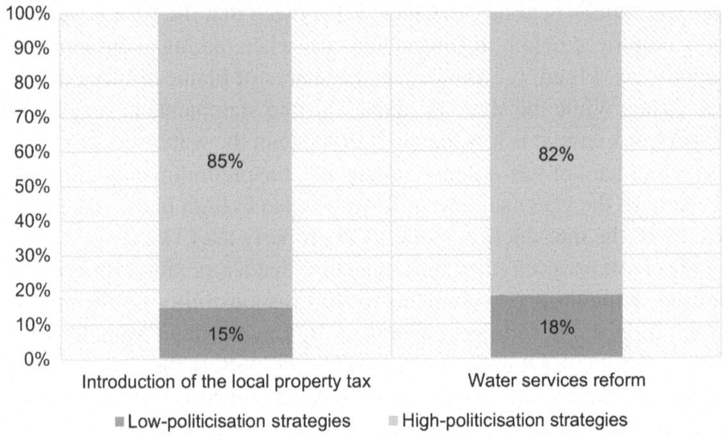

Fig. 6.8 High- and low-politicisation strategies in cases of varying reputation for policy support

high-politicisation strategies in more than 80% of the statements in both cases. Conversely, the share of low-politicisation strategies is consistently low for both the introduction of the property tax and the water services reform.

In sum, the second set of pairwise comparisons matches the theoretical framework's expectations for governments' blame avoidance behaviour in cases of varying reputation for policy support. As the cases within each comparison share a similar level of politicisation, the governments' choice of blame avoidance strategies was similar regarding the use of high- and low-politicisation strategies but varied in the evaluation of the policy. The Irish and Portuguese governments both faced low politicisation of the reforms of the Irish wage setting system and the regulated professions in Portugal. Consequently, in line with the theoretical framework, the Irish government's share of circle the wagons statements was more than three times larger than that of the Portuguese government. Conversely, the share of problem denial statements was considerable larger in the latter case. The Irish government faced significant headwinds when introducing the local property tax and the water services reform. Consequently, the share of blame shifting statements is in the local property case is more than twice as high as in the water services reform case. Conversely, the share of self-defence statements is twice as high in the latter case. Both pairwise comparisons thus exhibit clear variation in the evaluation of the analysed policy.

Furthermore, the comparisons support the conjecture that the degree of politicisation influences governments' strategy choice. The Irish and Portuguese governments consistently focused on low-politicisation strategies when discussing the reforms of the Irish wage setting system and the regulated professions in Portugal. Conversely, the Irish government mainly employed high-politicisation strategies when talking about the introduction of the property levy and the water service reform, where it faced considerable headwinds. The results of the pairwise comparisons thus lend overall support to the theoretical framework.

6.3 Alternative Explanations

The last two sections confirmed the empirical fit of the theoretical framework in the analysed cases. Together with the in-case evidence presented in Chaps. 4 and 5, this strengthens my confidence that the two independent variables, politicisation and reputation for policy support, indeed shape governments' choice of blame avoidance strategies when they have to comply with EU conditionality. To further support my conjectures, I will now evaluate the explanatory power of alternative explanations, focusing on sequential strategy choice, government ideology and the style of policymaking, and governments' compliance.

A Sequential Strategy Choice

First, a prominent proposition in the literature is that governments follow a sequential approach of choosing strategies according to their potential for blame avoidance (Hood et al., 2009). This approach suggests that governments always start out with strategies that manipulate the harm dimension. They move on to strategies that accept the perceived harm of a policy and aim to manipulate the agency dimension only when the former proves insufficient to avoid blame. If this conjecture applied, I would expect governments to focus predominantly on the harm-denying approaches of self-defence and problem denial from the onset. If blame shifting and circle the wagons statements are employed, they become predominant only later in the process of blame avoidance. This pattern should be observable in all cases.

Figure 6.9 shows that this expectation only partially applies. The Irish and the Portuguese government employed statements that denied the negative consequences of the reforms in more than 50% of their statements in only three cases: the reform of the wage setting system and the water services reform in Ireland, and the labour market reforms in Portugal. Conversely, the Irish government employed more blame shifting and circle the wagons statements from the onset when introducing the local property tax and increased the share of harm-denying strategies over time. Furthermore, in the case of the reforms of regulated professions the Portuguese government's blame avoidance pattern shows a temporary decrease in self-defence and problem denial statements in 2013 that is incompatible with a sequential approach.

Therefore, a sequential approach cannot account for all analysed cases of blame avoidance. What is more, a differentiation between harm-denying and harm-accepting strategies runs the risk of ignoring significant differences between the cases. While the reform of the collective bargaining system and the water services reform in Ireland, and the labour market reforms in Portugal look very similar in this comparison over time, the additional differentiation between strategies that centre or blur responsibility makes visible essential differences between the cases.

The Style of Policymaking and Government Ideology

Second, scholarship on welfare retrenchment and blame avoidance has highlighted that the style of policymaking and governments' ideology affect governments'

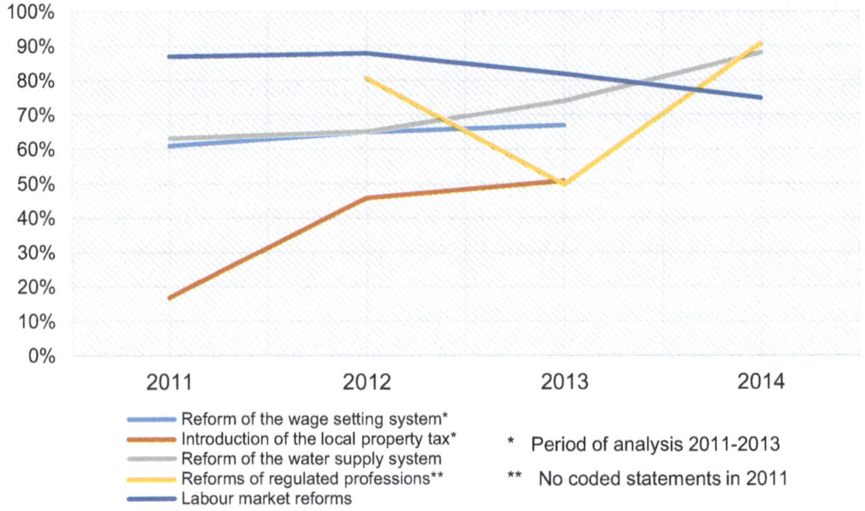

Fig. 6.9 Statements denying the perceived harm from policy by year

choice of blame avoidance strategies. A consensual style of politics and the formation of coalition governments are more amenable to blame dispersion than more conflictual politics (Green-Pedersen, 2002; Hering, 2008; Vis & van Kersbergen, 2007). Ireland and Portugal lean more towards consensus democracy than majoritarian democracy (Lijphart, 2012). Consequently, I would expect to see a clear tendency towards strategies that blur responsibility in all cases.

Furthermore, conservative and liberal governing parties should be more likely than left-wing incumbents to positively portray austerity and retrenchment measures, as these policies are closer to the parties' preferred policies. Incumbent left-wing parties are more likely to highlight the responsibility of other actors (Sommer, 2020). In both Ireland and Portugal, at least the larger party in the governing coalition was located right of centre of the political spectrum (Dukelow, 2015; Lütz et al., 2019). Consequently, I would expect that the Irish and Portuguese governments mostly lean towards strategies that deny the negative consequences of the policies introduced under EU conditionality. When taking these two conjectures together, this would suggest an overall dominance of problem denial statements in all cases.

Figure 6.10 displays the share of problem denial statements in all five cases and disproves this expectation. Only the Portuguese government focused predominantly on a problem denial approach when discussing the reforms of regulated professions introduced under EU conditionality. The other cases vary in the occurrence of problem denial statements. While the Irish and Portuguese governments employed problem denial in around 30% of their blame avoidance statements in the cases related to wage setting in Ireland and the Portuguese labour market, the Irish government used this strategy circa 15% of the time when talking about the introduction of the local property tax and the reform of the water supply system.

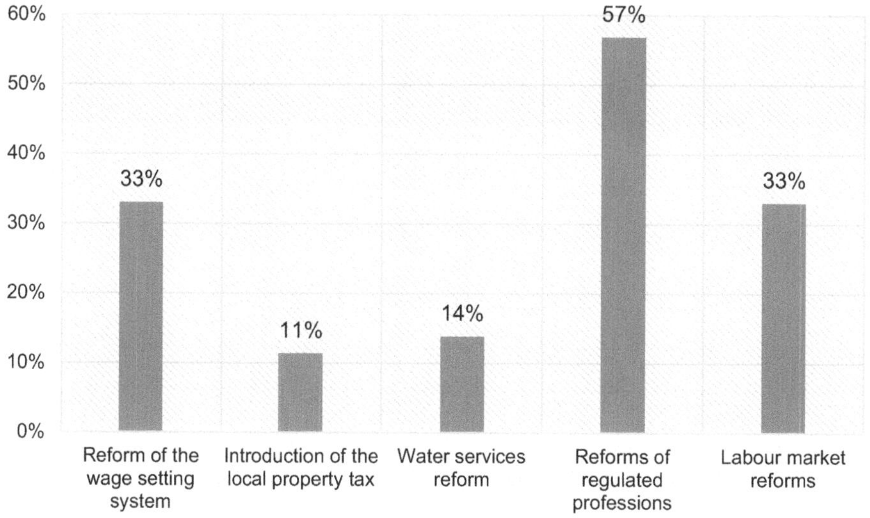

Fig. 6.10 Share of problem denial statements by case

Therefore, the observed patterns of blame avoidance do not confirm the expectations derived from the style of policymaking and governments' ideology. These conjectures can only account for one out of five cases. In sum, these factors cannot account for the variance in blame avoidance strategies or the comparatively low share of problem denial statements in most cases.

Governments' Compliance Record

Finally, I investigate whether governments' use of blame avoidance strategies is linked to their compliance record. Scholarship on international lending has long highlighted the potential for governments to use lending conditionality as a means to tie their hands and introduce reforms against strong domestic opposition (Drazen, 2001; Dreher, 2009; Vreeland, 2003). The potential of external constraints to empower governments to overcome domestic constraints is also well established in the context of the EU (Bolukbasi, 2009; Dyson & Featherstone, 1996; Featherstone, 2014; Moravcsik, 1994). More recently, scholars have highlighted that those governments that came under pressure from EU conditionality still had room for meaningful policy choice (Cioffi & Dubin, 2016; Hick, 2018; Moury & Gago, 2018; Moury & Standring, 2017). Consequently, one explanation for variation in compliance with conditionality is that governments used conditionality to introduce policies they favoured while being less stringent on those measures they opposed. Their compliance record should then serve as a direct proxy for governments' policy preferences.

Regarding governments' choice of blame avoidance strategies, this could imply that governments portray more favourably those policies with a good compliance record while accepting more readily the negative consequences of policies they

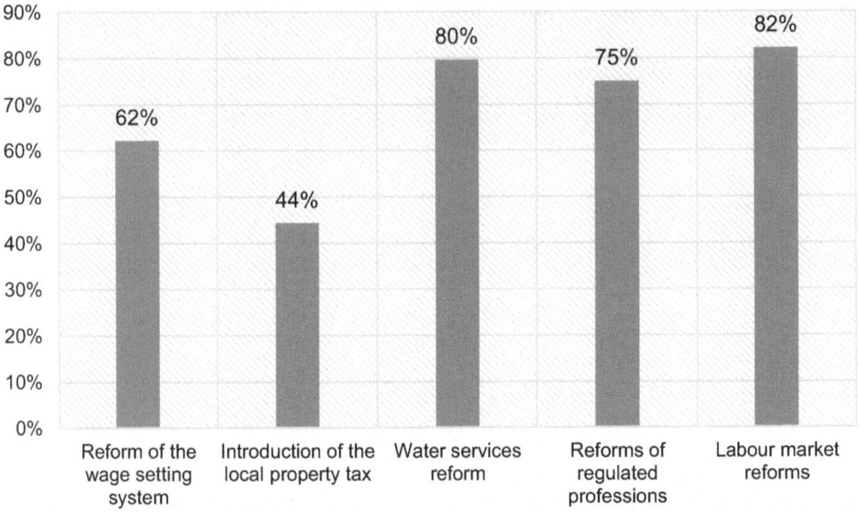

Fig. 6.11 Share of statements denying the perceived harm from a policy

oppose. The Irish and Portuguese governments both showed a strong commitment to the Economic Assistance Programmes signed with the EU in general (Dukelow, 2015; Henning, 2017; Lütz et al., 2019; Theodoropoulou, 2015). Yet, a look at the EU's post-Programme evaluation of governments' compliance records shows that they followed the EU requirements to varying degrees. As I laid out in Chaps. 4 and 5, the Commission was satisfied with the governments' compliance with the requirements to introduce a local property tax and reform the wage setting system in Ireland and reform the Portuguese labour market. Contrariwise, the Commission criticised a lack of progress regarding the reform of the Irish water supply system and the Portuguese reforms of regulated professions in their evaluation after the official end of the Programme. Using compliance as an indicator for governments' policy preferences thus leads me to expect that the Irish and Portuguese governments focused on strategies that deny negative consequences of the introduction of a local property tax and the reform of the collective bargaining system in Ireland, and the reform the Portuguese labour market. Conversely, they should focus predominantly on strategies that accept harmful consequences of the reform of the Irish water supply system and the Portuguese reforms of regulated professions.

Figure 6.11 shows that the observed choice of blame avoidance strategies does not confirm these expectations. First, while the share of statements that deny the negative consequences from the measures introduced under EU conditionality exceeds 50% in the cases of the reform of wage setting in Ireland (65%) and the Portuguese labour market reform (82%) as the compliance conjecture expects, the Irish government used less harm-denying statements than harm-accepting statements when talking about the introduction of the local property tax (48%). Second, the governments predominantly used harm-denying statements when discussing the reform of water services in Ireland (80%) and the reform of regulated professions in

Portugal (82%), thus refuting the expectations. In sum, three out of five cases do not match the pattern suggested by the compliance conjecture. Furthermore, this conjecture does not yield specific expectations regarding the centring or blurring of responsibility, thus missing out on significant variation between the cases.

In sum, the observed pattern of blame avoidance strategies in the five cases did not match the expectations derived from the three alternative conjectures on governments' choice of blame avoidance strategies. Furthermore, at least two of the raised alternatives had difficulties accounting for variation between statements centring and blurring of responsibility and harm-accepting and -denying statements simultaneously. I conclude this chapter by contrasting the theoretical framework's explanatory power with the alternative explanations.

6.4 Critical Appraisal

This chapter aimed to evaluate the empirical fit of the theoretical framework in two ways. First, I went beyond the in-case evidence presented in Chaps. 4 and 5 and evaluated whether the theoretical framework can account for the variation in governments' choice of blame avoidance across the five analysed cases. To this end, I compared the cases in four most similar pairwise comparisons. Second, I evaluated the match between the observed patterns of blame avoidance strategies and three alternative explanations. How did the theoretical framework fare in these two endeavours?

First, the four pairwise comparisons showed that the observed variance in governments' choice of strategies confirms the expectations derived from the theoretical framework. The observed variation in governments' use of blame avoidance strategies matched the expectations derived from the theoretical framework in all four case comparisons. In a nutshell, governments engaged more in blame shifting and self-defence when policies were highly politicised, whereas the shares of circle the wagons and problem denial was higher when governments faced little headwinds when introducing measures required by EU conditionality. Furthermore, governments systematically focused more on harm-denying strategies of self-defence and problem denial as their dominant strategy when they had a reputation for policy support and relied more heavily on harm-accepting approaches when they did not. Taken together, the level of politicisation of the policy and the government's reputation for policy support correctly predicted the differences in government's pattern of blame avoidance strategies.

Second, the observed pattern of governments' choice of blame avoidance strategies only partially matched three alternative accounts. While three cases matched the expected initial focus on harm-denying strategies, the cases of the local property tax in Ireland and reforms of the regulated professions in Portugal did not match the expectations of a sequential approach. Furthermore, only the Portuguese government's strategy choice in the regulated professions case matched the expectations derived from the style of policymaking and governments' ideology. Finally, only the observed pattern of blame avoidance strategies in the case of the reform of wage setting in Ireland and the Portuguese labour market reform matched the expectations from the compliance conjecture. The proposed alternative theoretical explanations thus could thus not account for the observed blame avoidance behaviour in the five cases.

Beyond the empirical fit of the alternative accounts, the sequential and compliance conjectures had difficulties accounting for variation between statements centring and blurring of responsibility and harm-accepting and -denying statements simultaneously. Therefore, they provide a less fine-grained account of governments' blame avoidance behaviour.

In sum, together with the in-case evidence in Chaps. 4 and 5, the four comparisons thus showed that the observed patterns of blame avoidance match the theoretical expectations both within each of the analysed cases, as well as across the cases. The analysis of blame avoidance strategies in each case showed that the governments' predominant choice of strategy was in line with the theoretical expectations in all cases. Furthermore, governments' use of high- and low-politicisation strategies followed the expected pattern. Finally, the results were stable over time in four out of five cases. Solely the Irish government's choice of blame avoidance strategies when talking about the reforms of the wage setting system changed over time due to an external event.

Table 6.1 summarises the findings on the framework's empirical fit. It underlines that the observed pattern of blame avoidance strategies matches the theoretical expectations and underlines that its empirical fit exceeds alternative accounts. The theoretical framework I developed in Chap. 2 thus provides more fine-grained expectations about governments' choice of blame avoidance strategies and better fits the observed blame avoidance patterns.

Table 6.1 Summary of the empirical fit of the theoretical framework and alternative explanations

Case	Theoretical framework	Sequential approach	Policymaking style and government ideology	Compliance
Reform of the wage setting system in Ireland	(✓)	✓	×	✓
Introduction of a local property tax in Ireland	✓	×	×	×
Reform of the water supply system in Ireland	✓	✓	×	×
Reform of regulated professions in Portugal	✓	×	✓	×
Labour market reform in Portugal	✓	✓		✓

References

Bolukbasi, H. T. (2009). On consensus, constraint and choice: Economic and monetary integration and Europe's welfare states. *Journal of European Public Policy, 16*(4), 527–544. https://doi.org/10.1080/13501760902872551

Cioffi, J. W., & Dubin, K. A. (2016). Commandeering crisis: Partisan labor repression in Spain under the guise of economic reform. *Politics and Society, 44*(3), 423–453.

Dáil Éireann. (2011). *9 June 2011: Official Report - Unrevised* (Parliamentary Debates), *735* (1).

Drazen, A. (2001). *Conditionality and ownership in IMF lending: A political economy approach.*

Dreher, A. (2009). IMF conditionality: Theory and evidence. *Public Choice, 141*(1-2), 233–267. https://doi.org/10.1007/s11127-009-9486-z

Dukelow, F. (2015). 'Pushing against an open door': Reinforcing the neo-liberal policy paradigm in Ireland and the impact of EU intrusion. *Comparative European Politics, 13*(1), 93–111.

Dyson, K., & Featherstone, K. (1996). Italy and EMU as a 'Vincolo Esterno': Empowering the technocrats, transforming the state. *South European Society and Politics, 1*(2), 272–299.

Featherstone, K. (2014). External conditionality and the debt crisis: The 'Troika' and Public Administration Reform in Greece. *Journal of European Public Policy, 22*(3), 295–314.

Green-Pedersen, C. (2002). *The politics of justification: Party competition and welfare-state retrenchment in Denmark and the Netherlands from 1982 to 1998. Changing welfare states.* Amsterdam University Press. https://doi.org/10.2307/j.ctt46n1h4

Henning, C. R. (2017). *Tangled governance: International regime complexity, the Troika, and the Euro Crisis.* Oxford University Press.

Hering, M. (2008). Welfare state restructuring without grand coalitions: The role of informal cooperation in blame avoidance. *German Politics, 17*(2), 165–183. https://doi.org/10.1080/09644000802075757

Hick, R. (2018). Enter the Troika: The politics of social security during Ireland's bailout. *Journal of Social Policy, 47*(1), 1–20. https://doi.org/10.1017/S0047279417000095

Hood, C., Jennings, W., Dixon, R., Hogwood, B., & Beeston, C. (2009). Testing times: Exploring staged responses and the impact of blame management strategies in two examination fiasco cases. *European Journal of Political Research, 48*(6), 695–722.

Lijphart, A. (2012). *Patterns of democracy: Government forms and performance in thirty-six countries* (2nd ed.). Yale University Press.

Lütz, S., Hilgers, S., & Schneider, S. (2019). Games borrower governments play: The implementation of economic adjustment programmes in cyprus and Portugal. *West European Politics, 42*(7), 1443–1463.

Moravcsik, A. (1994). Why the European union strengthens the state: Domestic politics and international cooperation. *CES Working Paper*(52), Harvard University.

Moury, C., & Gago, A. (2018). *Fallacious arguments in a three-level game: Discursive strategies of Irish and Portuguese executives during the financial crisis* (Paper Presented at the ECPR Joint Sessions in Nicosia, 10–14 April 2018). Paper Presented at the ECPR Joint Sessions in Nicosia, 10–14 April 2018.

Moury, C., & Standring, A. (2017). 'Going beyond the Troika': Power and discourse in Portuguese austerity politics. *European Journal of Political Research, 56*(3), 660–679.

Sommer, M. (2020). Blame-shifting in times of permanent austerity: Evidence from Spain and Greece in the Eurozone crisis. *Journal of Common Market Studies, 58*(3), 562–579. https://doi.org/10.1111/jcms.12926

Theodoropoulou, S. (2015). National social and labour market policy reforms in the shadow of EU bail-out conditionality: The cases of Greece and Portugal. *Comparative European Politics, 13*(1), 29–55.

Vis, B., & van Kersbergen, K. (2007). Why and how do political actors pursue risky reforms? *Journal of Theoretical Politics, 19*(2), 153–172. https://doi.org/10.1177/0951629807074268

Vreeland, J. R. (2003). *The IMF and economic development.* Cambridge University Press.

Chapter 7
Conclusion

EU conditionality in the Euro crisis has resulted in considerable hardship in those member states that had to introduce austerity measures and structural reforms in exchange for financial support. Conditionality has exacerbated the responsibility-responsiveness dilemma for the affected governments: To remain in the Eurozone, they had to comply with EU conditionality. Yet, the measures governments had to introduce in compliance with EU requirements were unpopular domestically as they implied the loss of material benefits and rights. Thus, governments had difficulties signalling to their electorate that they were responsive to their interests and faced the threat of electoral punishment.

Governments can mitigate this dilemma by disentangling the link between their actions and the hardship imposed on their electorate via blame avoidance strategies. The aim of this study was to explain governments' choice of blame avoidance strategy under EU conditionality. In this last chapter, I show that the study was successful in this regard and highlight how the theoretical and empirical insights contribute to scholarship on blame avoidance, the Euro crisis, and, more generally, government responsiveness in view of the increasing authority of international institutions. Furthermore, I point out the potential for further research that this study opens up.

7.1 The Policy-Specific Choice of Blame Avoidance Strategy

Chapter 2 began by explaining the relevance of blame avoidance strategies for governments who want to stay in office. For policy outcomes to become politically consequential, they need to be linked to policymakers' deliberate actions or omissions. The process of attributing responsibility, and thus drawing this causal link, is politically contested. It can have important implications for perceptions of responsiveness, as well as policymakers' reputation, legitimacy, and electoral success.

L. Kriegmair, *Responsiveness and Responsibility in the Euro Crisis*, Contributions to Political Science, https://doi.org/10.1007/978-3-031-84473-7_7

Governments whose goal is to stay in office thus have an incentive to signal responsiveness to their electorate by claiming credit for popular policies while avoiding blame for unpopular ones. The latter aspect takes precedence, as both governments and their electorate fall victim to negativity bias. Governments who have to introduce austerity measures and structural reforms to comply with EU conditionality should thus draw on blame avoidance strategies to evade blame and electoral repercussions.

The toolkit of blame avoidance strategies available to governments comprises agency strategies, policy strategies, and presentational strategies. However, under EU conditionality, only presentational strategies are available to governments. The budgetary constraints, short timeframe, and specific policy requirements impede agency strategies, which aim to shift formal policymaking competencies and policy strategies, which work on policy design. Thus, EU conditionality is an important scope condition for government's strategy choice.

Based on these conjectures from the scholarship on responsibility attributions, economic voting, and blame avoidance, I developed a typology of four presentational blame avoidance strategies available to governments under EU conditionality. This framework points out significant differences in blame avoidance approaches. First, governments' presentational blame avoidance strategies can work on the harm dimension, which concerns the perceived loss or harm that occurs due to the introduced policy. Governments can either deny or accept the adverse effects of a policy. Second, blame avoidance strategies can tackle the agency dimension, which concerns the responsibility for the adverse consequences of the policy. Governments choose to blur responsibility among actors or keep it centred. Combining both choices yields four different strategies:

- **Circle the wagons**, whereby governments accept the adverse consequences of a policy introduced in compliance with EU conditionality and blur responsibility by diffusing it among several actors.
- **Blame shifting**, whereby governments do not deny the negative consequences of a policy but shift responsibility onto other plausible targets, such as the troika institutions or the predecessor government.
- **Self-defence**, whereby governments challenge the perception of adverse consequences of the policy and accept the responsibility for the policy introduced under EU conditionality.
- **Problem denial**, whereby governments deny negative consequences of a policy and blur responsibility by diffusing it among several actors.

Which strategy governments choose upon introducing a policy in compliance with EU conditionality depends on the policy-specific context. I argued that the *degree of politicisation* and governing parties' *reputation for policy support* shape governments' decisions. First, the degree of politicisation influences the viability of responsibility-blurring approaches. Governments are free to diffuse responsibility among several actors under conditions of low politicisation. Yet, the more potential blame makers enter salient policy debates and the more polarised they become, the more the government finds itself in the spotlight of public criticism and has to rely on approaches that centre responsibility. Second, under EU conditionality, governments do not have the time and resources to reframe a policy. Instead, they need to draw on their previous issue reputation. Governments without a prior record of supporting a measure must accept the adverse consequences of a policy introduced under EU conditionality and plausibly shift the blame to third actors. These considerations allowed me to formulate specific expectations regarding governments' choice of blame avoidance strategy:

- When politicisation is low and governing parties have no reputation for policy support, they will predominantly opt for a **circle the wagons** approach rather than other blame avoidance strategies when introducing measures required by EU conditionality.
- When governments face a highly politicised policy required by EU conditionality and they have no reputation for policy support, they primarily focus on **blame shifting** than other blame avoidance strategies.
- When politicisation is high and governing parties have a reputation for supporting a policy that they are required to introduce under EU conditionality, they will adopt a **self-defence** approach more often than other blame avoidance strategies.
- When politicisation is low and governing parties have a reputation for policy support, they will focus their blame avoidance efforts on a **problem denial** approach rather than other strategies when introducing measures required by EU conditionality.

These theoretical conjectures make important contributions to the literature on blame avoidance that go beyond the context of EU conditionality. First, this theoretical framework highlights the importance of the policy-specific context for governments' strategy choice. Existing accounts focusing on governments' blame avoidance preferences (Gerhards et al., 2009; Schlipphak & Treib, 2017; Traber et al., 2020; Vasilopoulou et al., 2014) or the institutional policymaking context (Heinkelmann-Wild et al., 2020; Heinkelmann-Wild & Zangl, 2020; Hobolt & Tilley, 2014) highlight the opportunities for shifting blame to the European level in the context of EU conditionality. Indeed, the institutional setup is conductive for doing so, as the Commission and the ECB, in their function of troika institutions, are closely involved with the development and monitoring of EU conditionality. This expectation is further supported by scholarship highlighting the potential for governments to use external constraints as a means to tie their hands and introduce reforms against strong domestic opposition in the context of conditional lending by International Financial Institutions (Drazen, 2001; Dreher, 2009; Vreeland, 2003) as well as in the EU (Bolukbasi, 2009; Dyson & Featherstone, 1996; Featherstone, 2014; Moravcsik, 1994). These literatures thus assume at least implicitly that governments can alleviate the risk for blame and electoral repercussions by shifting the responsibility for unpopular policies to external actors. While these accounts lead us to expect that governments frequently engage in blame shifting to the EU, I show that the policy-specific context influences whether they do so or turn to other strategies instead. The study thus confirms previous findings that governments shift blame to the EU less frequently than assumed by large parts of the literature (Hobolt & Tilley, 2014) and provides an explanation for this phenomenon.

Second, I highlight other strategies beyond blame shifting that governments have at their disposal to alleviate the responsibility-responsiveness dilemma. The typology includes blame avoidance strategies that aim at positively reframing policies that bear a blame risk. These strategies are well known in the literature on welfare retrenchment (Elmelund-Præstekær et al., 2015; Elmelund-Præstekær & Emmenegger, 2013; Hinterleitner, 2017; Vis, 2016), but have so far received less attention in the context of blame avoidance in the EU (but see König, 2016a, b; Roose et al., 2018). Highlighting the different options available to governments emphasises that their choice is more complex than the decision for or against blame shifting to the EU.

These insights should apply beyond the context of EU conditionality. Today, governments often find themselves facing the responsibility-responsiveness dilemma. Since the end of the Second World War, governments have increasingly relied on international institutions to provide common goods they cannot achieve alone. Today, the authority of these international institutions has reached unmatched heights (Hooghe et al., 2017), and national governments sometimes find themselves in the position of having to take actions that go against their preferences (Zürn et al., 2007, 2012). For instance, the World Trade Organisation (WTO) international dispute settlement procedures ensure state compliance with their obligations under the international trade regime (Zangl, 2008). Moreover, the International Monetary Fund (IMF) has a long history of levering policy change by linking financial assistance to macroeconomic conditionality (Drazen, 2001; Dreher, 2009; Dreher et al., 2013; Nelson, 2009; Stone, 2008; Vaubel & Willett, 1991; Vreeland, 2007). Within the EU, Integration processes have extended supranational influence on member state policies overtime. Especially in the Eurozone, the EU intrusiveness and conditionality present a vital component of EU policymaking as long as fiscal and structural policies are decided at the national level (Bini Smaghi, 2015, p. 756). EU influence was significantly extended with the introduction of the European Semester, which allows the Commission to issue more and more binding policy recommendations in diverse set of policy fields (Kreuder-Sonnen, 2016; La Porte & Heins, 2015; Laffan, 2014; Lobo & Karremans, 2018; Savage & Verdun, 2016). This applies especially for those member states of the Eurozone that come under special surveillance of the Economic Deficit Procedure (EDP) or the Macroeconomic Imbalance Procedure (MIP). More recently, NGEU, which is the biggest stimulus package in the EU's history, relies on conditionality to change member states' macroeconomic policy (La Porte & Jensen, 2021). In sum, national governments now frequently encounter situations where they cannot control the domestic political agenda and face the responsibility-response dilemma (Kriegmair et al., 2022).

Theorising how EU conditionality limits governments' strategy choice allows for some considerations on the broader applicability of the framework. Making explicit that the limitations under EU conditionality arise from budgetary constraints, the specificity of the conditions and the short timeframe under which measures have to be introduced allows for specific expectations for broadening the framework's scope. Theorising these constraints, the study adds to scholarship on the limits of government responsiveness (Hagemann et al., 2017; Mair, 2007, 2011; Schneider, 2020). The theoretical framework should be applicable to lending conditionality beyond the EU and policymaking in the context of the European Semester, especially under the EU's EDP and MIP.

In sum, the insights into how governments mitigate the responsibility-responsiveness dilemma have the potential to hold beyond the realm of EU conditionality and should thus be valuable for a broader audience of scholars interested in the legitimacy and politicisation of international institutions in general and the EU specifically.

7.2 Variance in Blame Avoidance Strategies Under EU Conditionality

This study analysed blame avoidance strategies in the parliamentary arena, where governments are summoned to explain and justify their policy choices. Governments cannot evade topics in this realm and are forced to take up a position because opposition parties, as prominent blame generators, play a central role in holding governments accountable. This makes parliamentary debates the ideal territory to study how governments dealt with the responsibility-responsiveness dilemma during the Euro crisis and employed blame avoidance strategy in this regard.

The analysis of five cases of reforms introduced under EU conditionality has confirmed that the theoretical frameworks can account for governments' specific choice of blame avoidance strategy in each case study and the variation in strategies across the cases. The politicisation of the measures required by EU conditionality and governing parties' reputation for supporting these measures shaped governments' strategy to navigate the blame pressures they faced under the spectre of EU conditionality.

This study shows that the choice of strategy varied for each government depending on the policy and the theoretical expectations mostly held true. The Irish government mostly focused on self-defence when introducing the highly politicised reform of the Irish water services, which one of the governing parties had championed prior to the Programme. Instead, it chose to focus its blame avoidance efforts on blame shifting when introducing the highly politicised levy on residential property, which it had no record of supporting. When it came to the reform of the Irish wage setting system, the Irish government, which faced little headwinds and had no reputation of supporting the measure, mainly employed a circle the wagons approach. Similarly, the Portuguese government focused on a self-defence approach when introducing the highly politicised labour market reform for which it had a reputation of policy support chose a problem denial approach when reforming regulated professions, a measure that was not politicised and for which the government had a reputation of policy support.

The four pairwise comparisons further underline the policy-specific differences. On the one hand, governments engaged more in blame shifting and self-defence when policies were highly politicised, whereas the shares of circle the wagons and problem denial statements were higher when governments faced minor headwinds against the introduction of measures required by EU conditionality. On the other hand, governments systematically focused more on harm-denying strategies of self-defence and problem denial when they had a reputation for policy support and relied more heavily on harm-accepting strategies when they did not. In sum, governments' strategy choice was responsive to the context in which they introduced measures to comply with EU conditionality. These insights qualify existing accounts of blame avoidance in the Euro crisis, which have pointed out government-specific (König, 2016b; Moury & Standring, 2017; Sommer, 2020) or country-specific (Roose et al., 2017, 2018; Vasilopoulou et al., 2014) patterns of blame avoidance.

Furthermore, the case studies revealed important insights beyond the scope of the theoretical framework. First, in the case of the reform of the wage setting system, the Irish government employed harm-denying strategies to a similar extent as the circle the wagons approach the theoretical framework would have expected as the dominant strategy. A disaggregation over time showed that the government's choice of strategy changed due to an external event. A High Court ruling in July 2011 declared the existing wage-setting system unconstitutional and changed the discourse from reform to reinstatement of the system. This allowed the government to employ a strategy of self-defence, which then allowed it to claim credit for the reinstatement of the wage-setting system in the long run. This episode shows that while contextual constraints limit governments strategy choice, they still adjust their blame avoidance behaviour when the opportunity arises.

Second, the Portuguese government consistently employed a high share of harm-denying statements when reforming both the labour market and the system of regulated professions. This choice may suggest that the high ownership for the reforms and the Programme as a whole drove the government's choice of blame avoidance strategies in both cases. This insight suggests that differences in terms of Programme commitment may influence governments' strategy choice in addition to the degree of politicisation and the governing parties' reputation for policy support.

Third, Chaps. 4 and 5 showed that the Irish and Portuguese governments engaged in blame avoidance strategies less frequently in the cases of the wage setting system in Ireland and the reform of regulated professions in Portugal compared to the three other cases. One implication of this finding may be that low politicisation requires governments to engage in blame avoidance less frequently. This somewhat qualifies the assumption that governments cannot avoid unpopular reforms under EU conditionality (Traber et al., 2020). While governments are still required to take a position on these measures in Parliament, they have to do so less frequently than in highly politicised cases.

In sum, the study could point to interesting variations in governments' choice of blame avoidance strategies that have so far gone unnoticed and explain the observed variance. These findings thus show the merits of the typology and the theoretical framework in generating deeper insights into governments' blame avoidance behaviour during the Euro crisis.

7.3 Further Research

The theoretical framework and the empirical findings I summarised in the last two sections highlight several avenues for further research. The study invites research that probes extensions of the scope of the argument, as well as additions to the framework. Moreover, the study highlights the value of theorising the trade-off between blame avoidance and credit claiming motives and investigating the effectiveness of blame avoidance strategies.

First, the applicability of the theoretical argument beyond the context of EU conditionality should be probed in additional studies analysing international lending conditionality, as well as the broader context of EU policymaking. The theoretical framework should have explanatory leverage in the context of lending conditionality by international financial institutions beyond the EU and cases in which the EU has significant influence on domestic policymaking member states. The systematic typology of four blame avoidance strategies that differ in two dimensions and the theoretical framework building on the combination of two independent variables lend themselves to a more large-scale analysis of governments' blame avoidance behaviour. These extensions can contribute to a better understanding of how governments mitigate the responsibility-responsiveness dilemma that comes with the increasing authority of international institutions.

Second, further research should investigate additional factors that may influence governments' strategy choice. In the previous section, I highlighted that the Portuguese governments' reliance on harm-denying strategies stands out and cannot be accounted for by the theoretical framework. Systematic differences between governments, such as their overall Programme commitment, may influence the choice of blame avoidance strategies and should be further investigated to understand better how governments communicated the introduction of measures that carried considerable blame risk during the Euro crisis. What is more, in privileging internal validity, this study has focused solely on the realm of structural reforms required by EU conditionality. Structural reforms were an important aspect of EU conditionality because they led to long-term changes in member states' legislation. Instead, budgetary cuts stood out in the EU's conditionality because they lead to immediate derogations in domestic living standards. It remains open whether this difference systematically influenced governments' choice of blame avoidance strategy.

Third, further research should investigate the relationship between blame avoidance and credit claiming opportunities. Along with existing scholarship on blame avoidance (Hood, 2011; Hood et al., 2009), I claimed that harm-denying strategies make it easier for governments to claim credit for reforms in the long-run. This additional benefit should make harm-denying strategies especially attractive to governments. The case of the reform of the Irish wage setting system showed that the

Irish government indeed opted for harm-denying strategies when an external event allowed it to positively reframe the reform despite a lack of reputation for policy support. Similarly, the Irish government often combined blame shifting and self-defence strategies when talking about the introduction of the local property tax. One explanation for the combination of strategies could be that the government is balancing short-term and long-term advantages. Further research needs to theorise the trade-off between blame avoidance and credit claiming governments face when opting for different blame avoidance strategies and investigate how governments navigate this trade-off.

Finally, an important question that has so far remained unanswered is whether governments' efforts to avoid blame via presentational strategies are successful. In Chap. 2, I argued that the contested nature of responsibility attributions in the public provides a strong incentive for governments to engage in attempts to shape public responsibility judgements. Yet, this does not mean that their efforts are crowned by success. Governments are not the only actors involved in these processes. Members of the opposition, the media, and civil society organisations all play an important role in the public construction of responsibility attributions (Gerhards et al., 2009; Hinterleitner, 2020; Hobolt & Tilley, 2014; Hood, 2011; Roose et al., 2017, 2018). Further analysis of public responsibility discourses is necessary to gain a better understanding of the effectiveness of governments' blame avoidance: Are certain contexts more conductive to successful blame avoidance? Do specific strategies have a higher prospect of success?

In sum, the study contributes to a better understanding of how governments employed blame avoidance strategies under the spectre of EU conditionality in the Euro crisis and thus yields important insights into how governments mitigate the responsibility-responsiveness dilemma. It furthermore opens up avenues for further insightful research. Finally, I want to highlight two important normative implications of this study for governments' political accountability.

First, the economic voting literature posits that diffuse responsibility and lacking clarity of responsibility impede the link between unpopular policy outcomes and electoral outcomes (Anderson, 2000; Hobolt et al., 2013; Powell & Whitten, 1993). This casts a critical light on governments' efforts to blur responsibility. While such strategies may well be an effective means for blame avoidance, they constitute a problem for political accountability. The theoretical framework in Chap. 2 links governments' ability to blur responsibility to the degree of politicisation. The more players in- and outside Parliament oppose a policy, raise public attention to the measure and criticises the government for its policy, the harder it is for the latter to escape accountability by blurring responsibility. This highlights a positive effect of the politicisation of policies on accountability (De Wilde, 2011; Rauh & De Wilde, 2018).

Second, the constraining effect of politicisation and governments' reputation for policy support rests fundamentally on the requirement that governments' statements be plausible to resonate in the public: When governments make claims that can easily be refuted by other actors taking part in the public responsibility discourse, they do not stand a chance of shaping public responsibility judgements. Along with others (Heinkelmann-Wild et al., 2020; Heinkelmann-Wild & Zangl, 2020; Rittberger et al., 2017; Schwarzenbeck, 2017), I argue that governments anticipate this plausibility requirement and, thus, reflect contextual constraints in their strategy choice. This underlines the importance of free speech and open access to public discourse: Only when members of the opposition, the media and civil society can check and counter government statements are the latter bound by the plausibility requirement. Under these circumstances, blame avoidance is part of a process of public 'account giving' (Bovens, 2007; Rauh & De Wilde, 2018). When governments restrict the access of critical voices to public discourse, as is currently visible in several Eastern European countries, they become entirely free in their choice of blame avoidance strategy. They can shift blame to internal opponents and supranational actors at will, thus 'playing the blame game on Brussels' (see Schlipphak & Treib, 2017) in an unrestricted manner.

References

Anderson, C. J. (2000). Economic voting and political context: A comparative perspective. *Electoral Studies, 19*(2–3), 151–170. https://doi.org/10.1016/S0261-3794(99)00045-1

Bini Smaghi, L. (2015). Governance and conditionality: Toward a sustainable framework? *Journal of European Integration, 37*(7), 755–768. https://doi.org/10.1080/07036337.2015.1079372

Bolukbasi, H. T. (2009). On consensus, constraint and choice: Economic and monetary integration and Europe's welfare states. *Journal of European Public Policy, 16*(4), 527–544. https://doi.org/10.1080/13501760902872551

Bovens, M. (2007). Analysing and assessing accountability: A conceptual framework. *European Law Journal, 13*(4), 447–468. https://doi.org/10.1111/j.1468-0386.2007.00378.x

de La Porte, C., & Heins, E. (2015). A new era of European integration? Governance of labour market and social policy since the sovereign debt crisis. *Comparative European Politics, 13*(1), 8–28.

de La Porte, C., & Jensen, M. D. (2021). The next generation EU: An analysis of the dimensions of conflict behind the deal. *Social Policy and Administration, 55*(2), 388–402.

De Wilde, P. (2011). No polity for old politics? A framework for analyzing the politicization of European integration. *Journal of European Integration, 33*(5), 559–575. https://doi.org/10.1080/07036337.2010.546849

Drazen, A. (2001). *Conditionality and ownership in IMF lending: A political economy approach.*

Dreher, A. (2009). IMF conditionality: Theory and evidence. *Public Choice, 141*(1–2), 233–267. https://doi.org/10.1007/s11127-009-9486-z

Dreher, A., Sturm, J.-E., & Vreeland, J. R. (2013). Politics and IMF conditionality. *Journal of Conflict Resolution, 59*(1), 120–148. https://doi.org/10.1177/0022002713499723

Dyson, K., & Featherstone, K. (1996). Italy and EMU as a 'Vincolo Esterno': Empowering the technocrats, transforming the state. *South European Society and Politics, 1*(2), 272–299.

Elmelund-Præstekær, C., & Emmenegger, P. (2013). Strategic re-framing as a vote winner: Why vote-seeking governments pursue unpopular reforms. *Scandinavian Political Studies, 36*(1), 23–42. https://doi.org/10.1111/j.1467-9477.2012.00295.x

Elmelund-Præstekær, C., Klitgaard, M. B., & Schumacher, G. (2015). What wins popular support? Communicating or obfuscating welfare state retrenchment. *European Political Science Review, 7*(3), 427–450. https://doi.org/10.1017/S1755773914000253

Featherstone, K. (2014). External conditionality and the debt crisis: The 'Troika' and public administration reform in Greece. *Journal of European Public Policy, 22*(3), 295–314.

Gerhards, J., Offerhaus, A., & Roose, J. (2009). Wer ist verantwortlich? Die Europäische Union, ihre Nationalstaaten und die massenmediale Attribution von Verantwortung für Erfolge und Misserfolge. In F. Marcinkowski & B. Pfetsch (Eds.), *Politik in der Mediendemokratie*: [Politics in the media democracy] (pp. 529–558). VS Verlag für Sozialwissenschaften. doi:https://doi.org/10.1007/978-3-531-91728-3_22.

Hagemann, S., Hobolt, S. B., & Wratil, C. (2017). Government responsiveness in the European Union: Evidence from council voting. *Comparative Political Studies, 50*(6), 850–876. https://doi.org/10.1177/0010414015621077

Heinkelmann-Wild, T., & Zangl, B. (2020). Multilevel blame games: Blame-shifting in the European Union. *Governance, 33*(4), 953–969. https://doi.org/10.1111/gove.12459

Heinkelmann-Wild, T., Kriegmair, L., & Rittberger, B. (2020). The EU multi-level system and the Europeanization of domestic blame games. *Politics and Governance, 8*(1), 85–94.

Hinterleitner, M. (2017). Reconciling perspectives on blame avoidance behaviour. *Political Studies Review, 15*(2), 243–254.

Hinterleitner, M. (2020). *Policy controversies and political blame games. Cambridge studies in comparative public policy*. Cambridge University Press.

Hobolt, S. B., & Tilley, J. (2014). *Blaming Europe? Responsibility without accountability in the European Union* (1st ed.). Oxford University Press.

Hobolt, S. B., Tilley, J., & Banducci, S. A. (2013). Clarity of responsibility: How government cohesion conditions performance voting. *European Journal of Political Research, 52*(2), 164–187.

Hood, C. (2011). *The blame game: Spin, bureaucracy, and self-preservation in government*. Princeton University Press.

Hood, C., Jennings, W., Dixon, R., Hogwood, B., & Beeston, C. (2009). Testing times: Exploring staged responses and the impact of blame management strategies in two examination fiasco cases. *European Journal of Political Research, 48*(6), 695–722.

Hooghe, L., Marks, G., Lenz, T., Bezuijen, J., Ceka, B., & Derderyan, S. (2017). *Measuring international authority: A postfunctionalist theory of governance* (First edition). *Transformations in governance: Vol. 1*. Oxford University Press.

König, P. (2016a). Communicating austerity measures during times of crisis: A comparative empirical analysis of four heads of government. *The British Journal of Politics and International Relations, 18*(3), 538–558.

König, P. (2016b). Unpopular policies and the imperative of justification: Putting the Monti Government's reform communication in a comparative perspective. *Journal of Comparative Policy Analysis: Research and Practice, 18*(2), 176–194.

Kreuder-Sonnen, C. (2016). Beyond integration theory: The (Anti-) constitutional dimension of European crisis governance. *Journal of Common Market Studies, 54*(6), 1350–1366.

Kriegmair, L., Rittberger, B., Zangl, B., & Heinkelmann-Wild, T. (2022). Dolce far niente? Non-compliance and blame avoidance in the EU. *West European Politics, 45*(5), 1153–1174.

Laffan, B. (2014). Testing times: The growing primacy of responsibility in the Euro Area. *West European Politics, 37*(2), 270–287.

Lobo, M. C., & Karremans, J. (2018). Revisiting the politicization of the EU: A three-dimensional approach. In M. C. Lobo, F. Carreira da Silva, & J. P. Zúquete (Eds.), *Changing societies: Legacies and challenges. Citizenship in crisis* (pp. 51–71). Imprensa de Ciências Sociais.

Mair, P. (2007). Political opposition and the European Union. *Government and Opposition, 42*(1), 1–17.

Mair, P. (2011). Bini Smaghi vs. the parties: Representative government and institutional constraints. *EUI Working Papers*(RSCAS 2011/22). https://cadmus.eui.eu/handle/1814/16354

Moravcsik, A. (1994). Why the European Union strengthens the state: Domestic politics and international cooperation. *CES Working Paper*(52), Harvard University.

Moury, C., & Standring, A. (2017). 'Going beyond the Troika': Power and discourse in Portuguese austerity politics. *European Journal of Political Research, 56*(3), 660–679.

Nelson, S. C. (2009). *Creating credibility: The international monetary fund and the neoliberal revolution in the developing world* [A Dissertation Presented to the Faculty of the Graduate School of Cornell University].

Powell, G. B., & Whitten, G. D. (1993). A cross-national analysis of economic voting: Taking account of the political context. *American Journal of Political Science, 37*(2), 391–414. https://doi.org/10.2307/2111378

Rauh, C., & De Wilde, P. (2018). The opposition deficit in EU accountability: Evidence from over 20 years of plenary debate in four member states. *European Journal of Political Research, 57*(1), 194–216. https://doi.org/10.1111/1475-6765.12222

Rittberger, B., Schwarzenbeck, H., & Zangl, B. (2017). Where does the buck stop? Explaining public responsibility attributions in complex international institutions. *Journal of Common Market Studies, 55*(4), 909–924.

Roose, J., Sommer, M., Scholl, F., Kousis, M., Kanellopoulos, K., & Loukakis, A. (2017). Debating responsibility on the Eurozone crisis in traditional media newspaper reporting in Greece and Germany under a social media lens. In M. Barisione & A. Michailidou (Eds.), *Palgrave studies in European political sociology. Social media and European politics: Rethinking power and legitimacy in the digital era* (Vol. 31, pp. 267–290). Palgrave Macmillan.

Roose, J., Sommer, M., & Scholl, F. (2018). Verantwortungszuschreibungen in der Eurozonen-Krise. In J. Roose, M. Sommer, & F. Scholl (Eds.), *Bürgergesellschaft und Demokratie. Europas Zivilgesellschaft in der Wirtschafts- und Finanzkrise: Protest, Resilienz und Kämpfe um Deutungshoheit* (Vol. 10, pp. 43–73). Springer VS.

Savage, J. D., & Verdun, A. (2016). Strengthening the European Commission's budgetary and economic surveillance capacity since Greece and the Euro area crisis: A study of five directorates-general. *Journal of European Public Policy, 23*(1), 101–118.

Schlipphak, B., & Treib, O. (2017). Playing the blame game on Brussels: The domestic political effects of EU interventions against democratic backsliding. *Journal of European Public Policy, 24*(3), 352–365. https://doi.org/10.1080/13501763.2016.1229359

Schneider, C. J. (2020). Public commitments as signals of responsiveness in the European Union. *The Journal of Politics, 82*(1), 329–344.

Schwarzenbeck, H. (2017). *Politische Verantwortung: Der Einfluss von Governance-Design auf die öffentliche Zuweisung von Verantwortung* [Political responsibility. The influence of governnance design on the public attribution of responsibility]. *Internationale Beziehungen: Vol. 24*. Nomos.

Sommer, M. (2020). Blame-shifting in times of permanent austerity: Evidence from Spain and Greece in the Eurozone crisis. *Journal of Common Market Studies, 58*(3), 562–579. https://doi.org/10.1111/jcms.12926

Stone, R. W. (2008). The scope of IMF conditionality. *International Organization, 62*(4), 589–620.

Traber, D., Schoonvelde, M., & Schumacher, G. (2020). Errors have been made, others will be blamed: Issue engagement and blame shifting in Prime Minister speeches during the economic crisis in Europe. *European Journal of Political Research, 59*(1), 45–67.

Vasilopoulou, S., Halikiopoulou, D., & Exadaktylos, T. (2014). Greece in crisis: Austerity, populism and the politics of blame. *Journal of Common Market Studies, 52*(2), 388–402. https://doi.org/10.1111/jcms.12093

Vaubel, R., & Willett, T. (Eds.). (1991). *The political economy of international organizations: A public choice approach*. Westview.

Vis, B. (2016). Taking stock of the comparative literature on the role of blame avoidance strategies in social policy reform. *Journal of Comparative Policy Analysis: Research and Practice, 18*(2), 122–137. https://doi.org/10.1080/13876988.2015.1005955

Vreeland, J. R. (2003). *The IMF and economic development*. Cambridge University Press.

Vreeland, J. R. (2007). *The international monetary fund: Politics of conditional lending*. Routledge.

Zangl, B. (2008). Judicialization matters! A comparison of dispute settlement under GATT and the WTO. *International Studies Quarterly, 52*(4), 825–854. https://doi.org/10.1111/j.1468-2478.2008.00528.x

Zürn, M., Binder, M., Ecker-Ehrhardt, M., & Radtke, K. (2007). Politische Ordnungsbildung wider Willen. *Zeitschrift Für Internationale Beziehungen, 14*(1), 129–164.

Zürn, M., Binder, M., & Ecker-Ehrhardt, M. (2012). International authority and its politicization. *International Theory, 4*(1), 69–106. https://doi.org/10.1017/S1752971912000012

Appendix

In the following, I give an overview of the processes of data collection and analysis. The first section concerns the case selection (A1). Subsequently, I present the coding rules used for the analysis of Parliamentary debates from Ireland and Portugal in five case studies (A2). The third section presents the fine-grained results of the content analysis and discusses their reliability (A3). Lists of all collected and analysed debates (A4), and of all coded statements (A5) are provided in separate Excel files.

A.1 Case Selection

To answer the question of how governments chose blame avoidance strategies under EU conditionality, I collected a total of 700 Parliamentary debates in the five cases chosen for analysis. The following section provides a detailed account of the selection of suitable cases and their temporary delamination.

As detailed in Chap. 3, I selected cases in line with a most similar systems design. All cases are instances of reforms introduced under EU conditionality during the financial and Euro crisis and, in addition, share further important contextual similarities, while varying in a limited number of dimensions. Table A1 summarises the dimensions of similarity and difference between the cases.

The analysis focuses on how a specific government justifies the introduction of reforms required by EU conditionality. The *starting point* of the analysis thus depends on two factors. First, a loan agreement between the EU and a borrowing government needs to be in place that specifies reforms as a precondition for loan disbursement. Second, the government that is tasked with implementing EU conditionality needs to be officially in office. In the case of both Ireland and Portugal, Parliamentary elections took place just after financial assistance programmes were

L. Kriegmair, *Responsiveness and Responsibility in the Euro Crisis*, Contributions to Political Science, https://doi.org/10.1007/978-3-031-84473-7

Table A1 Overview of cases

Case	Period of analysis	Style of policy making	Government	Government ideology	Government type	Reform context	Type of conditionality	Compliance with EU conditionality	Policy contestation	Reputation for policy support
Wage setting system reform in Ireland	09/03/2011–31/12/2013	Consensus democracy	Fine Gael/Labour Party	Centre	Coalition, absolute majority	EU conditionality	Structural conditionality	Complete troika satisfaction	Low	No
Property tax introduction in Ireland	09/03/2011–31/12/2013	Consensus democracy	Fine Gael/Labour Party	Centre	Coalition, absolute majority	EU conditionality	Structural conditionality	Complete troika satisfaction	High	No
Water supply system reform in Ireland	09/03/2011–31/12/2014	Consensus democracy	Fine Gael/Labour Party	Centre	Coalition, absolute majority	EU conditionality	Structural conditionality	Lack of progress	High	Yes
Regulated professions reform in Portugal	21/06/2011–31/12/2014	Consensus democracy	PSD-CDS	Centre-right	Coalition, absolute majority	EU conditionality	Structural conditionality	Lack of progress	Low	Yes
Labour market reform in Portugal	21/06/2011–31/12/2014	Consensus democracy	PSD-CDS	Centre-right	Coalition, absolute majority	EU conditionality	Structural conditionality	Complete troika satisfaction	High	Yes

signed with the EU. The period of analysis in all five cases therefore starts with the newly elected governments' term of office. In Ireland, the coalition government consisting of Fine Gael and the Labour Party took office on 9 March 2011. In Portugal, the centre-right PSD-CDS coalition government took office on 21 June 2011.

The *end point* of the analysis, again, depends on two factors. On the one hand, the reforms required by EU conditionality have been introduced by the respective government. On the other hand, the borrowing country has completed the Programme. The period of analysis ends when both factors are present. While reforms are typically completed before the Programme's end, sometimes the implementation of reforms exceeds the Programme's duration. For instance, the water services reform in Ireland were only completed after the Ireland exited the financial assistance Programme. Yet, the troika institutions kept on monitoring compliance with EU conditionality in the post-programme period. Therefore, the period of analysis goes beyond the Programme's duration in this case. In each case, the period of analysis ends at the end of the year in which both factors are present for the first time. The period of analysis in each case is contained in Table A1.

A.2 Coding Rules

I conduct a qualitative content analysis of the relevant debates. I coded the debates with the help of the content analysis software MaxQDA Analytics Pro 2020 (Release 20.4.1). Additionally, I used the automatic translation software DeepL Pro (Version 2.5.1) to translate Portuguese Parliamentary debates into English. Debates in each case were coded in random order to avoid coding bias over time. The coding process took place in two steps. First, statements by government actors referring to the respective policies were categorised according to their evaluation of the policy ('positive' or 'negative') and according to the targets, to whom responsibility was assigned. In a second step, I went back over the coded statements and assigned them to the four types of blame avoidance strategies based on the categories assigned in the first step. In the following section, I give a detailed overview of the coding rules. The relevant coding rules are summarised at the end of each paragraph and followed by coding examples. Finally, I present the results of the analysis.

A.2.1 Identification of a Statement

In the analysis of governments' blame avoidance strategies, the sender of attributions remains constant and is limited to representatives of the relevant government. Furthermore, the attribution object is limited to the specific policy under analysis. These two attributes, government membership of the sender and reference to the relevant policy, connect all statements that are coded for the analysis. Yet, a statement is only complete when the sender assigns responsibility to one or several targets.

Thus, all statements have three necessary parts: a government sender (i), who makes references to the case-specific relevant policy (ii), and assigns responsibility to one or more targets (iii).

A statement **starts**, when a government representative starts to talk about the respective policy. To collect as much context information as possible, the statement typically starts at the beginning of the paragraph, in which the policy is first mentioned.

Three features signal the **end** of a statement. First, a statement ends when a senders' speech act ends. One exception from this rule is that a statement continues when a sender gets interrupted by interjections. Second, a statement ends when the sender stops referring to the policy under analysis and switches to another issue. Third, a statement ends when a change in the evaluation of the attribution object or the properties of the attribution target takes place.[1] Therefore, several statements can be coded within one speech act when the sender switches between different blame avoidance strategies.

Take, as an example the following excerpt from the debate in the Irish parliament on 14 February 2013:

Excerpt

Deputy Brendan Howlin: All of Deputy Kelleher's finger-pointing and shouting cannot deny the fact that two years ago a new Government came in to pick up the pieces of the broken economy and is now well on the way, step by step, with the help of the people to fix the destruction Fianna Fáil left behind in its wake.

We do need to broaden the tax base because Fianna Fáil left us in a situation where we could not pay for day-to-day expenses and we are borrowing at the rate of over €1 billion a month.

Deputy Billy Kelleher: The Minister was promising to cut taxes and so forth.

Deputy Brendan Howlin: Up to 30% of our tax base collapsed because Fianna Fáil had shrunk it. We need to broaden the tax base.

Deputy Billy Kelleher: The Minister was promising to cut taxes when he was in opposition.

Deputy Brendan Howlin: Part of that is to have a property-based tax that is analogous to every other developed country across the world.

Deputy Billy Kelleher: So the Minister supports it.

Deputy Brendan Howlin: The detail of the property tax will be brought through step by step-----

Deputy Billy Kelleher: So it is not the troika that wants it.

Deputy Brendan Howlin: The Deputy can shout me down all he likes. The tax will be debated in this House step by step. It will be done in as fair a way as we can in the circumstances Deputy Kelleher's party left this country.

Deputies: Hear, hear.

[1] A change in the target does not end a statement. Rather, this is an indication that responsibility is blurred among several actors.

Deputy Barry Cowen: Why is the Government only giving 20 min to debate it?

Deputy Brendan Howlin: The Deputies opposite have no shame.

Deputy Barry Cowen: Will the Government give us half an hour for this debate?

Deputy Mary Lou McDonald: The Minister will agree the leaking of the draft report of the inquiry into the death of Savita Halappanavar before her husband Praveen had sight of it was an act of gross insensitivity to her family. It seems from what we read in the press that the report vindicates what Praveen has been saying all along. It seems to indicate that little attention was paid to the risk of infection and that there was a failure to intervene even when it was clear that miscarriage was inevitable. It is fair to say the Halappanavar family, and Praveen in particular, has been treated disgracefully and appallingly throughout this entire process. [...]

From: Dáil Éireann. (2013). 14 February 2013: Official Report—unrevised (Parliamentary Debates), 792 (3), pp. 680-681.

In this passage, the coded statement is underlined. Deputy Minister for Public Expenditure and Reform, Brendan Howlin, argues that a property tax is needed to broaden the tax base, as the predecessor government has left the country in severe financial and economic difficulties. The Deputy Minister first mentions the case-specific policy, the local property tax in the second paragraph. This is where the coded statement starts. In this case, the coded statement does not end at the end of the Deputy Minister's statement, as he engages in a back-and-forth with opposition MPs and reiterates his point in his next four statements. The statement then ends as the topic of the debate changes, when an MP raises another issue. The rules to identify a statement are summarised in the following box.

Identification of Relevant Statements

Three necessary elements of statements:

- Attribution sender: Government representative
- Attribution object: Case-specific policy
- Attribution target: Responsibility is assigned to one or several targets

Statement start:

- Sender talks about relevant policy

Statement end:

- Sender statement ends (Exception: Interjections, back-and-forth!)
- Sender switches topic
- Sender changes evaluation of policy

A.2.2 Identification of Blame Avoidance Strategy

In a next step, the kind of blame avoidance statement is identified. The statements vary in the evaluation of the attribution object, for which responsibility is attributed and with regard to the target, to whom responsibility is attributed. First, blame avoidance statements can either accept negative perceptions of a policy, or challenge these perceptions and reframe the policy in a positive way. Second, statements can either centre responsibility on an actor or blur it among several actors. These differentiations yield the four blame avoidance strategies introduced in Chap. 2. In the following, I give instructions for the identification of all four types of blame avoidance statements and provide coding examples and explanations for coding decisions (Tables A2–A5).

Identification of Circle the Wagons Statements

- Sender accepts negative perception of policy.
- Sender does not deny government involvement in policymaking.
- Sender blurs responsibility, either horizontally (among national actors) or vertically (by emphasising international influences), or by appealing to the government's role as a public delegate.[2]
- Target categories include the troika institutions, the predecessor government, general EU commitments, and social partners. They are extended inductively as required.

Identification of Blame Shifting Statements

- Sender accepts negative perception of policy.
- Sender denies government's role in policymaking process.
- Sender underlines the role of others in policymaking, and thus shift responsibility, via horizontal diffusion, by underlining past mitigating circumstances or by drawing on both international and domestic actors.
- Target categories include the troika institutions, the predecessor government, general EU commitments, and social partners. They are extended inductively as required.

Identification of Self-Defence Statements

- Sender accepts or even underlines the government's role in policymaking.
- Sender does not attribute responsibility to other actors.
- Sender reframes the policy in a positive way by highlighting past or future benefits, the fairness of the policy, or current policy failures that will be ameliorated by the policy.

[2] Senders can, theoretically, also negate agency via counterfactual arguments by arguing that 'it would have happened anyways'. For instance, they can point out international developments, such as globalisation or crisis, that make necessary certain policy choices. However, these kinds of statements were not observed.

Table A2 Examples for circle the wagons statements

Circle the wagons arguments	Statement	Explanation
Horizontal diffusion	**Deputy Pearse Doherty** (All names and positions are reported as are in the official transcripts)**:** Is it the intention of the Government to bring forward legislation that will dissect legally binding employment legislation [sic!] orders? […] **Deputy Brendan Howlin:** […] there is a commitment in the programme for Government to review the JLC structure. A comprehensive report, which was authorised by the previous Government, was conducted by Mr. Duffy and Dr. Walsh and has been published by the Government. It will form the basis for the discussions that will take place between the Department and the social partners and the Minister will have his own views (Dáil Éireann. (2011). 26 May 2011: Official Report - unrevised (Parliamentary Debates), 733 (3), 485).	The Deputy Minister for Public Expenditure and Reform, Brendan Howlin, does not contradict that legally binding Employment Registration Orders (ERO) will be reversed by government reforms. Instead, he highlights that the government-led reform process was initiated by the predecessor government and is supported by expert knowledge. The Deputy minister thus does not deny the government's involvement, but blurs responsibility for the changes in employment legislation among several actors.
Vertical diffusion	**The Secretary of State for Employment:** […] I would like to say that the Government has every interest in ensuring that this proposal receives the broadest possible consensus. It is an initiative that stems from international commitments entered into by the Portuguese State, it is obviously subject to the restrictions that result from those commitments, but in any case, we certainly have every interest in trying to ensure that this proposal has the broadest and widest possible consensus. Regarding the more specific questions you addressed to me, I would like to mention that this proposal was discussed within the scope of the Commission for the Regulation of Access to Professions, which, as you know, includes in its composition representatives of all social partners (Diário da Assembleia da República. (2012). Reunião Plenária de 4 de Julho de 2012 (I Série - Número 129), 20–21).	The Secretary of State for Employment, Pedro Silva Martins, does not advertise reforms of regulated professions, but instead highlights international commitments and the involvement of several domestic actors in the transposition of the professional qualification directive. The Secretary of State thus does not deny the government's involvement in the reforms, but blurs responsibility among several actors.

(cotinued)

Table A2 (continued)

Circle the wagons arguments	Statement	Explanation
Public delegate	**The Taoiseach:** [...] For 2012, we will be well within our deficit target agreed with the troika. In May, the Irish people voted overwhelmingly to ratify the fiscal stability treaty. This much needed reform will ensure that governments now and in the future will manage the public finances appropriately and sustainably, so that what happened in the past will never recur. In recognition of mistakes made by previous governments, this budget has broadened the tax base. For too long, successive governments have relied on a very narrow source of revenues. The introduction of a fair, progressive and proportionate property tax will help us to address the budget deficit and will help to avoid additional taxes on income (Dáil Éireann. (2012b). 6 December 2012: Official Report - unrevised (Parliamentary Debates), 785 (3), 695).	In his speech on the government's budget, the Irish Prime Minister, Enda Kenny, argues that the introduction of a property tax was made necessary by previous governments' unsustainable tax policy. He reminds the Parliament that Ireland had voted in favour of and supported an agenda of fiscal stability. He thus does not deny the government's decision to introduce a property tax, but diffuses responsibility by arguing that this move was made necessary by the omissions of previous governments and is in the interest of the general public.

Identification of Problem Denial Statements

- Sender reframes the policy in a positive way by highlighting benefits, the fairness of the policy, or comparing it to other cases. Alternatively, sender portrays the policy as a necessary or technical solution.
- Sender does not deny government involvement in policymaking.
- Sender blurs responsibility by highlighting cooperation, or portraying policymaking process in a technical way quasi-independent from the actors involved.
- Target categories include the troika institutions, the predecessor government, general EU commitments, and social partners. They are extended inductively as required.

Table A3 Examples for blame shifting statements

Blame shifting arguments	Statement	Explanation
Vertical blame shifting (troika commitment)	**Minister for the Environment, Community and Local Government (Deputy Phil Hogan):** In addressing this matter we should begin with first principles. Ireland is committed, under the EU-IMF programme, to the introduction of a property tax. We must put the funding of locally-delivered services on a sound financial footing, improve accountability and better align the cost of providing services with the demand for such services, as Deputy McNamara has rightly pointed out. It was considered, in light of the complex issues involved, that a local property tax would take time to introduce and accordingly to meet the requirements of the EU-IMF programme, the Government decided to introduce a household charge in 2012 as an interim measure (Dáil Éireann. (2012). 6 November 2012: Official Report - unrevised (Parliamentary Debates), 781 (1), p. 55).	The Environment Minister Phil Hogan does not deny previous criticism that the administration of the household charge was problematic. Instead, he underlines that the commitments arising from Ireland's Financial Assistance Programme made necessary the introduction of a property tax, and as an intermediate measure, the introduction of a household charge. By highlighting Ireland's international commitments, he signals that the government's hands are bound on the issue, thus shifting the responsibility for the decision to Ireland's international lenders, the EU and the IMF.
Past mitigating circumstances (predecessor commissions and omissions)	**Deputy Gerry Adams:** Is this not another scandal? [...] The Government is saying there are limited protections and the Minister will not be able to introduce emergency legislation [...] **The Taoiseach:** The Deputy is aware that the court decision deemed the structure in place to be unconstitutional. [...] It would not be possible for the Minister to rectify an issue that has been struck down constitutionally with legislation as complex and as robust as would be required between now and the start of the summer recess. [...] However, elements of legislation that have been there for quite some time have been struck down as unconstitutional. There were indications, many years ago, that something should be done about those elements but nothing was done (Dáil Éireann. (2011). 12 July 2011: Official Report - unrevised (Parliamentary Debates), 738 (2), p. 193).	The Irish Prime Minister, Enda Kenny, does not deny that the Constitutional Court's ruling on Employment Regulation Orders leaves workers unprotected until reforms are introduced. He deflects blame that the government is not acting fast enough to rectify issues arising from the ruling. He blames the predecessor government for its omission to improve upon the legal wage setting framework even though issues about its constitutional fit were known for a long time. In this way, he shifts the blame for the workers' situation to the predecessor government.

(cotinued)

Table A3 (continued)

Blame shifting arguments	Statement	Explanation
Borderline case: Combination of troika commitment and commissions or omissions of previous government	**Minister for the Environment, Community and Local Government (Deputy Phil Hogan):** I can assure the House that no one wants to pay taxes. [...] The options are very limited when one is in a troika agreement and our economic sovereignty was ceded by our predecessors. It is not easy to ask the people for a further contribution to bail us out, but that is what we have to do to retrieve the economic situation we inherited (Dáil Éireann. (2013b). 12 June 2013: Official Report - unrevised (Parliamentary Debates), 806 (2)).	The Environment Minister Phil Hogan concedes that the introduction of a property tax is unpopular, but underlines that the commitments arising from Ireland's Economic Assistance Programme, which was agreed by the predecessor government, make it necessary. He thus shifts blame to both, the troika and the predecessor government. → This counts as blame shifting, as the government is not included in the circle of blame worthy actors.
Borderline case: Government uses limited room for manoeuvre	**Deputy Phil Hogan:** Before I conclude, it is worth recalling that when this Government took office we were required to implement commitments given by the previous Government to the EU, the IMF and the European Central Bank. One of those commitments provided for the introduction of domestic water charges with no provision for metering by the end of 2012. This Government decided that water charges should be based on metered consumption, as this is the fairest way to charge for water, and we have put in place the measures and structures to achieve this (Dáil Éireann. (2014a). 6 May 2014: Official Report - unrevised (Parliamentary Debates), 840 (1), p. 93).	Talking about the costs of water charges for Irish households in his speech on the amendment of the water services act, the Environment Minister Phil Hogan frames the government's policy as the best option under the tight constraints given by the troika's requirements. He highlights that these were agreed with the previous government. In this way, it shifts responsibility for the blameworthy aspects of the policy to these actors. → This counts as blame shifting. What differentiates this from a circle the wagons statement is that a clear distinction is made between the government's actions, which is portrayed in a positive way, and the assignment of blame for the negative actions of others.

Table A4 Examples for self-defence statements

Self-defence arguments	Statement	Explanation
Present benefits	**Deputy Gerald Nash:** [...] In the first instance, the decision to restore the national minimum wage to €8.65 per hour with effect from 1 July 2011, together with the decision to put the joint labour committee system on a more secure legal and constitutional footing and reinstate a robust system of protection for workers, represented a significant commitment by the Government to protect the lowest paid and most vulnerable workers (Dáil Éireann. (2014d). 17 December 2014: Official Report - unrevised (Parliamentary Debates), 862 (2), p. 12).	Countering criticism that the government's recovery plan disadvantaged workers, the Irish Minister of State, Gerald Nash, portrays the government's reform of the JLC system as a measure to protect low paid workers. Instead of denying the government's role in policymaking, he thus underlines the positive aspects of its policy.
Future benefits	**Deputy Fergus O'Dowd:** [...] We want to ensure that if people want to create employment, the right quality water will be there. That is what this Bill is about. It is about ensuring our environment is protected, health is protected and that we have a proper supply everywhere. Therefore, we must ensure we get everybody on board (Dáil Éireann. (2013a). 14 February 2013: Official Report - unrevised (Parliamentary Debates), 792 (3), p. 780).	In a debate about the Water Services Bill, the Irish Minister of State, Fergus O'Dowd, highlights that the government's reforms of the water supply system have tangible benefits for the environment, for water quality and the economy. He does not deny the government's role in policymaking and refrains from talking about the introduction of water charges, but highlights positive aspects of the policy.
Remedy for current policy failure	**Minister of Economy and Employment:** [...] In recent decades, labour legislation has perpetuated an unsuitable economic model, left unresolved problems of competitiveness, aggravated imbalances and, with them, injustices. The laws governing the labour market today are an obstacle to the competitiveness of our companies and to job creation. Many of these rules were drafted at a time when they had nothing to do with the complexity and dynamism that now characterise world economies. Today their rigidity is a real burden on employers and workers, an impediment to the growth of our economy. [...] Therefore, [...] the Government is presenting here today one of the most profound structural reforms of recent years (Diário da Assembleia da República. (2012a). Reunião Plenária de 28 de Março de 2012 (I Série - Número 89), pp. 16–18).	In a debate on the reform of the Portuguese Labour Code, the Portuguese Economic Minister, Álvaro Santos Pereira, argues that the outdated Portuguese labour laws are a burden for economic growth and contribute to unemployment. He portrays the status quo as untenable and underlines that the government's reforms are meant to tackle these rigidities to foster employment and growth, thus underlining the positive aspects of the government's policy.

(cotinued)

Table A4 (continued)

Self-defence arguments	Statement	Explanation
Fairness	**The Taoiseach:** I understand the challenge any introduced charge brings for many. We have tried to make this as affordable, fair and equitable as possible in the interests of providing proper facilities and high quality water for the entire country. It is different in many places in rural Ireland, where people may have paid for water for years because of the necessity to engage in pipework and so on, instead of having to bore wells on bad land, for example. Therefore, it is an issue. We have tried to make it fair, affordable and equitable, as we need to invest in and fix infrastructure and repair treatment works (Dáil Éireann. (2014b). 15 October 2014: Official Report - unrevised (Parliamentary Debates), 854 (2), p. 9).	Countering remarks on the financial burden on Irish households, the Irish Prime Minister, Enda Kenny, argues that criticism of the water charge turns a blind eye to the costs some Irish citizens are already paying for water supply. He is not denying the government's role in policymaking, but frames the reform of the system as an issue of fairness.
Borderline case: deny cost or put them into perspectives	**The Taoiseach:** I agree with Deputy Adams that the imposition of any new charge is always difficult for people. We recognise that, but I also recognise that 18,000 people have to boil drinking water every day. [...] I recognise that the infrastructure in so many places is grossly inferior to what it should be, so people have to deal with inferior, infrequent and poor supplies. The only way that can be dealt with is by having an entity that is entitled to borrow money to provide that infrastructure, construction jobs and facilities for business and domestic consumers alike. [...] the Government is required to discuss and decide the details of how we can make this affordable, equitable and as fair as possible (Dáil Éireann. (2014c). 16 April 2014: Official Report - unrevised (Parliamentary Debates 838 (2), p. 47).	The Irish Prime Minister, Enda Kenny, responds to the statement of an opposition MP, who criticised the water charge as a burden to low-income families, by underlining the hardship caused by the current system of water supply. He does not deny the government's role in policymaking, nor does he negate that the reform comes at a costs. Instead, he argues that these costs are low comparable to the negative aspects of the status quo.

Table A5 Examples for problem denial statements

Problem denial arguments	Statement	Explanation
Underline cooperation	**Mr. Minister of Solidarity, Employment and Social Security:** I want to reaffirm the importance of the concertation agreement we were able to conclude with the social partners. The Commitment to Growth, Competitiveness and Employment represented a milestone of enormous added value for Portugal. Never before had an agreement with the social partners been so structural, so extensive and so profound as this one, and it was thanks to it that Portugal advanced in a profound set of reforms to achieve a labor market that is more prodigal in job creation, more capable of adjusting to the pace of change in the global economy, and more friendly to innovation, investment and entrepreneurship. But the social dialogue did not end on January 18, 2012, with the signing of this agreement, but intensified in its implementation. It is in close dialogue that we have been honoring the Commitment to Growth, Competitiveness and Employment (Diário da Assembleia da República. (2014). Reunião Plenária de 28 de Junho de 2014 (I Série - Número 101), p. 28).	The Minister of Solidarity, Employment and Social Security, Pedro Mota Soares, underlines the positive aspects of the labour market reforms, such as a climate conductive to the creation of jobs. He does not claim this as the government's attainment, but underlines the close cooperation with the social partners, thus blurring responsibility among several actors.
Technical issue	**Mr. Secretary of State for Infrastructure, Transport and Communications:** [...] The bill we are presenting today follows the first stage of the legislative process that transposed Directive 2008/96/EC on road safety management [...] These audits and inspections are thus part of a set of intervention instruments on the road infrastructure and their main objective is to mitigate the risk and consequences of accidents on road infrastructures, [...] Several entities collaborated in this diploma, in a working group constituted for the revision of the regulatory model of the road sector, which included, besides a vast set of entities, the Orders of Engineers and Technical Engineers. I would also like to emphasize that international experience in this matter has shown the efficiency and benefits that unequivocally result from the performance of these audits to reduce the occurrence of accidents in road infrastructures, [...] I would like to point out the vital importance of this draft law in establishing road safety audits as a technical instrument that is absolutely fundamental to the pursuit of an interest that belongs to all and is certainly shared by all: the safety and reduction of accidents on our roads (Diário da Assembleia da República. (2014). Reunião Plenária de 27 de Fevereiro de 2014 (I Série - Número 53), p. 14).	The Portuguese Secretary of State for Infrastructure, Transport and Communications, Sérgio Monteiro, portrays the introduction of regulations regarding professions managing road safety management as a technical matter of transposing an EU Directive. He pre-empts criticism of the measures by portraying the reforms as safety measures, which technical experts nationally and internationally agree save lives. He does not underline the government's role in policymaking, but highlights the close cooperation with experts, thus blurring responsibility among several actors.

(cotinued)

Table A5 (continued)

Problem denial arguments	Statement	Explanation
No alternative to policy	**Deputy Minister for Public Expenditure and Reform:** […] There are Deputies opposite who will support no tax, no charge and no cut. It is Darby O'Gill economics by which people will not be fooled. […] People want this economy to recover and they know the path to recovery is a hard path. They will not be fooled by people pretending we can fund local government with magic money. The final point is that we need certainty on this funding (Dáil Éireann. (2012). 29 March 2012: Official Report - unrevised (Parliamentary Debates), 758 (1), p. 6).	Deputy Minister for Public Expenditure and Reform, Brendan Howlin, argues that the government's decision to introduce a local property tax is a choice without viable alternatives. The tax the only way to economic recovery. Other policy choices are framed as 'magic money'. Portraying this as a common knowledge, he suggests that this policy would most likely be introduced irrespective of the policymakers in charge, thus blurring responsibility.
Common sense	**Assistant Secretary of State and National Defence:** In Portugal, the activity of lifeguard has been exercised as a seasonal occupation, limited to the summer period and usually performed by young people who take a specific course and work one or two summers in this area. However, today's times dictate other demands. The increase of coastal areas accessible to bathers, the economic growth associated to nautical activities, the legal possibility of changing the length of the bathing season, […] force us to look at this activity in a different way. […] The exercise of the activity of lifeguard has a strong impact on the defence, safety and protection of life and welfare of citizens, so this activity must be subject to a procedure of verification and certification of professional qualifications required for situations of this nature. This is imposed by EU regulations, but it is also common sense and experience that call on us to improve the existing internal regulations regarding this profession. […]. This is an activity that can represent the difference between life and death. That is why the procedure for certification and attribution of these qualifications requires that all these courses are taught and oriented by entities duly certified for that purpose (Diário da Assembleia da República. (2014). Reunião Plenária de 13 de Fevereiro de 2014 (I Série - Número 50), p. 23).	Assistant Secretary of State and National Defence, Berta Cabral, argues that the existing regulations for lifeguards are no longer sufficient and need to be reformed in order to life up to current safety for people and the environment. While he admits that EU regulations require the amendment of current Portuguese law, he argues that these changes in a profession that saves life are 'common sense'. He thereby suggests this policy would most likely be introduced irrespective of the policymakers in charge, thus blurring responsibility

A.3 Results of the Content Analyses

The content analysis of Parliamentary debates in the five cases yields a total of 645 blame avoidance statements. Table A6 summarises the results by giving the absolute frequency of the four types of blame avoidance strategies for each case. This summary shows that the absolute number of statements found varies significantly in the five cases. However, as I am not comparing differences in the frequency of government statements across the cases, these differences do not influence the validity of the findings.

In the following, I present the detailed results for each of the five case studies, breaking down the results by year. Furthermore, I present a breakdown of the targets of blame shifting statements to find out when the EU and especially the troika institutions are made responsible for reforms.

A.3.1 Wage Setting System Reform in Ireland

Table A7 shows that the Irish government's use of blame avoidance strategies changed significantly over time. The absolute number of statements decreases steeply from 68 statements in 2011 to only six in 2013. Furthermore, while the government most frequently relied on a circle the wagons approach overall, this strategy was not dominantly used in any of the years under analysis. In 2011, the government employed problem denial in 37% of statements, whereas it used a circle the wagons approach in 35% of cases. Conversely in 2012 and 2013, the government relied on a self-defence approach in 34% and 67% of statements, whereas circle the

Table A6 Overview of blame avoidance statements

	Blame shifting	Circle the wagons	Self-defence	Problem denial	Total
Wage setting system reform in Ireland	4	35	30	34	103
Property tax introduction in Ireland	46	3	29	10	88
Water supply system reform in Ireland	49	13	200	42	304
Regulated professions reform in Portugal	7	4	8	25	44
Labour market reform in Portugal	11	8	52	35	106
Total	*117*	*63*	*319*	*146*	*645*

Table A7 Wage setting system reform in Ireland—results by year

	Blame shifting	Circle the wagons	Self-defence	Problem denial	Total
2011	3 (4%)	24 (35%)	16 (24%)	25 (37%)	68
2012	1 (1%)	9 (31%)	10 (34%)	9 (31%)	29
2013	0	2 (33%)	4 (67%)	0	6
(2014)	(0)	(0)	(9)	(1)	(10)
Total (2011–2013)	*4 (4%)*	*35 (34%)*	*30 (29%)*	*34 (33%)*	*103*

Table A8 Wage setting system reform in Ireland—blame shifting statements by actor

Troika institutions	Predecessor government	Troika institutions and predecessor government	Total
2 (50%)	2 (50%)	0	4

wagons statements account of 31 and 33% of statements respectively. Overall, the only strategy that is consistently scarcely used is blame shifting. Table A7 includes statements for 2014, which are indicated in brackets, as this year was excluded from the period of analysis.

Table A8 disaggregates the Irish government's blame shifting statements by target, listing only those target categories found in the statements. Due to low number of statements, these results yield little insight.

A.3.2 Introduction of Property Tax in Ireland

Table A9 shows that the Irish government's use of blame avoidance strategies increased over the period of analysis from 12 statements in 2011 to 37 statements in 2012 and 39 in 2013. The absolute number of statements then steeply decreases again in 2014. These results are given in brackets, as 2014 is outside the period of analysis.

The disaggregation by year shows that, in line with theoretical expectations, blame shifting is consistently the most frequently used strategy in all years, with its share ranging from 75% in 2011 to 49% in 2012 and 2013. Furthermore, self-defence is consistently the strategy the Irish government employed second most frequently, with the share of statements ranging between 17% in 2011 and 35% in 2012. The shares of low-contestation strategies are consistently low and ranges at or below 15% in all years.

Table A10 disaggregates the Irish government's blame shifting statements between 2011 and 2013 by target, listing only those target categories found in the statements. Government senders have chosen to shift blame to the predecessor government and the troika institutions in tandem in 46% of cases. The troika institutions alone were additionally targeted in 37% of cases. The EU institutions as part

Table A9 Property tax introduction—results by year

	Blame shifting	Circle the wagons	Self-defence	Problem denial	Total
2011	9 (75%)	1 (8%)	2 (17%)	0	12
2012	18 (49%)	2 (5%)	13 (35%)	4 (11%)	37
2013	19 (49%)	0	14 (36%)	6 (15%)	39
(2014)	(1)	(0)	(3)	(4)	(8)
Total (2011–2014)	*47 (49%)*	*3 (3%)*	*32 (33%)*	*14 (15%)*	*96*

Table A10 Property tax introduction—blame shifting statements by actor

Troika institutions	Predecessor government	Troika institutions and predecessor government	Total
17 (37%)	8 (17%)	21 (46%)	46

of the troika thus received the bulk of blame attributions for the introduction of the Irish property tax.

A.3.3 Water Supply Services Reform in Ireland

Table A11 shows that the Irish government's use of blame avoidance strategies was relatively stable from 2011 to 2013 and steeply increased in 2014. Still, the results are consistent and in line with expectations. The Irish government most frequently employed a self-defence approach, with shares ranging from 54% in 2012 to 72% in 2014. Furthermore, blame shifting statements are the second most frequent type of statement between 2011 and 2013 until there are overtaken by problem denial statements in 2014.

Table A12 disaggregates the Irish government's blame shifting statements by target, listing only those target categories found in the statements. Government senders have chosen to shift blame to the troika institutions 59% of cases. An additional third of all blame shifting statements attributes responsibility for the water services reform to both, the troika institutions and the predecessor government. The latter is hardly ever singled out as the sole culprit (8%). The EU institutions as part of the troika thus received the bulk of blame attributions for the Irish water services reform.

A.3.4 Regulated Professions Reform in Portugal

Table A13 shows that the Portuguese government's use of blame avoidance strategies varies over time. Significantly, no statements were found in 2011. The absolute number of statements is relatively low and decreases from 2012 to 2014. The overall

Table A11 Water supply services reform—results by year

	Blame shifting	Circle the wagons	Self-defence	Problem denial	Total
2011	12 (32%)	2 (5%)	22 (58%)	2 (5%)	38
2012	12 (22%)	7 (13%)	29 (54%)	6 (11%)	54
2013	6 (18%)	3 (9%)	21 (62%)	4 (12%)	34
2014	19 (11%)	1 (1%)	128 (72%)	30 (17%)	178
Total	*49 (16%)*	*13 (4%)*	*200 (66%)*	*42 (14%)*	*304*

Table A12 Water supply services reform—blame shifting statements by actor

Troika institutions	Predecessor government	Troika institutions and predecessor government	Total
29 (59%)	4 (8%)	16 (33%)	49

Table A13 Regulated professions reform in Portugal—results by year

	Blame shifting	Circle the wagons	Self-defence	Problem denial	Total
2011	0	0	0	0	0
2012	1 (5%)	3 (14%)	4 (19%)	13 (62%)	21
2013	6 (50%)	0	3 (25%)	3 (25%)	12
2014	0	1 (9%)	1 (9%)	9 (82%)	11
Total	*7 (16%)*	*4 (9%)*	*8 (18%)*	*25 (57%)*	*44*

Table A14 Regulated professions reform in Portugal—blame shifting statements by actor

Troika institutions	EU commitment	EU commitment and troika institutions	Total
1 (14%)	4 (57%)	2 (29%)	7

low number of statements makes the interpretation of the results difficult. Overall, and in line with expectations, the Portuguese government predominantly relied on a problem denial approach. This observation holds for 2012 and 2014 when disaggregating the data. The disaggregation of blame avoidance statement by years shows some outliers, such as the share of blame shifting statements in 2013, which amount to 50% of all statements that year. Yet, the low absolute number of statements makes the interpretation of the results difficult.

Table A14 disaggregates the Portuguese government's blame shifting statements by target, listing only those target categories found in the statements. Remarkably, all statements shift blame to the European Union, while refraining from targeting the predecessor government. The EU is blamed not merely as part of the troika, but also as a policymaker in general, with 57% of all statements referencing general EU commitments, such as Directives that require transposition into national law. Yet, the overall number of statements is low, so that it is difficult to draw general inferences from these findings.

Table A15 Labour market reform in Portugal—results by year

	Blame shifting	Circle the wagons	Self-defence	Problem denial	Total
2011	2 (13%)	0	7 (47%)	6 (40%)	15
2012	0	4 (13%)	15 (47%)	13 (41%)	32
2013	2 (9%)	2 (9%)	10 (43%)	9 (39%)	23
2014	7 (19%)	2 (6%)	20 (56%)	7 (19%)	36
Total	*11 (10%)*	*8 (8%)*	*52(49%)*	*35 (33%)*	*106*

Table A16 Labour market reform in Portugal—blame shifting statements by actor

Troika institutions	Predecessor government	Troika institutions and predecessor government	Total
5 (42%)	2 (17%)	5 (42%)	12

A.3.5 Labour Market Reform in Portugal

Table A15 shows that the Portuguese government's use of blame avoidance strategies is relatively infrequent and fluctuates over time, ranging between 15 statements in 2011 and 36 statements in 2014. The results are consistent over time. In line with expectations, the Portuguese government consistently employs self-defence as its dominant blame avoidance strategy, with shares ranging between 43% in 2013 and 56% in 2014. Moreover, problem denial is consistently the second most frequent strategy ranging between 19 and 41% of all statements.

Table A16 disaggregates the Portuguese government's blame shifting statements by target, listing only those target categories found in the statements. Government senders have chosen to shift blame to the troika institutions 59% of cases. An additional third of all blame shifting statements attributes responsibility for the labour market reform to both, the troika institutions and the predecessor government. The latter is hardly ever singled out as the sole culprit (8%). The EU institutions as part of the troika thus received the bulk of blame attributions for the Portuguese labour market reform.

A.3.6 Reliability of Coding Results

How reliable are the results of the conducted content analysis? Typical requirements of reliability are hard to transfer to qualitative content analysis.[3] Yet, appropriate measures can be taken to avoid biases in coding and increase the confidence in the reliability of the results. Several measures in coding process ensure stable, reproducible results and avoid biases.

[3] Mayring, P. (2015). Qualitative Inhaltsanalyse: Grundlagen und Techniken (12., überarb. Aufl.). Beltz Pädagogik. Beltz, p.124.

First, the coding process was designed to avoid that learning processes bias the results. While learning over time would not have affected the comparability between the cases, it would have impeded claims about the stability of the results over time. Therefore, the debates in each case were coded in random order. The coding sequence can be found in the list of collected debates (A 4). Furthermore, the two-step coding process ensured that I revisited each coding to check for consistency in the application of the coding rules.

Second, the coding process was designed to avoid coder-related bias. As only one coder was involved in the coding process, the variation across cases does not derive from different applications of the coding rules by different coders (Kuckartz, 2014, p. 47). This approach raises the question of reproducibility. In content analyses, this is oftentimes measured by intercoder tests. Yet, intercoder agreement is hard to interpret for qualitative content analyses for two reasons. First, qualitative content analysis does not work with predefined textual units, such as sentences or paragraphs.[4] This makes it hard to define thresholds of agreement between codings. Second, when coded categories contain complex, latent concepts, intercoder agreement is typically rather low in comparison to quantitative approaches, making it hard to define acceptable levels of intercoder agreement.[5] As there are thus no clear guidelines as to how to interpret intercoder agreement, no intercoder test was conducted for this study. Instead, throughout the coding process, special care was taken to ensure a consensual coding approach, whereby uncertain or questionable coding decisions are discussed with other researchers to ensure unambiguous coding rules and plausible individual coding decisions.

A.4 List of Collected Debates

Separate excel file upon request.

A.5 List of Coded Blame Avoidance Statements

Separate excel file upon request.

---

[4] Kuckartz, U. (2014). Qualitative Text Analysis: A Guide to Methods, Practice & Using Software. Sage, pp.46-7.

[5] See for instance: Gerhards, J., Offerhaus, A., & Roose, J. (2007). Die Öffentliche Zuschreibung von Verantwortung: Zur Entwicklung eines inhaltsanalytischen Instrumentariums. Kölner Zeitschrift Für Soziologie Und Sozialpsychologie, 59(105–124); Heinkelmann-Wild, T., Rittberger, B., & Zangl, B. (2018). The European Blame Game: Explaining Public Responsibility Attributions in the European Union. In A. Kruck, K. Oppermann, & A. Spencer (Eds.), Political Mistakes and Policy Failures in International Relations (pp. 171–189). Palgrave Macmillan. https://doi.org/10.1007/978-3-319-68173-3_8.

The manufacturer's authorised representative in the EU is Springer Nature Customer Service Centre GmbH, Europaplatz 3, 69115 Heidelberg, Germany. If you have any concerns regarding our products, please contact ProductSafety@springernature.com

Printed and bound by CPI Group (UK) Ltd, Croydon, CR0 4YY
01/10/2026
02225954-0013